Captive Insurance Deskbook for the Business Lawyer

taxation • reinsurance • securities • underwriting • tax controversy
employee benefits • commercial transactions • actuarial science

David J. Slenn
Editor

AMERICAN BAR ASSOCIATION
Business Law Section

Cover design by Catherine Zaccarine/ABA Publishing.

Page layout by Quadrum Solutions.

Printed in the United States of America.

22 21 20 19 18 5 4 3 2 1

ISBN: 978-1-64105-085-2

Table of Contents

Foreword ... ix

Contributors ... xi

Chapter 1: Introduction and Types of Captives ... 1
Jay D. Adkisson

I. Introduction ... 1

II. Tax Categories of Captives ... 2

III. Ownership Categories of Captives ... 2

IV. Underwriting Categories of Captives ... 3

V. Domicile Categories of Captives ... 4

VI. Summary ... 4

Chapter 2: Captive Insurance Company Feasibility ... 5
Kevin Malbon, Thomas Morante, and David J. Slenn

I. Introduction ... 5

II. Captive Insurance Company Benefits ... 6
  A. Lower or Better Manage Overall Insurance Costs ... 6
  B. Create an Alternative to Costly Commercial Insurance or Price Increases ... 7
  C. Obtain Coverage Where It Is Difficult or Generally Unavailable, and Access Reinsurance ... 7
  D. Enhance Relationships with the Third-Party Customers ... 8
  E. Incubate Emerging Risks ... 8

III. Captive Feasibility Study ... 9

IV. Business Plan ... 10

V. Feasibility Studies and Federal Tax Issues ... 12

VI. Determining Premiums ... 13

VII. Owner's Financial Resources and Impact on Feasibility Factors ... 14

VIII. Captive Design ... 14

IX. Captive Domicile ... 15

X. Meeting with Regulator ... 16

XI. Captive Management ... 16

Chapter 3: U.S. Taxation of U.S. Captives 21
James L. Mannello, Jeffrey J. Webb, and Charles J. Lavelle

I. Introduction to Taxation and Qualification as an Insurance Company 21
A. Initial Summary 21
B. Preliminary Matters 22
C. Insurance Tax Tests 23

II. Qualifying as an Insurance Company 33

III. Alternative Captive Taxing Regime: Small Insurance Company—Section 831(b) Election 34
A. Summary of Section 831(b) 34
B. Caveat Regarding IRS Notice 2016-66 on Micro-Captives 35
C. Avrahami v. Commissioner 36
D. Section 831(b) Review 36

IV. Alternative Captive Insurance Regime: Exempt Insurance Companies—501(c)(15) 36

V. Taxation of Insurance Companies under Subchapter L 37

VI. Treatment of Prepaid Insurance by the Parent or Related Party 37

VII. State Taxation of Captive Insurance Companies 38

VIII. Failing to Qualify as a Captive Insurance Company 38

IX. Treatment of Dividends 39

X. Termination of Captive Insurance Companies 40

XI. Captive Insurance Company Takeaways 40

Chapter 4: U.S. Taxation of Non-U.S. Captives 41
P. Bruce Wright and Saren Goldner

I. Introduction 41

II. The Controlled Foreign Corporation (CFC) Rules 41
A. The General CFC Rules 42
B. The Insurance CFC Rules 45
C. The RPII CFC Rules 47
D. Special Rules for Tax-Exempt Owners of Insurance and RPII CFCs 49
E. Distributions Received from CFCs 50
F. Sales, Exchanges, or Redemptions of CFC Stock 50
G. U.S. Corporate Taxation as an Alternative to CFC Status 50
H. CFC Information Reporting 50

III. Non-CFC Status 51

IV. Passive Foreign Investment Company (PFIC) Rules 51

V. 953(d) Election 53

VI. U.S. Trade or Business Considerations 54
A. Imposition of U.S. Federal Tax 54
B. Definition of a U.S. Trade or Business and a Permanent Establishment 55
C. Customary Practical Operational Considerations 58

VII. Federal Insurance Excise Tax (FET) 58

VIII. Withholding Tax 60

IX. Information Reporting 60

X. Comparison of Non-CFC, CFC, and 953(d) Election 62

Chapter 5: Employee Benefits 65
Karin Landry

I. Introduction 65

II. Using a Captive to Fund Employee Benefits 65

III. Advantages of Placing Employee Benefits in Captives 67

IV. Employee Benefit Funding Opportunities 68

V. A Brief History of ERISA Benefit Captive Funding 70

VI. Using a Captive to Fund Retiree Medical Obligations 70

VII. Using a Captive to Fund Pensions 71

VIII. Critical Steps in the Captive Development Process 72
A. Establishing a Captive for Employee Benefits 72
B. Feasibility 72
C. Design 74
D. Implementation 75
E. Ongoing Development 75

IX. Using a Captive to Fund Medical Stop-Loss 76
A. How Medical Stop-Loss Captive Funding Works 76
B. Common Types of Stop-Loss Captives 79
C. Who Should Consider Medical Stop-Loss Captive Funding? 80
D. Cell Captives: The Right Fit for Many Businesses for Medical Stop-Loss Funding 80

Chapter 6: The Role of Corporate Counsel 83
Michael T. Scott

I. Introduction 83

II. Business Reasons to Have a Captive Insurance Company 83
A. Reduce the Reliance on Commercial Insurance 84
B. Provide Stability with Respect to Insurance Premiums, and Provide Loss Control Services 85
C. Provide Coverage That Is Not Otherwise Available 85
D. Allocate the Cost of Risk 85
E. Provide Improved Claim Handling and Control Over Claims .. 86
F. Investment Income 86
G. Opportunities to Write Related Third-Party Business and Tax Advantages 86

III. Corporate Counsel's Role within a Captive 86
A. Risk Manager/President of the Captive 87
B. Claims Manager 88
C. Board of Directors 88

IV. Managing Conflicts of Interest 89
A. Conflict of Interest in Setting Up Insurance Programs 89
B. Conflict of Interest in Claims Situation 90
C. Conflicts of Interest When Corporate Counsel Represents Both the Captive and the Parent Company as Legal Advisor ... 93

V. Conclusion 95

Chapter 7: The Role of the Domicile Regulator 97
David F. Provost

I. Introduction 97

II. Mission of the Vermont Department of Financial Regulation 97

III. Regulatory Approval Process 98
A. Meeting with a Regulator 98
B. Feasibility Study 98

IV. Performing Ongoing Financial Surveillance 99
A. Required Filings 100
B. Annual Meeting 100
C. Monitoring and Surveillance 100

V. Examinations 101

VI. IAIS Guidance 101

VII. Caveat Emptor 102

Chapter 8: Closing the Captive 105
Andrew Rothseid

I. Introduction 105

II. Dormancy 105

III. Run Off: Deadweight on the Business 106

IV. Options for Speeding Up Closure 106
A. Putting Run Off into Perspective 107
B. Closure Options Available to Solvent Insurers and Reinsurers in Run Off 108

V. The Case for Commutation 113

VI. Conclusion: From Passive to Active Run Off 117

Chapter 9: Captive Insurance Tax Controversy 119
Steven Miller and Meeren Amin

I. Introduction 119

II. IRS Examinations of Captive Insurance Companies 120
A. Key IRS Issues during a Captive Insurance Audit 120
B. Audit Process 121

III. The Appeals Process 125
A. Fast-Track 126
B. The Regular Appeals Process 127

IV. Captive Insurance Litigation 129
A. Definition of Insurance for Tax Purposes 130
B. Economic Substance Doctrine and Related Penalty 131
C. Penalties—IRC Section 6662 132
D. Expert Witnesses 133
E. Summons 133

V. Pre-Audit Strategies 134
A. Issue: Purpose for Formation of Captive 134
B. Issue: Coverages Provided and Risks Covered 135
C. Issue: Pricing of Premiums 136
D. Issue: Existence of Claims 136
E. Issue: Flow of Monies 136

Endnotes 139

Appendix: The Base Erosion Anti Abuse Tax ("BEAT")—Overview 157
Saren Goldner and P. Bruce Wright

Index 159

Foreword

Many lawyers who do not include captive insurance planning as a part of their practice could very well encounter a captive insurance issue at some point in their career. This is due to the fact that most of the Fortune 500s as well as many mid-sized (and even small) businesses and tax-exempt organizations participate in captive insurance structures.

As this book will demonstrate, captive insurance as field of practice can be portrayed pictorially as a Venn diagram, with various overlapping and subsuming circles representing legal and nonlegal practice areas such as taxation (domestic, foreign, state and local), insurance (regulatory, coverage, reinsurance, etc.), securities, commercial transactions, employee benefits, tax controversy, actuarial science, underwriting, etc.

A business lawyer might be required to give special attention to an M&A transaction where a target company participates in a "captive program," a term that might be foreign to the lawyer. Alternatively, a lawyer might be asked whether a client must hold a meeting related to its captive, and whether the meeting can be held in the place most convenient to the owners. The lawyer must most likely dig deeper upon further review to examine program documents, governing law of the captive program, and other insurance and tax issues. Or, a lawyer might be consulted regarding the deductibility of premiums paid to a captive because the lawyer specializes in taxation, requiring opening Subchapter L, perhaps for the first time. A client may contact a lawyer regarding a sales pitch involving a captive that will help the client save income taxes and pass wealth to family members. Perhaps the lawyer will be asked to sign off on documents related to the entry or exit of a captive structure, or respond to an IRS request for information related to the client's participation in a captive program.

This book will help the lawyer understand the issues involved with situations like this and much more. Although a single lawyer most likely cannot handle every issue that arises in the context of captive insurance, this book should help the lawyer identify the issue and if not address the issue, point the lawyer in the right direction to provide helpful assistance.

This book consists of contributions from accomplished and well-regarded professionals of various areas of expertise, with two chapters presented as first-person accounts of the Vermont captive regulator and former in-house counsel for a Fortune 500. This book begins with a discussion of types of captives, addresses how one would approach whether a captive makes sense for a business owner, and then focuses on various aspects of the captive's operation and management, from taxation, special uses, and regulation to eventual exit and potential tax litigation issues.

Many of the contributing authors have presented on these topics for the American Bar Association's Captive Insurance Companies Committee in the Business Law Section. The committee has accumulated these presentations for free access to its members. This book represents a compilation of many of these efforts; however, much more, including breaking news items, can be obtained through committee membership (open to all, including non-lawyers). It has been an absolute pleasure serving as a chair of the committee, and a truly captivating experience working with these co-authors.

David J. Slenn, Editor

Contributors

Jay D. Adkisson is a partner of Riser Adkisson LLP with offices in Las Vegas, Nevada, and Newport Beach, California. He is admitted to practice in Arizona, California, Nevada, Oklahoma, and Texas; is a former chair of the American Bar Association's Committee on Captive Insurance; authored a popular book on captive insurance companies; and was a partner in a captive management company in the British Virgin Islands.

Meeren Amin is a senior associate in alliantgroup's Washington, DC office. His practice focuses on representing clients during complex tax controversies in front of the Internal Revenue Service. Meeren has experience in a broad range of tax matters including captive insurance, R&D tax credits, reasonable compensation, section 1603 grants, whistleblower cases, and section 6700 investigations. He holds an LLM in taxation from Georgetown University and a JD from Wake Forest University School of Law.

Saren Goldner is a partner in the New York office of Eversheds Sutherland (U.S.) LLP and focuses her practice on international tax and insurance and insurance tax issues, including structuring non-U.S. operations, captive insurance companies, insurance characterization, and other insurance-specific tax issues. She advises clients on the structuring of international insurance operations (including the application of tax treaties, FATCA, the CFC, and PPIC rules and other tax issues arising as a result of cross border operations), the formation and operation of captives and cell companies, tax exempt issues, and public and private securities offerings (including ILS transactions).

Karin Landry, CEBS, GBA, ACI, CLTC, is managing partner for Spring Consulting Group, LLC, which is a leading consulting and actuarial firm whose core focus is developing integrated and innovative solutions in the areas of employee benefits, risk management, and wealth strategies. Karin holds a BSBA from Babson College and has pursued graduate studies in finance from Northeastern University. Karin currently holds a Certified Employee Benefit Specialist (CEBS), Group Benefits Administrator (GBA), Certified Long Term Care Consultant (CLTC) and an Associate in Captive Insurance (ACI) designation. She is a Licensed Insurance Advisor for Life, Health and Property and Casualty and also a licensed broker in several states. In the past, she has held NASD series 7 and 63 licenses.

Charles J (Chaz) Lavelle has been listed in the Captive Review's Power 50 and Enterprise Risk Captive Pioneer 20 and is a lawyer in the Louisville, Kentucky Office of Bingham Greenebaum Doll LLP. He regularly counsels clients in captive insurance matters and IRS defense. He is a frequent speaker and writer on captive insurance topics. Chaz was outside Tax Counsel for both Humana (brother-sister) and Ocean Drilling (unrelated business) in their captive insurance victories in the U.S. Court of Appeals. Among his civic and charitable activities, he is a past Chair of the Kentucky Chamber of Commerce.

Kevin Malbon, MBA, CMA, ARM, director, Actuarial & Analytics, Aon Global Risk Consultants. Kevin is responsible for delivering risk financing analysis and solutions to clients. He has extensive financial analysis experience in the insurance industry, starting with a base of ten years of finance and accounting for a multi-billion dollar insurance company, then 25 years in brokerage and consulting for a broad variety of clients. Kevin obtained an MBA from Loyola Marymount University and a bachelor's degree in business administration (marketing) from California State University at Northridge.

Jim Mannello is an Insurance Tax Partner based in Stamford and leads Deloitte's Health Insurance Tax Practice and also heads Deloitte's Captive Insurance Tax Practice. He has over 35 years of experience in public accounting working with insurance companies. Jim is a Certified Public Accountant and a member of the Connecticut Bar. Jim is active in various industry and professional organizations and is a frequent speaker at tax conferences. Jim received his Bachelor of Arts degree in mathematics and economics with honors from Wesleyan University and his J.D. from the University Of Connecticut School Of Law.

Steven T. Miller is alliantgroup's national director of Tax and served as the former IRS acting commissioner and deputy commissioner for Services and Enforcement, leading all IRS interaction with taxpayers. He was also commissioner of the Large and Mid-Size Business Division, overseeing IRS audits and other dealings with large taxpayers. With more than 25 years of experience at all levels of the IRS, Miller earlier served as commissioner of the Tax Exempt and Government Entities Division, where he supervised the IRS oversight of governments, tax exempt entities, and retirement programs. Miller also served as legislation counsel to the Congressional Joint Committee on Taxation. He holds an LLM in taxation from Georgetown University and a JD from George Washington University.

Thomas F. Morante is a partner in the Ft. Lauderdale/Washington, DC offices of Holland & Knight. Tom helps financial services companies navigate an increasingly complex global regulatory environment. He co-chairs the firm's Insurance Industry Team, representing insurers, reinsurers, captives, insurance wholesalers, insurance agents/brokers, funds and fund managers, and alternative capital providers. Toms' representative matters include domestic and foreign insurance company formation, U.S. and cross-border mergers and acquisitions (M&A), captive insurance structuring, policy coverage and analysis, agent/agency licensing, InsureTech and blockchain, fronting/reinsurance, variable product and insurance dedicated fund regulation. Tom obtained his JD from American University, Washington College of Law, his LLM (international and comparative law) from Georgetown University Law Center, and his BA from Union College.

David F. Provost, CFE, is deputy commissioner of Vermont's Captive Insurance Division, responsible for the regulation of captive insurance companies and risk retention groups. He has been with the Division since 2001, and was appointed deputy effective June 1, 2008. Mr. Provost has over 25 years of experience in captive insurance in both the private and government sectors. His prior experience includes work in the captive insurance arms of Johnson & Higgins, Sedgwick, and AIG, and he served as treasurer of the Vermont Captive Insurance Association. A lifelong Vermonter, Mr. Provost is a certified financial examiner and a member of the Society of Financial Examiners.

Andrew Rothseid is a lawyer, licensed to practice in Pennsylvania and New York, and the principal and owner of RunOff Re.Solve LLC, a specialist turnaround, restructuring, and advisory services firm serving the global insurance and reinsurance industry. Further information is available at www.runoffresolve.com.

Michael T. Scott is an attorney at Allison & Mosby-Scott where he heads the firm's Business Law practice and serves as president of Allison & Mosby-Scott Risk Management, the firm's risk management consulting practice. Michael's practice areas include business and commercial litigation; business organization and transactions; mergers and acquisitions; ERISA; contracts; and captive insurance company taxation, formation, and regulation. Michael leverages his 22 years of legal experience and his unique skills as a strategic thinker and problem solver to help clients solve complex legal issues and to achieve their strategic goals. Prior to joining the firm, Michael was vice president, Insurance & Risk Management at Archer Daniels Midland Company (ADM) and president and general counsel of Agrinational Insurance Company, the captive insurance company of ADM. Prior to his time at ADM, Michael served as a corporate attorney for State Farm Insurance Companies in Bloomington, Illinois. In addition to being licensed to practice law in Illinois, Michael holds the CPA, CRM, CPCU, CLU, ChFC, FLMI, ARM, ARC, AIC, AMIM, ARe, AIAF, AU, and CGMA designations. He is a graduate of the University of Illinois and Southern Illinois University School of Law.

David J. Slenn is a partner in the Tampa office of Shumaker, Loop & Kendrick, LLP. David concentrates his practice in tax, estate, and business planning with an emphasis on risk mitigation. Dave helps business owners from various industries, small to publicly-held, with decisions related to captive insurance feasibility, operational issues, tax audit exposure, as well as exit options and strategies. He is the immediate past chair for the Captive Insurance Committee in the Business Law Section of the American

Bar Association (ABA) and a past chair for the Asset Protection Planning Committee in the Section of Real Property Trusts and Estate Law of the ABA. Additionally, he was an ABA advisor to the Uniform Law Commission Drafting Committee for the Uniform Voidable Transactions Act (formerly the Uniform Fraudulent Transfer Act).

Jeffrey J. Webb is in the Financial Services practice of Deloitte Tax, LLP. He has over thirteen years of experience working with financial services companies, primarily focusing on the insurance and health plan industries. Jeff assists many companies with either establishing, maintaining, gaining efficiencies or integrating closely held insurance platforms. This assistance has been for domestic, outbound and inbound profiled companies. He received his Bachelor of Science degree in Accounting from the University of Connecticut. Jeff is a licensed Certified Public Accountant in New York and Illinois and a member of the AICPA, NYSSCPA, Illinois CPA Society and Wall Street Tax Association.

P. Bruce Wright is a partner in the New York office of Eversheds Sutherland (U.S.) LLP. Nationally recognized as an authority in the captive insurance industry, Bruce Wright counsels companies on a wide range of tax and insurance law issues, including formation of commercial offshore privately and publicly held entities. He also works with clients on the development of structured financial products such as securitizations, swaps, options, and similar products used as alternatives to conventional risk financing mechanisms such as "rent-a-captives" and "cell companies."

Chapter 1

Introduction and Types of Captives

Jay D. Adkisson

I. INTRODUCTION

A captive insurance company, often referred to as simply a "captive," is an insurance company whose license permits it to only underwrite insurance for certain businesses that are affiliated with the captive. Because the insurance company cannot underwrite insurance for the public at large, but is restricted only to affiliated businesses, it is said to be captive to those businesses, and therein is found the genesis of the term.

The primary goal of a captive is to fill an insurance need of the affiliated businesses, where insurance coverage is either not available or is more expensive than can be provided by the captive. A captive accomplishes the former by acquiring capital, operating profitably, and growing its reserves and surplus through its underwriting profits, just as any new insurance company would do. A captive often accomplishes the latter by cutting out the middleman, being the commercial insurance companies that ordinarily sell insurance to the businesses, and instead allows the business to acquire insurance direct from the wholesaler, which in the insurance industry means reinsurance companies.

Captives are regulated industries, much like a bank, and are subject to strict licensing and oversight by insurance regulators. Captive applications are quite complex and detailed, and require personal and financial information about their owners, directors, and officers. Captives must be audited annually, and most jurisdictions that authorize captives also require an examination of the captive to be performed every three years or so.

Many captives choose to be taxed as an insurance company for U.S. tax purposes, and, as discussed elsewhere in this book, if they choose to be taxed as an insurance company, they must meet not only the insurance company provisions under the U.S. Tax Code but also additional Treasury guidance that is specific to captives.

There are many types of captives, which may be pigeonholed into categories based on regulatory classifications, tax classifications, and classifications based upon their structure or usage.

From a regulatory viewpoint, all insurance companies typically fall into one of two major categories, which are known as "life companies" that underwrite life insurance, annuities, and the like, and "non-life companies" that underwrite all other forms of insurance, most predominantly property-casualty (P/C) insurance. Life captives, as they are sometimes called, are rarities; the vast majority of captives are non-life companies.

II. TAX CATEGORIES OF CAPTIVES

Changing to the tax perspective, it is important to understand at the outset that a substantial number of captive insurance companies do not seek to be treated as insurance companies for U.S. tax purposes. It is also important to know that the U.S. Tax Code does not itself define a "captive insurance company," but rather the authority for such companies is found variously in court opinions and Treasury guidance.

For those companies that do seek to be treated as an insurance company for tax purposes, the U.S. Tax Code has essentially two major categories of insurance companies: life insurance companies and non-life insurance companies. These categories are found in captives as well. Some states license captives as life insurance companies, so as to provide certain employee benefits or to act as reinsurance captives for life insurance companies that sell directly to consumers. By far the largest number of captives, however, are non-life captives which are also sometimes referred to as property-casualty captives.

Non-life captives may also be parsed based upon which treatment they elect and qualify for under the U.S. Internal Revenue Code. Non-life captives may be taxed as so-called ordinary insurance companies under Tax Code section 831(a), small insurance companies under Tax Code section 831(b) if they have total premium income of less than $2.2 million (this amount indexed against inflation), and exempt insurance companies under Tax Code section 501(c)(15) if the gross revenue of the captive and all affiliated companies is less than $600,000.

III. OWNERSHIP CATEGORIES OF CAPTIVES

Captives are often categorized for regulatory purposes based on their ownership.

A captive with a single owner, or which is owned by closely affiliated owners, is known as a "pure captive." This varietal constitutes by far the largest number of captives. A pure captive typically has a license that restricts the captive to underwriting only the business of its owner or closely affiliated businesses, such as subsidiaries. An example would be an oil company with many subsidiaries (refining, storage, exploration, etc.) that uses its wholly owned captive to underwrite environmental cover for its subsidiaries.

Where a captive has multiple unrelated owners who are utilizing the captive to spread risks among themselves, the captive is known as a "group captive." Such a captive will typically have a license that restricts the captive to underwriting only certain types of risks of its group members. An example of a group captive would be where several manufacturers of children's toys pool use a captive to cover their product liability exposure. However, insurance regulators will typically restrict the size of a group captive to a relatively small group.

For much larger groups, such as those with members running into the thousands, "risk retention groups" (RRGs) which are formed under the Liability Risk Retention Act of 1986 are used. Risk retention groups are very similar in their operation to mutual insurance companies, where the insured/owners are paid dividends based on the performance of the company as a whole.

Typically, but not always, used for businesses that require a captive insurance company but can pay only relatively low premiums, often lower than $500,000 annually, so-called sponsored-cell captives (or often just "cell captives") are effectively a pure or group captive that is legally organized within some other entity. Cell captives are organized as segregated business units (SBUs) within Series LLCs in states that allow that arrangement. The benefits of SBUs are lower costs, and sometimes the ability to use the surplus capital of the parent company or other SBUs. The downside to this structure is that, unlike a stand-alone captive, the captive owner does not fully control the destiny of its SBU and may be subject to controls of the parent. A variation of a cell captive is the "rental captive" or "rent-a-captive," whereby an existing captive allows a business to conduct its insurance business through the captive, but the risks and transactions of that particular insurance business are internally segregated away from other insurance of the captive.

"Agency captives" are insurance companies that are owned by insurance agencies or brokerage firms, and that seek to take advantage of the underwriting profits from their customers. Agency captives promise either by directly writing insurance to their customers, where allowed by insurance regulators, or often by reinsuring the risks of their customers by taking on a portion of the risks of the front-line large commercial carriers and being compensated by way of a reinsurance fee.

IV. UNDERWRITING CATEGORIES OF CAPTIVES

Captives may also be parsed by what sort of risks they underwrite. For instance, a "workers comp captive" will typically only insure that line of business. Some captives, known as "special purpose captives," are in fact formed to underwrite only a single large, one-time risk, such as a company that is transporting a particularly valuable oil rig across the oceans. These captives have varied advantages, from segregating liability away from the parent company to simply obtaining reinsurance more cheaply.

Captives may also be differentiated by what layers of risk they are taking on. A "deductibles captive" will cover only the deductible that is owed by a company before its commercial coverage kicks in; these captives typically allow the business to substantially increase its deductible level and thus lower its commercial insurance costs. By contrast, a "primary captive" will directly take over the main layer of risk. An "excess captive" takes on the layer of risk above that provided by the commercial carrier, that is, once the policy with the commercial carrier has been exhausted, the captive's coverage becomes available to the business.

V. DOMICILE CATEGORIES OF CAPTIVES

Finally, captives are often defined by the jurisdiction in which they are domiciled, that is, the jurisdiction where they are licensed and primarily regulated. From the U.S. view, a "domestic captive" means a captive that is domiciled in one of the U.S. states or territories that have passed captive-enabling legislation and licenses captives. By like token, a "foreign captive" (or often "alien captive") is a captive that is formed outside the United States, and an "offshore captive" is a foreign captive that is formed in one of the tax-haven countries, such as Bermuda or the Cayman Islands.

There are, of course, variations of these main themes. For instance, a "branch captive" is essentially a subsidiary or segregated business unit of a foreign-licensed captive.

VI. SUMMARY

As shown, captives come in many shapes, sizes, and flavors. This diversity is born of the many roles that captives play as an alternative risk management (ARM) tool. For captive planners, the process is not to simply choose a particular captive structure at the outset and then hammer the insurance business into it, but it is rather to fully understand the particular risk-management concerns of the insureds and then find an appropriate captive structure that efficiently fits that business. Such an evaluation requires a deep understanding and appreciation of a myriad of issues as will be discussed in the following chapters.

Chapter 2

Captive Insurance Company Feasibility

Kevin Malbon, Thomas Morante, and David J. Slenn

I. INTRODUCTION

The decision to form a captive insurance company (referred to as a "captive") is driven by many factors, with some factors having more importance than others, depending on the facts and circumstances. A captive insurance company is just one way to mitigate risk, and is often referred to as an alternative form of risk mitigation (with commercial insurance being a traditional form of risk mitigation.) The end result might be a captive that turns into a profit center with proper structuring, or it might be a captive that is primarily utilized to help reduce overall insurance costs. To understand what factors are more important when considering formation of a captive, it is necessary to understand the goals and objectives of the owners of the insured business (ranging from an individual to shareholders of a Fortune 500, all such owners are referred to as a "business owner").

The decision to form a captive is typically motivated to achieve a variety of goals and related benefits, such as to:

- Lower or better manage overall insurance costs
- Create an alternative to costly insurance or price increases
- Obtain coverage where it is difficult or generally unavailable
- Enhance relationships with third-party customers
- Incubate emerging risks

With these goals in mind, it is imperative to consider the future of the captive program, with expected claims and costs on an annual basis, and to analyze best and

The authors would like to thank Barbara Efraim for her assistance. Barbara has completed her final year of law school at American University, Washington College of Law, and joins Holland & Knight LLP as an associate in 2018 in the areas of international trade and financial services.

worst-case scenarios. Thus, the prospective business owner should consider the benefits of creating a captive program for the business and any subsidiaries (such businesses collectively are referred to as the "insured") and should also consider the consequences of exiting a captive, under various scenarios.

With a successful risk mitigation program, the business owner may receive distributions from the captive (subject to tax considerations more particularly discussed in Chapters 3 and 4.) that would have otherwise been paid for commercial coverage and never seen again. Over time, a properly designed and tax-compliant captive may build up surplus sufficient to make distributions to the owners or write additional or increased coverage. Since a driving force behind the decision to form a captive includes obtaining coverage not available or too costly to obtain otherwise and/or lowering the overall cost of insurance, it is important to identify and quantify the value of these goals. This, in turn, will then set in motion the use of time and money (i.e., the cost) to conduct a further analysis of a captive program, referred to as a captive "feasibility study," described in more detail in Section III of this chapter.

II. CAPTIVE INSURANCE COMPANY BENEFITS

A. Lower or Better Manage Overall Insurance Costs

A captive can help reduce overall insurance costs by pooling retained risks for multiple lines over multiple years. Each risk has its own volatility, which if treated individually would cause insureds to purchase more insurance than they may need. By pooling risks in a captive, a business owner can protect operations while diversifying risk exposure (i.e., the arbitrage that inheres from the business) and conserve premium dollars.

Commercial insurance premiums are written on an industry basis and then grossed up to include insurance profit loadings. As a result, insureds' commercial risk transfer premium expenses include underwriting risk and underwriting profit. The underwriting risk is based on industry loss history with only some modifications for unique risk profiles. When an insured has reason to believe that the premium expense in the commercial insurance markets will (in the short to medium term) exceed its budgetary considerations, the insured has several ways to recapture some of the excess expenses. One way is to increase retentions; another is to participate in the commercial insurer's profits through a profit-sharing arrangement. For instance, the insured can utilize a captive to write a quota share portion of insurance, on a form-following basis (i.e., to be sure that excess carrier coverage matches primary carrier coverage), for a specific layer of risk. This willingness to retain risk can also be an effective negotiating tool.

In a captive environment, owners select all their service providers (such as underwriters and actuary or claims administrators) individually. As a result, the owner is not bound to those assigned to them by their insurer in a commercial insurance context, thus permitting the owners to pick and choose the best providers for each service. Through this customization process, the business owner may be able to reduce the cost of insurance in comparison to insuring through a commercial insurance company. This is because there is a tendency to think of the insurance contract as primarily providing coverage against potential and eventual losses; however, the insurance contract addresses a number of other obligations, including claims adjusting, engineering, and loss control, elements that a captive might be better able to control by controlling the service providers.

B. Create an Alternative to Costly Commercial Insurance or Price Increases

By creating and owning a captive, the business owner has an alternative to the commercial market, which can help to insulate it from fluctuations in market pricing. If markets harden (i.e., premiums increase), the insured can opportunistically take risk into the captive or use the captive as leverage during negotiations with carriers. For insureds whose loss experience is better than the industry average, a captive can be used to provide coverage based on actuarial rates that are lower than those available commercially. Some coverages may be prohibitively expensive in the commercial market, in which cases a captive can be used to write (or "manuscript") policies to meet the insureds' needs.

C. Obtain Coverage Where It Is Difficult or Generally Unavailable, and Access Reinsurance

There are often certain risks with respect to which a business owner may have determined not to purchase commercial insurance for a variety of reasons. In other situations, insurance products are not available in the commercial marketplace. The decision to form a captive in these cases is usually associated with high rates on line (premium to limit), limited capacity, unattractive terms and conditions, or concern that insuring the exposure is against public policy (e.g., fraud).

When an insured chooses not to purchase insurance, the insured has selected an unfunded risk retention strategy requiring the use of current free cash flows or possible diversion of investments away from other planned opportunities, or issuing securities (e.g., selling bonds or commercial paper) to pay for future losses. A captive insurance company can offer a formal structure to finance retained risks on a pre-loss basis. Premiums may be paid to a captive to reduce the year-over-year volatility of the retained losses, from a cash flow perspective, by having the captive issue insurance policies to cover these risks. In other words, by setting funds aside to cover future losses, the financial impact of such future losses may be smoothed out over time in a tax efficient manner.

If an insured is not able to secure the right coverage for its risk exposure in the commercial insurance marketplace, it can use a captive to access the reinsurance marketplace. A reinsurer, by virtue of its charter or regulation, can only offer risk solutions to insurance companies. Given reinsurance coverage and premium options, a captive insurance company would give an insured the ability to deal directly with the reinsurance market. In such cases, the captive functions as a direct insurer of the insured such that virtually all of the risk can be immediately reinsured with a professional reinsurer.

This strategy can also be used to create an aggregate stop-loss program for a captive program (see Chapter 5 for an illustration of how a captive can be used to fund medical stop-loss). In a stop-loss program, the captive elects to pay a premium to a reinsurance company to cap the aggregate exposure in the captive. The insured should be able to manage the aggregate capacity; however, if the insured decides to increase the exposures in the captive, this reinsurance solution may give the insured the flexibility to integrate more risks in the captive while having the confidence that the captive will be protected from catastrophic loss. An aggregate stop-loss program can also be used by an insured in the early years of a captive program, before sufficient surplus has built up for the captive to withstand significant losses.

D. Enhance Relationships with the Third-Party Customers

In a highly competitive business environment, companies depend on the value they bring to their customers. Often these customers can a get a similar product or service from a variety of sources, so differentiating the product or service is a key to success. Some insureds utilize captive insurance to help differentiate their product or service, thus improving the customer experience and overall competitiveness. This can be seen in concept with existing "Extended Warranty" captives that have been around for many years.[1]

Some companies have determined that by offering individualized insurance products through these channels they can not only provide revenue stream but also increase customer "stickiness" . . . thus fending off competition.

E. Incubate Emerging Risks

Cyber risk is an example of an emerging risk that is a growing and significant concern for most insureds. A solution to a current threat is quickly eclipsed by a new threat that needs to be counteracted. Cyber events that started as retail or healthcare "records release" have now spread to machine-controlling software and denial of service for ransom (e.g., "Wanna Cry").

The insurance marketplace has encountered challenges keeping pace with these risks, and although numerous commercial insurers have entered the market, available coverages differ significantly with pricing that can be very volatile. This is due, in part, to the difficulty in determining the exposure and magnitude of losses arising.... resulting in mispricing or inadequate coverage. The use of captives as an alternative form of risk financing and risk mitigation for cyber threats continues to increase. In addition, the captive can craft coverage language and provide a "track record" or modeling that will provide a basis for alternative or future risk transfer opportunities in the cyber risk context.

III. CAPTIVE FEASIBILITY STUDY

The captive decision-making process begins with a feasibility study. The importance of undertaking a feasibility study is critical, not just for the purpose of determining the insured's objectives, but also because the study establishes a framework to facilitate achieving organization consensus and support, while also providing crucial components needed in connection with the insurance regulatory filing to create the captive. The feasibility study also provides analysis regarding the potential financial and strategic advantages that could be realized through the establishment of a captive. Furthermore, for companies that seek income tax benefits associated with captive formation (i.e., deductions for their premiums, as discussed in Chapter 3), the feasibility study can be used in court or an administrative proceeding to help support an argument that the captive is not a sham and/or does not lack a business purpose, thus minimizing the risk of a denial of deductions for the premiums paid to the captive insurance company.

The importance of a captive feasibility study is demonstrated in recent case law. For example, the captive feasibility study was reviewed in *Rent-A-Center, Inc. v. C.I.R.*,[2] a recent case establishing important legal precedent regarding tax treatment of captive insurance companies and confirming the value of a feasibility study.

> After successfully resolving petitioner's D & O insurance problem, Aon evaluated petitioner's risk management department. Petitioner, with Aon's assistance, improved risk management practices, switched from bundled to unbundled policies, and hired SRS as a third-party administrator. Aon proposed that petitioner form a captive, and petitioner determined that a captive would allow it to reduce its insurance costs, obtain otherwise unavailable insurance coverage, formalize and more efficiently manage its insurance program, and provide accountability and transparency relating to insurance costs. Petitioner engaged KPMG to prepare financial projections and evaluate tax considerations referenced in the feasibility study. Federal income tax consequences were considered, but the formation of Legacy was not a tax-driven transaction. *See Moline Props., Inc. v. Commissioner*, 319 U.S. at 439; *Britt v. United States*, 431 F.2d 227, 235–236 (5th Cir. 1970); *Bass v. Commissioner*, 50 T.C. 595, 600, 1968 WL 1442 (1968). To the contrary, in forming Legacy, petitioner made a business decision premised on a myriad of significant and legitimate nontax considerations. *See Jones v. Commissioner*, 64 T.C. 1066, 1076, 1975 WL 3065 (1975) ("A corporation is not a 'sham' if it was organized for legitimate business purposes or if it engages in a substantial business activity."); *Bass v. Commissioner*, 50 T.C. at 600.[3]

The iterative nature of the captive feasibility process can be described in Figure 2.1.

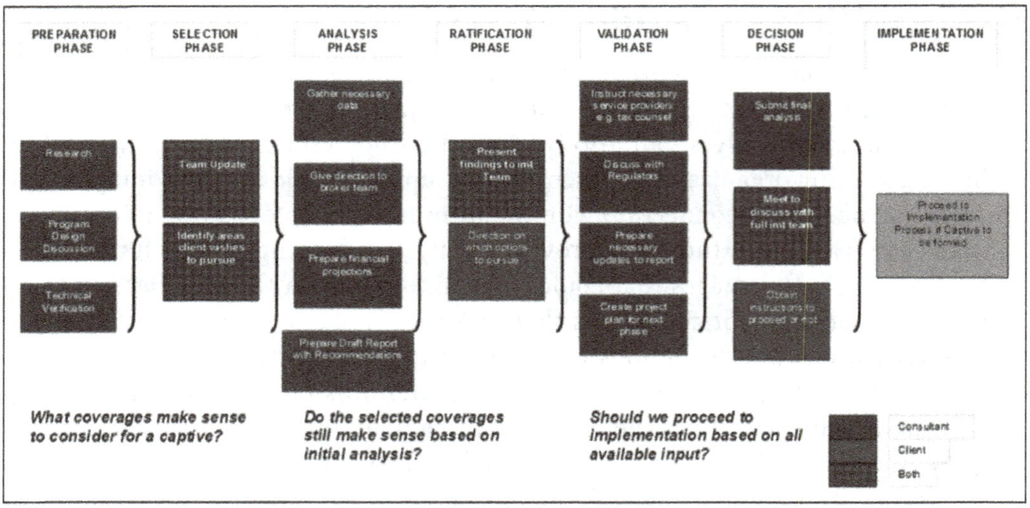

Figure 2.1 Captive Feasibility Process
Diagram courtesy of Aon Captive Insurance Managers.

The feasibility report highlights the reasons for forming a captive subsidiary of the insured and generally includes the following topics:

- General captive theory, the business owner's potential for captive participation, and key strategic benefits that a captive might bring from a qualitative standpoint;
- Financial benefits and likely frictional costs of a captive;
- Discussion of the contribution of business owner's business units to a captive, which lines of cover will be placed in the captive, potential levels of Self Insurance Reserve (SIR) retentions, and a domicile analysis;
- Overview of treating the captive as an insurance company for tax purposes, the potential tax benefits of doing so, and a synopsis of applicable revenue rulings;
- Comparison of potential domiciles using metrics important to the client; and
- Discussion of the long-term nature of a captive and assessment of the potential difficulties that could be encountered upon withdrawal.

IV. BUSINESS PLAN

The components of the feasibility study become the basis of the business plan submitted to the domicile state regulator for the captive, and will govern the captive activities—unless changed in a business plan amendment. The business plan generally contains the following sections:

Introduction. This section provides a high-level summary statement of the reasons why the captive is being formed.

Owner/insured overview. This section provides information about the ownership structure of the proposed captive and background on the insured and the owner of the captive (which may be different than the owner of the business), including its primary business, if applicable. Particulars such as the business owner/insured's web address (if applicable) and latest audited financial statements (if applicable) and an illustration of its corporate structure (if available) are included.

Business purpose of the captive. This section explains the business reasons for setting up the captive. It provides a description of the lines of business to be written/(re)insured by the captive, including the nature/location of the business/risks being underwritten. How the business will be sourced (e.g., via broker) and details of primary or fronting carriers and/or reinsurers (as the case may be) are included. If relevant, the reinsurance/retrocession cover to be purchased by the insured is described.

Reinsurance. This section provides details of the reinsurance to be secured by the captive. The names of possible reinsurers and their respective ratings, if known, are included. If reinsurance is not applicable to the proposed captive program, then a statement is made in this section that the business owner does not plan to reinsure any of the risks at this time although consideration of this will be reviewed from time to time.

Underwriting. This section is used to explain the underwriting policies/techniques that will be provided by the business owner to identify risk opportunities (i.e., a basic description of the underwriting approach). Information detailed in this section includes:

- A description of reserving policy and choice of approved actuary;
- Detailed descriptions of underwriting criteria and methods, including pricing and how premiums are being set;
- Loss ratio analysis, including what data is being used and actuarial reports if available;
- A brief description of investment policies;
- A discussion of how claims will be handled; and
- A description of the senior management team, especially in relation to insurance expertise.

Capitalization of the captive insurance company. This section describes how the captive will be capitalized, and the level or amount of capitalization is justified using pro forma financial projections to support the proposed funding.

Board of directors. Detailed biographical information about the captive board of directors is provided in this section. The proposed board of directors is often composed of both senior management of the business owner and experts from external companies. For issues related to overlapping roles and potential conflicts of interest issues, see Chapter 6.

Service providers. In this section, the service providers for the captive are detailed. This includes:

- Registered office. The captive's registered office is often that of the law firm selected to service the captive.
- Auditors. These are independent auditors to the insured who will audit the captive financials.
- Actuary. The actuary retained to analyze captive reserves and forecast future captive losses.
- Bankers. The insured's bank that will hold the funds used to pay captive claims.
- Attorney and corporate secretary. An attorney and corporate secretary are selected to handle the legal concerns and regulatory compliance of the captive.
- Captive manager. The proposed insurance manager and principal representative of the insured is the captive manager, who will oversee compliance with all statutory requirements, including the maintenance of all necessary insurance records.
- Other roles. Other roles may exist within the captive structure and may be assumed by parties that assume multiple roles, such as the captive manager or law firm, or by third parties. These roles include underwriter, claims administrator, and employee benefits specialist. (See Chapter 6 for the appropriateness of independent versus in-house claims administration, including potential conflicts of interest.)

V. FEASIBILITY STUDIES AND FEDERAL TAX ISSUES

Tax issues play an important role in the feasibility process, both for tax exempt organizations and for-profit business owners.[4] If the risk to be insured through a captive is determined not to be an insurance risk, significant tax problems can arise (more fully discussed in Chapters 3 and 9). If the underlying exposure to be covered through the captive is implausible or illusory, then the premium for such coverage will not be considered a payment for insurance. If not considered insurance for federal income tax purposes, then, premiums paid to the captive would not be deductible.[5]

Notwithstanding the foregoing, some business owners may obtain coverages that are associated with exposures that have never resulted in claims, do not make sense given the business owner's exposure, and are typically priced unusually high (especially when used as excess coverage) given such circumstances. For some, the motivation is driven purely by tax benefits; the cost to implement the captive insurance program without meaningful coverages is offset by the benefit of (1) an income tax deduction associated with a premium payment and corresponding tax rate arbitrage when a dividend is paid or the captive is liquidated and (2) the ability to sidestep transfer taxes by funneling premiums to family members or trusts for their benefit.[6] In *Avrahami v. Commissioner*,[7] the Internal Revenue Service (IRS or Service) challenged the premiums paid to a micro-captive that utilized a risk pool (offering terrorism coverage). The U.S. Tax Court held in favor of the Service, finding the captive did not provide insurance in the commonly accepted sense, and that the reinsurance structure did not provide risk distribution. Captive programs motivated by tax-driven considerations and exhibiting certain characteristics should continue to trigger scrutiny by the Service.[8]

Business owners should seek independent review of their feasibility study and carefully consider the reasons for forming a captive.[9] In tax controversies, it is not unusual for the court to review the genesis of the captive insurance program, noting that the interest in forming the captive arose as part of the taxpayer's risk management analysis and based on the feasibility report considered by management.[10] In a pending Tax Court case involving a section 831(b) captive,[11] the Service assigns weight to the fact that the captive originated with an estate planner and not a risk mitigation professional. This underscores the importance of securing a qualified insurance professional at the beginning of the feasibility process, or even earlier, in what is often referred to as a "pre-feasibility" study.

If either one of the aforementioned primary goals can be established and justified for business purposes, the next step is to consider various other factors related to implementation, such as (1) estimated premium amounts associated with the desired coverages; (2) resources available to create and maintain a captive insurance program; (3) available structures that can accomplish the primary goals; (4) the federal, state, and local tax consequences of the captive insurance program; (5) the appropriate domicile for the captive insurance program; (6) financing requirements to implement the captive insurance program; and (7) regulatory or business concerns associated with participating in a captive insurance program.

VI. DETERMINING PREMIUMS

The captive gives the insured the ability to tailor premiums to the underlying risk being underwritten in the captive. There are two different methodologies that can be used to ensure that the premiums are supportable by an audit.

The first method of calculating premium paid to a captive is to use market rates. By using commercial insurance rates, the captive can evidence "arms length" pricing. Generally, this will lead to excess premium being paid to a captive, which can be beneficial if the captive needs to accrue a surplus. This technique also eliminates the need for a captive to calculate pricing, and will to a large extent be accepted by regulators. However, there could be several drawbacks to this methodology: it can be difficult in the commercial market to get premium rates and quotes; the strategy may lead to an overpayment of premium since the data will reflect commercial carrier's profit loading and industry experience; and, this can create increased premium volatility.

In the second method, a captive can use the experience of the insured to tailor premium. Experience-based premiums can be calculated to generate target loss ratios or captive return on equity. Therefore, requiring the captive to use industry data in its analysis is essential. Experience-based premium charges should be balanced to ensure that the captive will be adequately funded to address adverse developments.

It should be noted that when a captive is formed it is generally desirable to conservatively fund the captive in the first few years. This helps build equity in the captive, creating a financial cushion that protects its assets in the case of a large loss or adverse experience, and avoids the need to recapitalize per statutory requirements.

The captive's board of directors has the ability to adjust the premiums within reasonable parameters in order to ensure that the premiums are right for the business units. Premiums can create incentives for the business units to heighten control of their losses. This makes certain that the premium allocation to the business units is fair and consistent.

VII. OWNER'S FINANCIAL RESOURCES AND IMPACT ON FEASIBILITY FACTORS

In electing a domicile (discussed in Section IX) and the appropriate structure for the captive, the insured owner must consider the insured's available resources. There are various types of captive structures and numerous available domiciles that can accomplish the same coverage goals, each with different costs to implement and maintain. In the captive structuring context, a pure captive might be possible given the insured owner's structure (see Chapter 1); however, the cost of implementing a pure captive might be cost-prohibitive when compared to a cell captive.[12]

Limited resources might also play a role in deciding where a captive should be domiciled, as one domicile might require capital of $250,000,[13] whereas another domicile might require nominal capitalization of $10,000.[14] Notwithstanding the allure of a very low capital requirement, selection of a domicile should not be based on the absolute lowest amount required to form a captive. Choice of domicile and the capital required should be determined by the insurance professionals preparing the feasibility report based on the business operations of the insured.[15] Further, for those who seek to use a captive and deduct premiums paid, the use of a domicile with an extremely low required capital amount, along with other lax requirements, could be perceived negatively by a court. In short, cheaper is not necessarily always better. Given the importance of ensuring that the captive is adequately capitalized and can accommodate solvency requirements, domiciles require a business plan, reflecting, among other items, projections and investment policies, which are subject to review and approval.

VIII. CAPTIVE DESIGN

In addition to financial considerations, the design of a captive might be driven by tax considerations. For example, if a business owner can justify the use of a pure captive, the use of a risk pool could be avoided. On the other hand, the structure of the business might not support a pure captive and if a reorganization is not feasible or desired, the business might decide to engage a captive manager to form a captive and establish reinsurance agreements with a pool of other captives to satisfy risk-shifting and risk-distribution requirements. If a tax-exempt organization is interested in a captive, a pure captive could be considered, or a similar cell captive could be used (such captive structures discussed in Chapter 1), but with restrictions in the participation agreement that would prohibit the sharing of risk (to help avoid the unrelated business income tax).

IX. CAPTIVE DOMICILE

There are over 60 jurisdictions worldwide that have specific captive legislation, many with a flexible regulatory framework in which a captive can operate. While the legislation in most U.S. states is similar, statutes and operating environments vary around the world, resulting in operating inequalities among captive domiciles. Captive jurisdictions can be separated into three broad categories: onshore-U.S. domiciles, offshore domiciles, and European Union (EU) based domiciles.

When considering a domicile, an insured should evaluate the reasons for and the benefits to hopefully be derived from forming the captive. Considerations should include coverage, regulatory environment, tax, administration, cost, and accessibility. Each domicile will have its own preferences and regulations concerning the coverage that can be in a captive.

Some domiciles will allow only first-party or affiliated-party coverages in a captive, whereas others will allow unrelated risk. In addition, domiciles differ in what risks can be insured through the captive. For example, only some domiciles allow government-supported terrorism coverage, employee benefits, and punitive damages.

It is important that the regulatory environment is supportive of the insured's captive endeavor. Therefore, it is essential to look at the stability of the regulatory team and their receptiveness to captive business, and to work with regulators who will be responsive to a captive's requests.

As noted above, tax issues must be carefully considered. Non-U.S. captives (i.e., established in offshore domiciles) may be subject to additional taxes and fees that can complicate how premiums and loans are treated. In addition, non-U.S. captives need to consider U.S. state insurance regulatory compliance issues in connection with engaging in insurance business in the United States. Domicile cost is an important consideration, but it needs to be understood in the context of the entire captive's purpose. Choosing a domicile location (domestic or foreign) based on its favorable tax scheme is not necessarily the best option, especially if it comes at the expense of the accessibility and flexibility of regulators. If a foreign domicile is chosen, one must consider the complexities involved with owning a foreign corporation, the application of the controlled foreign corporation income tax rules, tax reporting, and the consequences of an adverse finding by the IRS.[16]

The accessibility of a captive will facilitate the ability of management to leverage the captive. Accessibility includes geographic location, time zones, and required travel time for board meetings. Location of the captive may also drive other costs such as management and auditing fees.

X. MEETING WITH REGULATOR

Once a plan has been developed addressing the need for a captive, including an appropriate domicile to form the captive, a meeting with the regulator in the chosen domicile is typically required. A decision will be made as to whether to proceed, and if so, information will need to be gathered for the application process. Chapter 7 provides more detail about what transpires behind the scenes with a proposed captive from the viewpoint of the Vermont regulator. Among the items requested will be an actuarial report. As discussed in other areas of this book, this report is of vital importance, not only to help identify the viability of a proposed captive from the regulator's viewpoint, but to also withstand scrutiny from the IRS if the insured business is ever audited. Thus, choosing a domicile that both requires *and scrutinizes* an actuarial study should not be viewed as an impediment but rather as support for making an informed decision.

XI. CAPTIVE MANAGEMENT

Captives outsource establishment, management, and operation functions to captive managers. The captive manager typically acts to coordinate the various individuals and firms providing services to a captive. The captive manager is, in effect, the steward of the captive in the domicile, often acting as an extension of the regulatory to be sure that the captive activities follow the business plan.

The vast majority of captives are managed by third-party managers; it is the rare captive that is big enough to justify management via full-time employees. Captive managers are professional managers who function in much the same way as the management and accounting departments of a commercial insurer. They are generally trained as accountants and are typically licensed in the jurisdiction in which they operate. Captive managers are expert in local regulatory, financial, and administrative requirements of the captive operation, and often also have significant insurance expertise.

Figure 2.2 illustrates how captive managers generally operate, and demonstrates how they coordinate with other service providers.

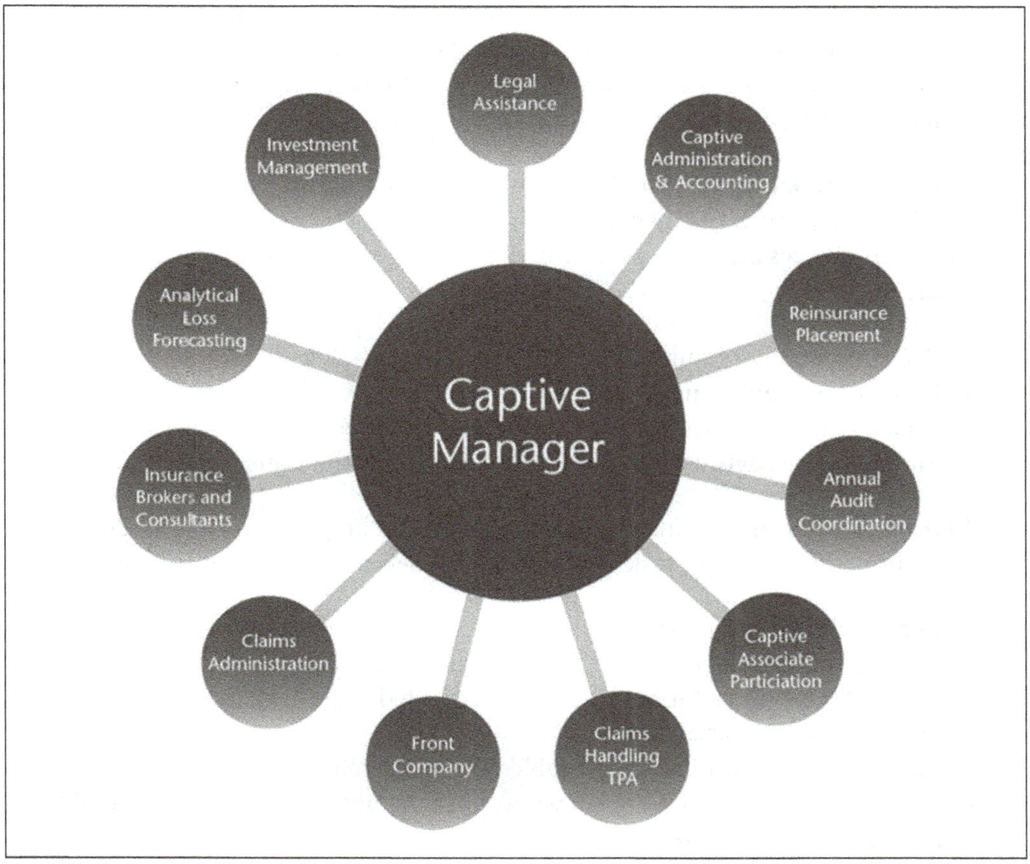

Figure 2.2 Captive Management Coordination
Diagram courtesy of Aon Captive Insurance Managers.

The duties of the captive manager include the following:

Regulatory compliance and corporate governance. The following items must be addressed to comply with regulations and corporate formalities:

1. Provide a director to serve on the captive board in order to demonstrate at least one outside director with insurance and captive knowledge.
2. Maintain all books and records to support the clean examination by the domicile department of insurance.
3. Assist auditors in the completion of the required annual audit of the captive financial records.
4. Provide loss information to the actuary to complete the required actuarial analysis of loss reserves.
5. Review the actuary's work for reasonableness.
6. Complete and file any other regulatory reports required on an annual/ quarterly basis.

7. Work with examiners to efficiently complete their examinations.
8. Arrange for the annual meeting of shareholders and directors, produce and distribute meeting materials, and invite the domicile regulator to part of the meeting if so desired.

Financial reporting. The captive should produce financial statements on a quarterly basis and report to the owner(s) their respective percentage share of the results.

Premium processing. The following duties are required for premium processing purposes:

- Record monthly premium.
- Record premium reinsured, if any.
- Establish and monitor unearned premium reserves.
- Monitor the provision of collateral/security from the reinsurers.

Claims processing. An insurance company must be prepared to process claims. Consequently, the following tasks must be addressed in claims processing:

- Record claims paid, loss reserves, and allocated loss expenses based on monthly loss reports received from the claims handler (TPA).
- Establish and update incurred but not reported (IBNR) reserves in line with management/actuarial advice.
- Monitor and record loss recoverables due from reinsurers.
- Loss reserves and IBNR are shown as gross liabilities, with loss recoverables from reinsurers as assets.
- Report losses recoverable from reinsurers to regulators.

Treasury and Investment Functions. Since the insurance company will receive funds, pay claims, and potentially cede risk to all reinsurers, the following items must be addressed:

- Monitoring of cash received by insured.
- Payment of reinsurance premiums.
- Monitoring of claims escrow account established with the claims handler (TPA) and claims paid on a monthly basis.
- Payment of quarterly estimated federal income tax deposits.
- Payment of quarterly premium taxes.
- Annual domicile state license fees paid.
- Recording of monthly accrued interest and bank fees.
- Monthly bank account reconciliation.

General and administrative expenses. The manager must also deal with expenses and the process for obtaining funds for payment of expenses. This entails preparing checks or wire transfers in accordance with pre-defined operating procedures, after receiving approval of expenditures. When the amount of a check or wire is above a pre-defined authority limit, the check or the wire transfer must be sent to the designated officer for a second signature or approval. The manager will also review invoices submitted for payment for reasonableness based on expected costs, (i.e., actuarial, audit, etc.).

Chapter 3

U.S. Taxation of U.S. Captives

James L. Mannello, Jeffrey J. Webb, and Charles J. Lavelle

Historically, a captive insurance company was an insurance company created and wholly owned by a non-insurance company to underwrite the risks for the operating subsidiaries and/or the parent company. This definition has been expanded over time to include assuming risks unrelated to the captive, most notably "controlled unaffiliated" risks, typically pool risks, customers or vendors. Captive insurance companies are typically formed to meet the risk-management needs of the owner and members; however, there may also be significant financial benefits associated with the structure. This chapter discusses captive insurance companies, including formation, qualifying as an insurance company for Federal income tax purposes, captive operations, alternative types of captive insurance companies, and termination of captive insurance companies. Unless otherwise specified, all Section or IRC references are to the Internal Revenue Code of 1986 (IRC), all "Treasury Regulation" references are to the regulations promulgated thereunder, both as amended through the date of this publishing.

I. INTRODUCTION TO TAXATION AND QUALIFICATION AS AN INSURANCE COMPANY

A. Initial Summary

Assuming a captive insurance company is feasible (as discussed in more detail in Chapter 2), the parent company that forms the captive will incur certain start-up costs related to the captive. Some of the start-up costs include captive manager and attorney fees for obtaining the captive's certificate of authority with the domiciliary captive insurance regulations, consulting fees for the feasibility study, and administrative fees for the state insurance applications. These start-up costs are generally eligible for current deduction, up to $5,000, with the remainder to be capitalized and amortized over 180 months as provided by Section 195. If the start-up expenditures exceed $50,000, this deduction is reduced by the excess and is then phased out dollar by dollar (up to $55,000).

The authors would like to thank Kristen Sorbera and Ross Cohen for their help in putting together this chapter.

In order to qualify as an insurance company for Federal income tax purposes, one must look to guidance from both the courts and the Internal Revenue Service (IRS or the Service). Qualifying as an insurance company for tax purposes largely rests upon a facts and circumstances analysis.[1] There are two preliminary matters: (1) non-tax business purpose and (2) the business of insurance. The Tax Court has described a three-pronged test for whether a transaction constitutes insurance, including whether: (1) there is risk shifting and risk distribution, (2) the transaction meets the "commonly accepted notions" of insurance, and (3) the presence of insurance risk. Should a captive qualify as an insurance company for Federal tax purposes, many benefits are afforded to the captive and insured, including deductible premiums and unpaid loss reserves as discussed in more detail later in the chapter.

B. Preliminary Matters

1. *Non-Tax Business Purpose*

While the courts have not formally articulated non-tax business purpose as a specific requirement of an insurance transaction, several cases have stated that the arrangement is not a sham or made similar references to business purpose.[2] All captive insurance arrangements would be best served to be established and maintained for non-tax business purposes.

2. *The "Business of Insurance"*

To begin, one must establish that the captive is conducting the business of insurance. The definition of an insurance company set forth in Treasury Regulation Section 1.801-3(a)(1) provides:

> The term "insurance company" means a company whose primary and predominant business activity during the taxable year is the issuing of insurance or annuity contracts or the reinsuring of risks underwritten by insurance companies. Thus, although its name, charter powers, and subjection to State insurance laws are significant in determining the business which a company is authorized and intends to carry on, it is the character of the business actually done in the taxable year which determines whether a company is taxable as an insurance company under the Internal Revenue Code.

Essentially, the character of the business activity actually performed in the taxable year determines whether an entity is an insurance company for U.S. Federal income tax purposes. If an entity is primarily engaged in the issuance of insurance or annuity contracts or the reinsuring of risks underwritten by insurance companies, then the entity should be subject to tax as an insurance company.[3]

Code Section 816(a) defines the term "insurance company" as "any company more than half of the business of which during the taxable year is the issuing of insurance or annuity contracts or reinsuring of risks underwritten by insurance companies." Section 831(c), which refers to 816(a), was added by The Pension Funding Act of

2004 (29 U.S.C. 1001) and now specifically applies the insurance company definition to property and casualty insurance companies, including captives.

It is important for captive insurance companies to be engaged in the typical operations of an insurance company.[4] These operations may include, but are not limited to, underwriting risk, earning investment income on premiums received from insured parties, and negotiating and entering into valid and binding insurance contracts. A captive insurance company should also be evaluating premium pricing and premium collection; managing investment activities; evaluating valuation of loss reserve adequacy; reporting and handling claims that include loss monitoring and loss prevention activities; and disbursing loss payments. Other activities, such as the meeting of the board of directors and administering record keeping, accounting, and financial reporting, should also be performed by the captive.

C. Insurance Tax Tests

The insurance tests are discussed in the following subsections:

1. *Risk Shifting*

Risk shifting involves one party transferring its risk of loss to another. The Joint Committee on Taxation has stated:[5]

> The concept of risk shifting refers to the fact that a risk of loss is shifted from one individual insured to the insurer (and the insurance pool managed by the insurer). For example under a fire insurance policy, the property owner's risk of loss from a fire (and the resulting damage costs) is shifted from the owner to the insurance company to the extent that the insurance proceeds from the contract will reimburse the owner for that loss.

Although the Code and Treasury Regulations define "insurance company," neither defines "insurance." Instead, case law defines insurance as involving risk shifting and risk distribution.[6] The earlier cases often spoke of risk shifting and risk distribution as one test, and often put more emphasis on risk shifting. Currently, the courts appear to accept that risk shifting has occurred if there is a transfer of risk to an insurance company with sufficient net worth to bear that risk, and no other person or entity has guaranteed the captive's performance; those courts appear to treat risk distribution as a more independent factor and place more emphasis on it. The following discussion of the earlier cases involving risk shifting reflects the case law as issued by the courts at the time.

Traditionally, in analyzing whether risk has indeed shifted and an arrangement constitutes insurance, it was necessary to analyze the affiliates and/or third parties that are being insured. With respect to insuring affiliates, courts have generally adopted a balance sheet and net worth approach to determine whether risk has shifted.[7] Under this balance sheet and net worth approach, a determination of whether risk has shifted depends on whether a covered loss affects the balance sheet and net worth of the insured.[8] With respect to third-party risk and risk shifting, courts and the Service generally adopt thresholds for what amount of third-party insured risk is sufficient for a captive arrangement to constitute insurance for parent-subsidiary captive arrangements.[9]

Originally, the IRS ruled that an arrangement will not be considered insurance when a captive insures the risks of its parent corporation.[10] However, the Service has provided guidance with respect to when a wholly owned captive subsidiary insuring the risk of its parent will qualify as insurance for Federal tax purposes. In Revenue Ruling 2002-89,[11] the Service addressed two situations in which a wholly owned captive insured the professional liability risks of its parent company, directly or through reinsurance, as well as homogeneous risks[12] of unrelated, third parties.

In situation 1 from Revenue Ruling 2002-89,[13] the premiums and risks assumed from the parent were 90 percent of the captive subsidiary's total risks for its taxable year, with the remaining 10 percent being unrelated risks. In this instance, the Service concluded that this arrangement was not insurance, because the requisites of risk shifting and risk distribution were not present because such a large portion of the premiums and risks were received from the parent.

In situation 2 from Revenue Ruling 2002-89,[14] the premiums and risks received from the parent were less than 50 percent of the captive subsidiary's total risks assumed for its taxable year, with the remainder of the risks being unrelated risks. Accordingly, the Service concluded that the arrangement was insurance and that the premiums paid by the parent were deductible as insurance premiums under Section 162. The ruling concedes that, assuming the remainder of the arrangement is appropriate, greater than 50 percent of unrelated risk establishes insurance between a parent and a captive subsidiary, while only 10 percent does not in the commissioner's view.

Carnation Co. v. Commissioner marked the first time that the Tax Court analyzed Parent-Subsidiary ("Parent-Sub Arrangement") captive arrangements.[15] In *Carnation*, the parties entered into two insurance contracts: an agreement between Carnation and an unrelated insurer, and a reinsurance agreement between the captive and the unrelated insurer (commonly referred to as a fronting arrangement). The unrelated insurer expressed concern to Carnation about the captive's financial stability and requested a letter of credit or other guarantee. In response, Carnation refused to provide a letter of credit or other guarantee, but did execute an agreement to provide $2,800,000 of additional capital on demand to the captive. The agreement was seen by the Tax Court as a form of parental guarantee of the operations of the captive, because the capital was available on demand. Due to this agreement, the Tax Court found that insurance risk did not exist and that risk had not shifted away from Carnation to the captive, as the ultimate risk still fell upon the parent.

Clougherty Packing Co. v. Commissioner was the Tax Court's next opportunity to analyze Parent-Sub arrangements.[16] In *Clougherty*, the parties entered into two insurance contracts: an agreement between Clougherty and an unrelated insurer, and a reinsurance agreement between the unrelated insurer and the captive (a fronting arrangement). The captive was a wholly owned subsidiary of the insured, Clougherty. There was no parental guarantee from Clougherty on the operations of the captive. The Tax Court analyzed Clougherty's balance sheet, and held that risk did not shift to the captive, because the risks borne by the parent were still on the parent's balance sheet as the captive reinsured the parent's risks.

Similar to *Carnation* and *Clougherty*, the Tax Court in *Humana Inc. & Subs. v. Commissioner* was faced with a captive arrangement. Specifically, the Tax Court considered the deductibility of premiums in two situations: premiums paid to a wholly owned captive subsidiary by the parent, known as a Parent-Sub arrangement, and premiums paid by affiliated subsidiaries to an affiliated sibling captive ("Brother-Sister Arrangement").[17] A total of three policies were issued during the taxable years in question, which provided coverage to 22 insured affiliates for years one and two, and 48 insured affiliates for year three.[18]

With respect to the Parent-Sub Arrangement, the Tax Court held that the premiums were not deductible because Humana did not shift risk to the captive.[19] The Brother-Sister arrangement presented an issue of first impression for the Tax Court. The Tax Court in *Humana* extended its rationale from *Carnation*[20] and *Clougherty*,[21] (both finding that a captive insuring the risks of a parent was not insurance) to the Brother-Sister Arrangement, because declining to do so "would exalt form over substance and permit a taxpayer to circumvent [the Tax Court's] holdings by simple corporate structural changes."[22]

On appeal, the Sixth Circuit affirmed the Tax Court's decision relating to a Parent-Sub Arrangement, but reversed the Tax Court's decision relating to a Brother-Sister Arrangement.[23] The Sixth Circuit stated that the test for determining whether a transaction can be classified as insurance is whether there is risk shifting and risk distribution. The Sixth Circuit adopted the Ninth Circuit's balance sheet and net worth approach in *Clougherty* to determine whether risk had shifted. Under this balance sheet and net worth approach, a determination of whether risk has shifted depends on whether a covered loss affects the balance sheet and net worth of the insured.[24]

The Sixth Circuit went on to address the Tax Court's assertion of form over substance by turning to the economic reality of the insurance arrangement between the Humana subsidiaries and reinsurance companies. In particular, the Sixth Circuit stated that where the subsidiaries own no stock in the reinsurance company and the reinsurance company owns no stock in the subsidiaries, the net worth of the Humana subsidiaries is not reduced when a loss occurs and is paid by the reinsurance company.[25] Relying on the Ninth Circuit's balance sheet and net worth analysis, the court held that "[t]he subsidiaries, balance sheets and net worth are not affected by the payment of an insured claim by [the captive]" and that "[i]n reality, therefore, when the Humana subsidiaries pay their own premiums under their own insurance contracts, as the facts show, *they shift their risk to* [the captive]" (emphasis added).[26]

In *Malone & Hyde*, similar to *Humana*, the captive assumed its parent's and brother-sister entities' risk; in *Malone & Hyde*, this was accomplished through a reinsurance agreement with a domestic fronting insurance company.[27] However, unlike the situation in *Humana*, where the parent had difficulty obtaining insurance from an unrelated carrier, the Appeals Court found that Malone & Hyde had no such problems. Rather, Malone & Hyde, "without any legitimate [business] reason, devised the circuitous scheme for realizing tax deductions."[28] Also in contrast to *Humana*, where the captive was fully capitalized under state law, Malone & Hyde's captive was capitalized only to meet the minimum requirements under Bermuda law, and Malone & Hyde entered into a "hold harmless" agreement with the fronting insurer, which provided that the fronting insurer was guaranteed not to be held responsible if the captive defaulted on its obligations as a reinsurer. With the existence of the "hold harmless" agreement, there was no risk shifting to the captive. The Appeals Court further found that there was no proof "that Bermuda exercised oversight similar to that which Colorado exercised over Humana's captive insurer."[29]

The Tax Court analyzed *Humana* in upholding a captive insurance arrangement between affiliated subsidiaries in *Rent-A-Center, Inc. and Affiliated Subsidiaries v. Commissioner.*[30] In *Rent-A-Center,* Rent-A-Center, Inc. (RAC) was the parent of approximately 4 to 15 affiliated subsidiaries depending on the year (see paragraph 58 of petitioner's opening brief). Through its subsidiaries, RAC rented, sold, and delivered home electronics, furniture, and appliances. From 2003 through 2007, RAC's subsidiaries owned between 2,623 and 3,081 stores, had between 14,300 and 19,740 employees, and operated between 7,143 and 8,027 insured vehicles. Faced with rising insurance costs, RAC, the holding company, formed Legacy Insurance Co., Ltd, a wholly owned Bermudan insurance company (Legacy).

From 2003 through 2007, the subsidiaries of RAC obtained unbundled workers' compensation, automobile, and general liability policies from Discover Re. The Discover Re policies provided the subsidiaries of RAC with coverage above a predetermined loss threshold and Legacy, in turn, wrote policies that covered RAC's workers' compensation, automobile, and general liability claims below the Discover Re threshold. The RAC subsidiaries could seek payment (depending on the amount of a loss) from Legacy, Discover Re, or both companies.

In order to meet certain solvency requirements under Bermudan law, Legacy utilized deferred tax assets and a guarantee from RAC. The Tax Court overruled its previous finding from *Humana* that insurance premiums in a Brother-Sister arrangement are not deductible.[31] Citing the Sixth Circuit's holding in the appeal from *Humana*, the Tax Court, in analyzing whether the arrangement possessed adequate risk shifting, narrowed its scrutiny to the economic impact of the arrangement between Legacy and RAC's subsidiaries and whether Legacy's policies did indeed shift risk.[32] In ruling for RAC, the Tax Court found that the policies at issue did shift risk from RAC's insured subsidiaries to Legacy and stated that Legacy (1) was formed for a valid business purpose; (2) was a separate, independent, and viable entity; (3) was financially capable of meeting its obligations; and (4) reimbursed RAC's subsidiaries when they suffered a loss. Moreover, a payment from Legacy to the subsidiaries did not reduce the net worth of the subsidiaries, because the subsidiaries did not own stock in Legacy.[33] Additionally, the Tax Court found that the guarantee of the deferred tax asset did not prevent risk from shifting because the guarantee was not on the insurance obligations and operations of Legacy, but on the unrelated deferred tax asset.[34] See also *Securitas v. Commissioner,* T.C. Memo 2014-225.[35]

2. *Risk Distribution*

Risk distribution involves the party onto whom risk is shifted spreading a portion of that risk among others. The Joint Committee on Taxation has stated that

> The concept of risk distribution . . . relies on the law of large numbers. That is, within a group of a large number of individual insureds who share a similar type of risk of loss, only a certain number will actually suffer the loss within any defined period of time. When a loss is suffered by any insured, each individual insured makes a contribution through the payment of premiums toward indemnifying the loss suffered.[36]

As defined by the courts, risk distribution is viewed from the insurer's perspective, through distributing risk amongst multiple risks and the application of the "law of large numbers." Risk distribution can be achieved by insuring a statistically significant number of risks; taxpayers believe this can occur without regard to the number of insured entities.[37]

In Revenue Ruling 2002-90,[38] the Service established a safe harbor rule that a captive arrangement that includes at least 12 sibling corporations would satisfy the risk-shifting and risk-distribution tests, where none of the operating subsidiaries' coverages constituted less than 5 percent, nor more than 15 percent, of the overall risk. The number 12 does not appear to be held out as a minimum standard, but is just one of a few factors outlined within the revenue ruling. There have been multiple cases in which the courts have decided that various numbers of policyholders constitute an adequate insurance risk pool for risk distribution purposes.[39]

In Revenue Ruling 2005-40,[40] the Service set forth four situations addressing whether amounts paid to a company that might qualify as an insurer are deductible as insurance premiums and whether the purported insurer qualifies as an insurance company for Federal income tax purposes.

In situation 1 of Revenue Ruling 2005-40, the taxpayer operates a courier transport business covering a large portion of the United States and entered into an arrangement with an unrelated domestic corporation whereby in exchange for an agreed amount of "premiums," the unrelated domestic corporation "insures" the taxpayer against the risk of loss arising out of the operation of its fleet in the conduct of its courier business. In situation 1, the Service found that while the arrangement may have shifted risks from one corporation to another, those risks were not distributed among other insureds or policyholders, and therefore the arrangement does not constitute insurance for Federal income tax purposes.

In situation 2 from Revenue Ruling 2005-40, the facts are the same as situation 1, except that, in addition to the unrelated corporation entering into an arrangement to insure one taxpayer, it also enters into an arrangement to insure an additional unrelated corporation. The second insured paid 10 percent of the premiums; the first insured paid 90 percent of the premium. The Service found that the arrangement with the second unrelated corporation did not change the conclusion that the arrangement between the first two unrelated corporations does not constitute insurance, as risk is not being distributed among multiple insureds.

Situations 3 and 4 of Revenue Ruling 2005-40[41] contain a fact pattern similar to *Humana*.[42] In these situations, the Service addresses if an arrangement constitutes insurance when a domestic corporation operates a business covering a large portion of the United States through 12 limited liability companies (LLCs). These LLCs own and operate a large fleet of automotive vehicles representing a significant volume of independent, homogeneous risks. The 12 LLCs entered into an arrangement with an unrelated corporation whereby in exchange for an agreed upon premium, the unrelated corporation insures the 12 LLCs against the risk of loss arising out of its operations. In both situations, none of the LLCs accounted for less than 5 percent nor more than 15 percent of the total risk assumed by the unrelated company. Both situations describe the same fact pattern, apart from the fact that (1) situation 3 involves LLCs that are disregarded for tax purposes[43] and (2) situation 4 involves LLCs that are regarded for tax purposes. The Service ruled that situation 4 distributed risk appropriately, as the entities were regarded as separate legal entities for tax purposes, whereas risk was not distributed where the entities were not separately regarded for tax purposes in situation 3.[44]

Outside income tax purposes, single member LLCs are often not disregarded (that is, they are treated as separate entities). A disregarded single-member LLC ("SMLLC") will not be disregarded for employment tax purposes.[45] Similarly, a disregarded SMLLC will not be disregarded for excise tax purposes. TAM 201116019 provides that a SMLLC cannot be disregarded for collection purposes. An SMLLC is not disregarded for estate and gift tax purposes.[46]

The other means of achieving risk distribution is via insurance of third-party or outside risk. As discussed earlier, Revenue Ruling 2002-89[47] provides guidance on the level of outside risk necessary for risk distribution to exist. In this ruling, the Service stated that risk distribution was present and that insurance premiums paid by the parent to the captive would be considered deductible insurance premiums provided the insurer underwrites at least 50 percent unrelated risk.

Courts have held that a different level of unrelated risk than specified in Revenue Ruling 2002-89 also satisfies the risk distribution requirement. Three such cases involved captives that underwrote at various times approximately 50, 29, and 99 percent unrelated risk, respectively.[48] In all three cases, the Tax Court held that the related party premiums paid were deductible, and the Seventh and Ninth Circuit Courts of Appeal affirmed these decisions. In *Ocean Drilling & Exploration Company v. United States*, the Federal Circuit affirmed per curium a decision of the now-Court of Federal Claims that 44 percent and 66 percent unrelated business was sufficient for risk distribution.[49] In *Avrahami v. Commissioner*,[50] the Tax Court found that the pooling entity was not a bona fide insurance company, and thus ignored the unrelated business that it insured with the captive. The Tax Court did not address the extent to which the captive had assumed the liability for those risks from an economic sense, and the effect on the risk distribution analysis.

In a Brother-Sister Arrangement, some cases have focused on the presence of a large number of risk exposures as sufficient element of insurance, rather than the number of insured entities. Risk distribution has generally been understood as involving the "law of large numbers," where, from a statistical view, as a sample size grows, its mean will get closer and closer to the average of the whole population.

The Tax Court in *Rent-A-Center*, discussed earlier, much like in *Malone & Hyde* and *Securitas*, did not address what specific number of insured entities is required for true insurance and what level of risk concentration amongst the insured subsidiaries is permissible.[51] Instead, and of note, the Tax Court looked at "the *actions of the insurer* because it is the insurer's, not the insured's, risk that is reduced by risk distribution."[52] In doing so, the Tax Court opined that risk is distributed where the insurer assumes numerous relatively small, independent risks that occur randomly over time, which allows the insurer to more accurately predict expected future losses. Given this, the Tax Court indicates that the "law of large numbers" does not look to the number of entities that are insured, but the unit of risk and the aggregate amount of insured activities. This is consistent with the Tax Court's opinion in *Malone & Hyde* (see footnote 36 above). In *Rent-A-Center,* the Tax Court found that the requirement of risk distribution was met, based on the thousands of store locations, employees, and vehicles that were insured.[53]

Recently, the Tax Court buttressed this view that the law of large numbers requires an analysis of the insured's operations (as opposed to strictly the number of insured entities) in *Securitas Holdings, Inc. and Subsidiaries v. Commissioner* by citing *Rent-A-Center* and finding that risk was properly distributed where the petitioner employed approximately 100,000 people and operated over 2,250 vehicles.[54] Specifically, the court stated that an insurer achieves risk distribution when it pools a large enough collection of unrelated risks, those not generally affected by the same circumstances. In *Securitas*, the taxpayer insured five types of risks for over 100,000 people in 20 different countries. The court also stated that risk distribution is viewed from the insurer's perspective, and as a result of the large and diverse number of employees, offices, vehicles, and services provided by Securitas, the company was exposed to a large pool of statistically independent risk exposures.

3. "Commonly Accepted Notions of Insurance"

In addition to the risk shifting and risk transfer requirements articulated earlier, courts have also looked to whether a company's arrangements are consistent with commonly accepted notions of insurance when determining insurance company status for Federal income tax purposes.[55] TAM 200827006 states "the 'commonly accepted sense' of insurance derives from all the facts surrounding each case, with emphasis on comparing the implementation of the arrangement with that of known insurance."[56]

In *Kidde Industries v. Commissioner*, Kidde was a broad-based, decentralized conglomerate with 100 wholly owned subsidiaries.[57] Kidde had insurance agreements with commercial insurers, but in the midst of a products liability insurance crisis, Kidde was informed that its products liability insurance policy would not be renewed. In order to procure insurance at a reasonable rate, Kidde created a captive insurance company. The Court of Federal Claims explicitly refuted the Service's contention that the captive arrangement in that case was inconsistent with the commonly accepted notion of insurance. The Federal Claims Court found that the captive met the commonly accepted notion of insurance requirement as the written insurance agreement had the effect of allocating risk, because premiums were determined through typical industry means (i.e., in reference to estimates of future claims), and because, from a claimant's perspective, the captive acted as any other independent insurance company.[58] The Court of Federal Claims also disagreed with the Service's claims that the captive's organizational structure and internal operation were inconsistent with the commonly accepted notion of insurance. The Court of Federal Claims stated:

> As to Kidde's control over [the captive], staffing [the captive] with Kidde employees suggests that Kidde not only wanted to take advantage of the expertise of its own employees in overseeing [the captive's] operation but also wanted to keep firm control over [the captive's] day-to-day operations. But assuming that such a close relationship between the insured and insurer is relatively rare, Kidde's aims would not be inherently inconsistent with [the captive] creating what amounts to a traditional insurer-insured relationship with respect to future claims against Kidde. As to [the captive] "contracting out" most typical insurance functions, it would not seem unreasonable for [the captive] to do so when [the captive] first entered the insurance business. Through such contracts, a new entrant into the industry could eliminate uncertainty as to the cost of performing certain services and thereby secure greater predictability as to its operational costs.[59]

As such, the Court of Federal Claims concluded that Kidde's captive arrangement was consistent with the commonly accepted notions of insurance, and outsourcing the operational aspects of the captive served to eliminate uncertainty in captive costs. See also, Revenue Ruling 2009-89, which provides that some of the operational aspects could be outsourced.

In *Harper Group*,[60] the Harper Group operated similarly to the captive insurance company in *Kidde*. The Harper Group was a California corporation that owned various subsidiaries in the United States and throughout the world. The subsidiaries engaged in a number of businesses related to the international shipment of cargo by air and sea, and incurred liabilities in numerous fashions. In 1974, Harper Group management decided to create a captive insurance company to provide insurance historically provided by commercial insurers to Harper. The Tax Court summarized a structure, which it held to satisfy this standard, as follows:[61]

> [The captive insurer] was both organized and operated as an insurance company. It was regulated by the Insurance Registry of Hong Kong. The adequacy of [the captive's] capitalization is not in dispute. The premiums charged by [the captive] to its affiliates . . . were the result of arm's-length transactions. The policies issued by [the captive] were valid and binding. In sum, such policies were insurance policies and the arrangements between [the insured affiliates] and [the captive] constituted insurance, in the commonly accepted sense.

By finding that Harper's captive operation contained the common notions of insurance, the Tax Court made it clear that being properly organized and operating as an insurance company, including adequate capitalization, arms-length premiums, and valid policies, is an integral part of qualifying as an insurance company for Federal income tax purposes.

In *Avrahami*, the Tax Court stated that in the prior cases, the Tax Court had looked at a number of factors in deciding if it "*looks* like insurance in the commonly accepted sense."[62] The *Avrahami* case reviewed: whether the captive was organized, operated, and regulated as an insurance company; whether it was adequately capitalized; whether the policies were valid and binding; whether the premiums were reasonable and the result of an arm's-length transaction; and whether claims were paid. The *Avrahami* opinion stated that some of these criteria were successfully met, but, overall, the arrangement was not insurance in its commonly accepted sense because the captive was not operated as an insurance company, the premiums were wholly unreasonable and the policies were unclear and contradictory. The *Avrahami* opinion states that prior Tax Court opinions in other cases had also looked at whether the policies covered typical insurance risks, and whether there was a legitimate business reason for acquiring insurance from the captive, but the *Avrahami* opinion did not address these two items.

4. *Presence of Insurance Risk*

It is generally accepted that insurance risk involves fortuity; the Service has stated that insurance risk "must contemplate the fortuitous [that is, uncertain] occurrence of a stated contingency."[63] In Revenue Ruling 2007-47, the Service provides guidance that insurance risk must be that of real fortuity and not a risk of "whether estimated present value of the cost of performing measures to fix a liability would accrue to exceed the cost of the greater of a company's cost to program the required measures or contract limit."[64] In Revenue Ruling 2007-47, the taxpayer was engaged in a hazardous business that required remediation upon its commencement; a nuclear power plant (requiring decommissioning upon termination) or strip mining (requiring reclamation upon termination) would be examples of such a business.

It is important to note that the Service's definition of insurance risk is narrower than the definition expressed by the courts. At times, the Service has attempted to limit the definition of insurance risk and exclude from the definition what it calls "business risk." The courts have excluded investment risk but, to date, have not excluded business risk from the definition of insurance risk. In ILM 201511021, the Service stated that "not all contracts that transfer risk are insurance policies, even where the primary purpose of the contract is to transfer risk."[65] The Service concluded an arrangement between members of a taxpayer group and the group's affiliated insurance company involving foreign currency fluctuations did not constitute insurance because the risk was merely an investment risk.[66] The Service stated that "insurance risk requires a fortuitous event or hazard, and not a mere timing or investment risk; a fortuitous event is at the heart of any contract of insurance."

Revenue Ruling 89-96,[67] also known as the MGM Fire ruling, further discusses insurance risk, where a company obtained retroactive liability insurance to provide coverage for a loss that had already occurred. The expected losses far exceeded the layer of coverage that was purchased. Although the contracts created certain risks for the insurer, those risks were seen as investment risks and not insurance risks. This is due to the fact that the only risks borne by the insurer were (1) that it would be required to make payments with respect to a known loss earlier than expected, and (2) that the available investment yield between the time of payment of the premiums and the time of payment of the claims will be lower than expected. As such, the IRS concluded the policies lacked the uncertainty and fortuity required for insurance risk. Compare CCA 200628018 (7/14/06) (an embedded express warranty is not an insurance risk) with CCA 200631002 (8/14/06) and PLR 200811009 (11/15/07) (extended warranties are insurance risks).

More recently, in *R.V.I. Guaranty Co.*, the taxpayer, R.V.I., sold contracts that insured against the risk that the residual value of a leased asset upon termination would be significantly lower than expected.[68] The IRS concluded that the policies offered by R.V.I. did not involve insurance risk, but investment risk. The Tax Court disagreed, stating that residual value policies carry a similar risk to mortgage guaranty or municipal bond insurance.[69] The court concluded that the policies contained insurance risk, as various macroeconomic events, such as a real-estate market collapse, or hazardous events, such as a car crashing, may occur and cause the policies to pay out their losses. R.V.I. was at risk for significant underwriting losses unrelated to its investment returns, because depending on the occurrence of fortuitous events, losses insured vary from zero to the full insured value.[70]

It is a commonly accepted practice to perform or obtain an actuarial study that considers whether sufficient risk transfer is present to constitute insurance.

FAS 113 paragraph 9[71] states:

> *Indemnification of the ceding enterprise against loss or liability relating to insurance risk in reinsurance of short-duration contracts requires both of the following, unless the condition I paragraph 11 is met:*
>
> *a. The reinsurer assumes significant insurance risk under the reinsured portions of the underlying insurance contracts.*
>
> *b. It is reasonably possible that the reinsurer may realize a significant loss from the transaction.*
>
> *A reinsurer shall not be considered to have assumed significant insurance risk under the reinsured contracts if the probability of a significant variation in either the amount or timing of payments by the reinsurer is remote.*

Specifically, the Paragraph 11 exception states:

> *Significance of loss shall be evaluated by comparing the present value of all cash flows, determined as described in paragraph 10, with the present value of the amounts paid or deemed to have been paid to the reinsurer. If, based on this comparison, the reinsurer is not exposed to the reasonable possibility of significant loss, the*

ceding enterprise shall be considered indemnified against loss or liability relating to insurance risk only if substantially all of the insurance risk relating to the reinsured portions of the underlying insurance contracts has been assumed by the reinsurer.

Actuarial guidance published by the American Academy of Actuaries Committee on Property and Liability Financial Reporting (COPLFR) issued a Practice Note (Reinsurance Attestation Supplement 20-1: Risk Transfer Testing Practice Note) in January 2007 on testing for risk transfer. The Practice Note provides guidance on when risk transfer for a reinsurance contract is reasonably self-evident. Page 15 of COPLFR's Practice Note states: "Risk transfer is reasonably self-evident in most traditional per-risk or per-occurrence excess of loss reinsurance contracts. For these contracts, a predetermined amount of premium is paid and the reinsurer assumes nearly all or all of the potential variability in the underlying losses, and it is evident from reading the basic terms of the contract that the reinsurer can incur a significant loss..." Reinsurance contracts that are reasonably self-evident for risk transfer do not require explicit risk transfer testing. Examples of this would be reinsurance for catastrophic events such as property reinsurance for hurricanes or product liability reinsurance coverage for mass tort pharmaceuticals.

For contracts where risk transfer is not reasonably self-evident a typical risk transfer analysis involves performing a statistical exercise to ensure that there is a sufficient transfer of timing and event risk from the insured to the insurer(s) and there is a reasonable possibility that the insurer(s) may incur a significant loss in present value on this contract. Neither accounting nor actuarial standards define the terms "reasonably possible" or "significant loss". However, the 10/10 rule is a frequently cited test for determining whether or not there is risk transfer. This rule defines a significant loss as a loss of at least ten percent of premium. It also defines this loss to be reasonably possible if there is at least a ten percent chance of such a loss. In other words, risk transfer would exist if there is at least a ten percent chance that the present value of losses exceeds 110 percent of the premium paid.

For contracts where risk transfer is not reasonably self-evident a typical risk transfer analysis involves performing a statistical exercise to ensure that there is a sufficient transfer of timing and event risk from the insured to the insurer(s) and there is a reasonable possibility that the insurer(s) may incur a significant loss in present value on this contract. For reinsurance, the CPAs judge whether there is a significant (10 percent) chance of a significant (10 percent) loss.

II. QUALIFYING AS AN INSURANCE COMPANY

Earlier, we identified two preliminary considerations in determining if an arrangement is insurance for Federal income tax purposes: (1) non-tax business purpose and (2) business of insurance. In addition, there is a three-pronged facts and circumstances-based analysis outlined by the courts, and guidance from the Service, discussed earlier. The three prongs of the test include (1) risk shifting and risk distribution, (2) commonly accepted notions of insurance, and (3) insurance risk. Should a company pass the two preliminary considerations and all three prongs of the tests, there is a greater likelihood of qualifying as an insurance company for Federal income tax purposes.

III. ALTERNATIVE CAPTIVE TAXING REGIME: SMALL INSURANCE COMPANY—SECTION 831(b) ELECTION

A. Summary of Section 831(b)

An alternative captive taxing structure, known as a small insurance company, or 831(b) captive, by making an election under Section 831(b), Alternative Tax for Certain Small Insurance Companies. If an insurance company qualifies for, and makes, the election, the company is taxed on its investment income alone.[72] Section 831(b) applies to all insurance companies other than life insurance companies,[73] if the net written premiums for the taxable year do not exceed $2,200,000, indexed for inflation, such company meets certain diversification requirements under Section 831(b)(2)(B), and such company elects the application of Section 831(b), as well as qualifies as an insurance company for tax purposes, as discussed in detail in the preceding pages.[74] In 2015, the Protecting Americans from Tax Hikes Act (PATH)[75] raised the allowable premiums threshold from $1,200,000 to $2,200,000 (indexed) and adding diversification requirements for all prospective 831(b) insurance companies, effective for taxable years beginning after December 31, 2016. Under Notice 2017-58, pursuant to the indexing, the cap is $2,300,000 for 2018.

The diversification requirements are met if (1) no more than 20 percent of net written premiums (or, if greater, direct written premiums) of such company for the taxable year is attributable to one policyholder (after attribution), or (2) no one person who holds an interest in such insurance company is a "specified holder" who holds interests in the company that are more than 2 percent higher than the percentage of interest held in the specified assets of the insurance company.[76] For the second requirement, a specified holder refers to any individual/natural person who holds an interest in the insurance company and is a lineal descendant and/or spouse of an individual who holds an interest in the assets of the insurance company,[77] and specified assets refers to the trades or business, rights, or assets with respect to which the net written premiums of such insurance company are paid.[78]

Additionally, all prospective Section 831(b) insurance companies must abide by the controlled group rules of Section 831(b)(2)(B). These rules state that all premiums received in a controlled group,[79] where a controlled group includes all members with more than 50 percent ownership by the parent, are to be counted together in determining the premium limit requirement. It should be noted that much IRS scrutiny has been seen in the 831(b) captive realm recently. Certain 831(b) captive structures that the IRS perceives as abusive have recently been on the IRS's "Dirty Dozen" list of tax items the Service has put under extra scrutiny.[80]

B. Caveat Regarding IRS Notice 2016-66 on Micro-Captives

On November 1, 2016, the IRS released Notice 2016-66 (the Notice), which alerts taxpayers and their representatives that certain "micro-captive" transactions have been identified as "transactions of interest." The Notice covers certain captive insurance transactions designed to take advantage of the IRC Section 831(b) election to be taxed on investment income only. Taxpayers who have entered into transactions described in the Notice, or substantially similar transactions, are now subject to certain reporting requirements under Treasury Regulation Section 1.6011-4(d).

The IRS's description of the micro-captive transaction of interest, found in Section 2.01 of the Notice, is as follows:

a. A person ("A") directly or indirectly owns an interest in an entity (or entities) conducting a trade or business and the business entity is the "Insured";
b. An entity or entities ("Captive") directly owned by A, Insured, or persons related to A or Insured, enters into a contract (or contracts) (the "Contracts") with Insured that Captive and Insured treat as insurance, or reinsures risks that Insured has initially insured with an intermediary, C;
c. Captive elects under § 831(b) to be taxed only on taxable investment income (the net premium written threshold for the election is $1.2 million through 2016 and increases to $2.2 million beginning in 2017);
d. A, Insured, or one or more persons related to A or Insured, directly own at least 20 percent of the voting power **or** value of the outstanding stock of Captive; **and**
e. One or both for the following apply:
   i. The amount of liabilities incurred by Captive for insured losses and claim administrative expenses during (in general) Captive's most recent five taxable years is less than 70 percent of Captive's premiums earned, less policyholder dividends paid; **or**
   ii. Captive has at any time during (in general) its most recent five taxable years directly or indirectly made financing available or otherwise "conveyed or agreed to make available or convey to A, Insured, or a person related to A or Insured, in a transaction that did not result in taxable income or gain to the recipient," any portion of the payments (premiums) under the Contract such as through a guarantee, loan, or other transfer of Captive's capital.

The Notice makes clear that a transaction described in Section 2.01 of the Notice is identified as a transaction of interest regardless of whether the transaction has characteristics of an abusive transaction. The Notice is part of the IRS's ongoing campaign to eliminate transactions being entered into for tax avoidance purposes. The IRS's increased focus on captive arrangements places additional stress on taxpayers to ensure they have valid, non-tax business purposes for establishing new captive arrangements and maintaining such arrangements. The IRS's designation of micro-captives as a new "campaign" issue of the Large Business & International (LB&I) unit ensures that controversies will continue to arise; therefore, having strong facts and circumstances is critical.

C. Avrahami v. Commissioner

In the first case involving an insurance company electing to be taxed under IRC Section 831(b), the Tax Court held in *Avrahami*, that the taxpayer's insurance arrangement was not insurance for Federal income tax purposes. The court found that there was no risk distribution (looking only at related insurance, there were not enough entities nor enough exposure units; there was no unrelated business because the pooling entity was not a bona fide insurance company), nor was the arrangement insurance in its commonly accepted sense (the captive was not operated like an insurance company, the premiums were wholly unreasonable, and the policies contained unclear and contradictory terms). No penalty was assessed against the insurance deduction because the taxpayers relied on their long-term estate planning lawyer and it was an area in which there was not previously guidance that was on point.

D. Section 831(b) Review

Accordingly, ongoing review of any captive that elects to be taxed on investment income only under Section 831(b) will be critical to identifying the captive's IRS reporting obligations. Any company continuing to conduct a captive Insurance Program must be able to prove that it entered into, and maintained, the arrangement for good non-tax business purposes, shifted and distributed insurance risks in an arrangement that was insurance in its commonly accepted sense. In today's environment, taxpayers must assume that they will not receive the benefit of the doubt, and their proof must be very persuasive.

IV. ALTERNATIVE CAPTIVE INSURANCE REGIME: EXEMPT INSURANCE COMPANIES—501(c)(15)

An alternative captive tax regime is available under Section 501(c)(15) that makes the captive exempt from Federal income tax. Under Section 501(c)(15), insurance companies where (1) controlled group gross receipts for the taxable year do not exceed $600,000, and (2) more than 50 percent of such gross receipts consist of premiums, are known as "exempt insurance companies." For mutual insurance companies (certain companies owned entirely by their policyholders), the gross receipts for the taxable year cannot exceed $150,000, and more than 35 percent of such gross receipts must consist of premiums. Should a company qualify as an "exempt insurance company," such company is exempt from income taxes under Section 501(c).[81]

V. TAXATION OF INSURANCE COMPANIES UNDER SUBCHAPTER L

An insurance company is a per se corporation under Section 7701(a)(3) and is taxable as a corporation even if it is not a corporation under state law.[82] Under Section 831(a), an insurance company is taxed on gross income minus deductions. Gross income, under Section 832(b), means the sum of gross amounts earned from investment income and underwriting income, as well as all other items constituting gross income under Subchapter B. Investment income refers to the gross amount of income earned during the taxable year from interest and dividends, and underwriting income refers to premiums earned on insurance contracts, less losses incurred and expenses incurred. Deductions allowed under Section 832(c) includes all ordinary and necessary expenses incurred, as provided in Section 162, as well as interest, taxes, and all other items deductible under Subchapter B.

When calculating premiums under Section 832(b)(4), insurance companies must take into account the concept of unearned premiums (UPR). Unearned premiums are the portion of the gross written premium allocable to the unexpired term of a contract. Premiums earned during the taxable year are calculated as follows: gross written premiums plus 80 percent of UPR at the prior year-end minus 80 percent of UPR at the current year-end. This is known as a 20 percent UPR haircut.

When calculating loss reserves, insurance companies must take into account loss reserve discounting under Section 846. For tax purposes, losses are discounted at set rates presented yearly by the IRS.[83] This discounting creates a book-tax difference that reverses as losses are paid.

VI. TREATMENT OF PREPAID INSURANCE BY THE PARENT OR RELATED PARTY

When a parent or related party pays a premium covering a future policy period to a captive insurance company, a prepaid insurance account is set up on the parent's or related party's books. Treasury Regulation 1.264(a)-4 provides guidance on the general rule of amounts paid to create intangibles, under which prepaid insurance falls. Generally speaking, when premiums are paid to the captive for a future policy period, an intangible of prepaid insurance is created, and such intangible must be capitalized. However, under the guidance provided in Treasury Regulation 1.264(a)-4(f), a taxpayer is not required to capitalize amounts of prepaid insurance where the benefit for the taxpayer does not extend past the earlier of 12 months after the first date on which the taxpayer realized the right or benefit or the end of the taxable year following the taxable year in which the payment is made. As such, premiums for prepaid insurance for one year or less, or up to the taxable year-end, is not required to be capitalized, and is taken as a tax deduction.[84]

VII. STATE TAXATION OF CAPTIVE INSURANCE COMPANIES

Captive insurance companies may be subject to taxation in their domiciles. These taxes include premium or surplus lines taxes. Many states impose a premiums tax on direct premiums written by admitted or licensed insurance companies. In general, the domiciliary state of the captive may impose a premiums tax based on the amount of premiums paid to the captive insurer.

Some states may also impose a self-procurement tax, where the insured, whether a parent or other related party, must pay taxes on insurance premiums that were independently procured and paid to a non-admitted insurer (i.e., an insurer that is not regulated by the domicile state of the insured and not on a surplus lines list). Generally, a self-procurement tax is only imposed on insureds, whether related or unrelated to the captive, which procure insurance from non-admitted insurers. In the captive context, this tax arises when the captive is not in the home state of the insured. This is an area where the industry expects increasing collection activity by the states in the future. If an arrangement is not insurance, a state may try to subject it to income tax.

VIII. FAILING TO QUALIFY AS A CAPTIVE INSURANCE COMPANY

Under Revenue Ruling 2005-40 and Revenue Ruling 2008-8, 2008-1 C.B. 340, if a captive insurance company fails to qualify as an insurance company due to lack of risk distribution, any premiums paid into the captive may be re-characterized as contributions of capital (to the extent of the value, if any), a deposit arrangement, a loan or an indemnity agreement that is not an insurance contract, or otherwise.[85] Presumably, payments under an indemnity agreement that is not an insurance contract are deductible by the insured as an ordinary and necessary business expense because the insured received a promise of indemnification which was of value, even if not technically insurance, and is income to the insurance company, but reserve deductions cannot be taken with respect to it.

In *Crawford Fitting Co. v. United States*, Crawford was a manufacturer of valves used by power plants and oil rigs.[86] The captive, Constance Insurance Company, was created due to Crawford's inability to secure insurance at a reasonable price and without substantial limitations on the types and amounts of risk. Constance insured more than 45 subsidiaries and five individuals, as well as 115 independent distributors, of which none had ownership of the captive.[87]

The Service disallowed the deduction for premiums paid to Crawford's captive, reasoning that the risks had been retained at the insured subsidiaries, and that the premiums constituted capital, not expenses.[88] However, the court found that the captive insurance company was a separate and independent corporate entity that provided insurance for Crawford that was unavailable or available only at higher rates.[89]

The court stated that diversity of ownership and just a few policyholders can create deductible premiums, even where one policyholder was responsible for indemnifying the others, and, as such, the taxpayer had shifted the risk of loss outside its economic family.[90] As such, the premiums were deductible as ordinary business expenses under Section 162, and not capital contributions.

However, had the premiums not been deductible as ordinary business expenses, they may have been seen as contributions to the capital of a corporation. Per Section 118, the general rule for contributions of capital is that the gross income of a corporation does not include any capital contributions. Instead of going into income, contributions of capital would increase the equity of the captive insurance company, being recorded to the balance sheet instead of the income statement, and as such, increasing the tax basis in the company. This is in contrast to *Crawford*, where premiums were deductible under Section 162.

As noted, alternatives to treatment as a capital contribution, should a captive insurance company fail to qualify as an insurance company, include the premium paid can be accounted for as a loan or a deposit by the insured entity. The basic concept of deposit accounting is that the amount paid to the captive insurance company is treated as a deposit and is reported on the balance sheet as an asset and a corresponding liability. The insured would treat the transaction as a reduction to cash with a corresponding receivable recorded. There is no income statement activity in the initial payment of the premium on either the insured or insurance company side.

Perhaps most importantly, should a captive fail to qualify as an insurance company for Federal tax purposes, it would not be able to establish and deduct loss reserves. Corporations generally follow the general provision provided under Section 461 to deduct insurance-type liabilities (i.e., workers compensation) on a paid basis. Qualifying captive insurance companies establish a deductible loss reserve under the insurance provisions of the Code in Subchapter L, Section 832, in the year that the loss is incurred, though it may take many years for the loss to be fully paid out.

IX. TREATMENT OF DIVIDENDS

Dividends are distributions of property, typically in the form of cash, paid by a corporation. Dividends can be received by both corporations and individuals, and must be paid out of the earnings and profits (E&P) of a corporation. Corporations that receive dividends are subject to a "double taxation" of the dividend: once at the corporate level and once at the shareholder level. In order to reduce this double taxation, Section 243 allows for a dividends received deduction, which allows a corporation to take a deduction equal to 50 percent, 65 percent, or 100 percent of the dividend received, based on the corporation's ownership in the company paying the dividend.

It is important to note that there are two different types of dividends for individual taxation: qualified and non-qualified. Qualified dividends, for individuals, are taxed at the lower long-term capital gains rates, whereas non-qualified dividends are taxed at the higher, ordinary income rates. Generally speaking, a dividend distribution from an onshore captive or a non-U.S. captive with a valid Section 953(d) election, will be a qualified dividend, subject to favorable long-term capital gains tax rate.

X. TERMINATION OF CAPTIVE INSURANCE COMPANIES

When winding down captive structures, it is important to consider the requirements and consequences of their dissolution. One item of importance is the treatment of the current policies in-force. Two options available for the treatment of policies in-force are (1) commutation, or exchange, to another insurance company, or (2) allowing the policies to run off. With either choice, all policies should be identified and catalogued, and no insurance liabilities should remain. In addition, it is important to take note of potential regulatory implications of the winding down as well as tax implications. Regulatory considerations may include discussions with the insurance state regulators in order to demonstrate that all obligations have been satisfied. Tax considerations include the gain/loss on the liquidating distributions of property, gain/loss on the sale of the company, or gain/loss on converting the current C-corporation captives into S-corporations. With all options, there will be required tax forms and disclosures required to be filed with the IRS and the state taxing authority.

XI. CAPTIVE INSURANCE COMPANY TAKEAWAYS

After formation, two preliminary items (non-tax business purpose and business of insurance) and a three-pronged test are applied to determine whether the captive is an insurance company for Federal income tax purposes. This test includes (1) risk shifting and risk distributions, (2) the commonly accepted notions of insurance, and (3) insurance risk. There are alternative types of captives available for small insurers, exempt insurance organizations, group captives, pooling facilities, cell scenarios, and a host of other structures. It is important for each company, entity, and individual or otherwise to understand its Insurance Program first, then understand if an alternative risk facility could be a good fit for its business.

Chapter 4

U.S. Taxation of Non-U.S. Captives[1]

P. Bruce Wright and Saren Goldner

I. INTRODUCTION

Non-U.S. captive insurance companies owned by U.S. persons are subject to a myriad of U.S. federal tax rules. In addition, even if such captives are ultimately owned only by non-U.S. persons, if the captive writes U.S. risks, some of the rules discussed in this chapter will apply. The application of many of these rules will depend on whether the transactions of the captive are characterized as insurance for federal income tax purposes,[2] and careful consideration should be given to this determination in order to properly apply the rules described in the following sections.

As discussed in more detail later, a non-U.S. captive is likely to be characterized as a controlled foreign corporation, (a CFC), and subject to U.S. withholding tax and the federal insurance excise tax. It will need to be careful to operate so that it is not characterized as engaged in a U.S. trade or business and therefore subject to U.S. federal income tax as well as the branch profits tax. Alternatively, a non-U.S. captive may (in certain circumstances) choose to make an election to be characterized as a U.S. domestic company for all federal tax purposes. After a separate discussion of each of these topics, there is a chart comparing CFC status to non-CFC status and the domestic election.

II. THE CONTROLLED FOREIGN CORPORATION (CFC) RULES

In general, under the CFC rules, certain U.S. persons[3] that have specified ownership interests in a non-U.S. corporation[4] characterized as a CFC are required to include amounts earned by the CFC in their U.S. federal gross income for the year the CFC earns the income.

There are three separate types of CFCs: a general CFC, an insurance CFC, and a related person insurance income or "RPII" CFC, and the income inclusion rules apply differently for each type of CFC. There are also special elections that non-U.S. insurance companies can make for alternate U.S. federal taxation regimes.

A. The General CFC Rules

1. *What Is a General CFC?*

A non-U.S. corporation is considered a general CFC if 10% U.S. Shareholders (as defined in the following paragraph) own (directly, indirectly through non-U.S. entities, or by application of the attribution rules of section[5] 958(b) (i.e., constructively)),[6] more than 50 percent of the total combined voting power of all classes of voting stock of such non-U.S. corporation or more than 50 percent of the total value of all stock of such corporation.[7]

A "10% U.S. Shareholder" is a U.S. person who owns (directly, indirectly through non-U.S. entities or constructively) at least 10 percent of the total combined voting power of all classes of stock entitled to vote of the non-U.S. corporation.[8]

Example 1

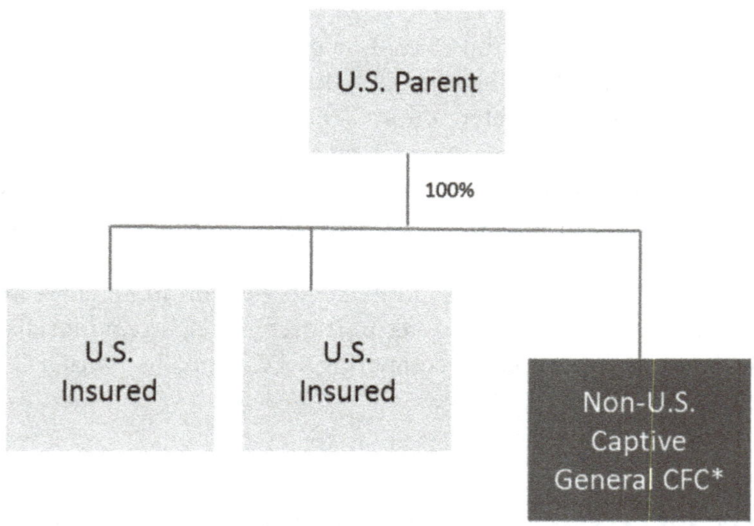

*Also insurance CFC, if earns insurance income; see also RPII rules.

Figure 4.1 Example of CFC Status

Example 2

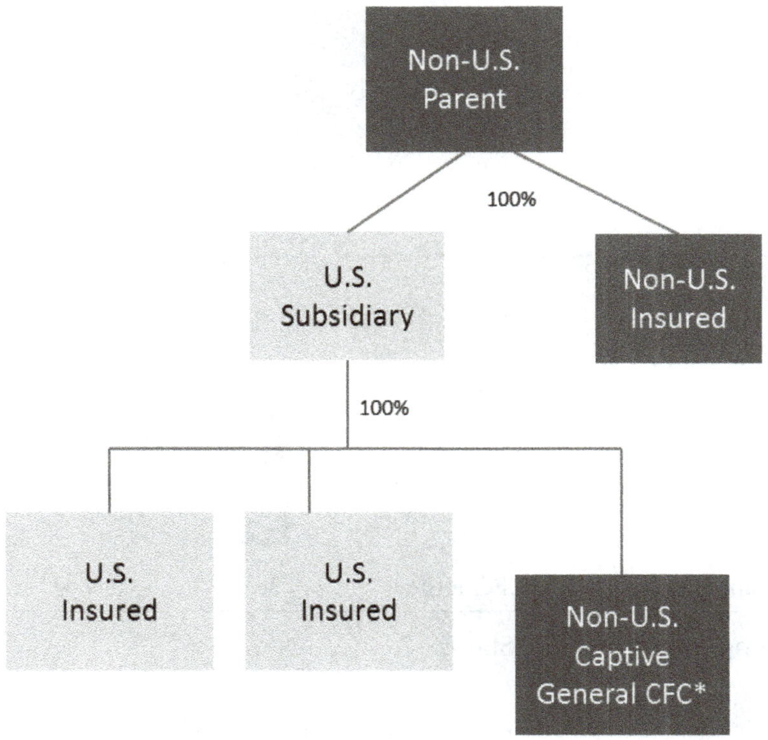

*Also insurance CFC, if earns insurance income; see also RPII rules.

Figure 4.2 Example of CFC Status

Example 3

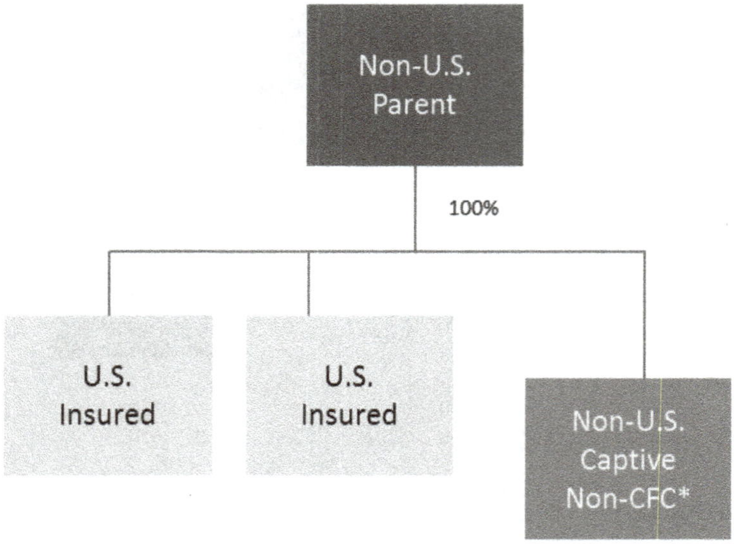

* Not an insurance CFC or RPII CFC either.

Figure 4.3 Example of Non-CFC Status†

2. Income Inclusions by General CFC Owners

Each 10% U.S. Shareholder of a non-U.S. corporation that is a CFC for an uninterrupted period of 30 days or more during a taxable year,[9] who owns shares in the non-U.S. corporation, directly or indirectly through non-U.S. entities,[10] on the last day of the non-U.S. corporation's taxable year on which it is a CFC must include in its gross income for U.S. federal income tax purposes its "pro rata share" of the CFC's "subpart F income," even if the subpart F income is not distributed.[11]

The pro rata share of such income is generally the amount that would have been distributed to the shareholder if all of the CFC's earnings and profits (as computed for U.S. federal income tax purposes) were distributed.[12] For these purposes, subpart F income of a non-U.S. captive will typically include foreign personal holding company income (such as dividends, interest, notional principal contract income, and other passive income) and/or insurance income (if the non-U.S. company earns insurance income).[13]

If a CFC has losses in one year and earnings in a later year, 10% U.S. Shareholders may be able to offset the later year earnings with prior year losses (i.e., deficits in earning and profits) for purposes of computing the amount they must include in their U.S. federal gross income,[14] provided the shareholder was also a 10% U.S. Shareholder during the earlier loss year.

† Under the provisions of the Act, the captive is a CFC, but no U.S. shareholder has income inclusions.

B. The Insurance CFC Rules

1. *What Is an Insurance CFC?*

If a non-U.S. corporation is characterized as earning insurance income, it may be characterized as an insurance CFC. Such characterization would occur if more than 25 percent of the total combined voting power of all stock or more than 25 percent of the total value of such corporation is owned (directly, indirectly through non-U.S. entities or constructively) by 10% U.S. Shareholders on any day of its taxable year.[15]

Example 1

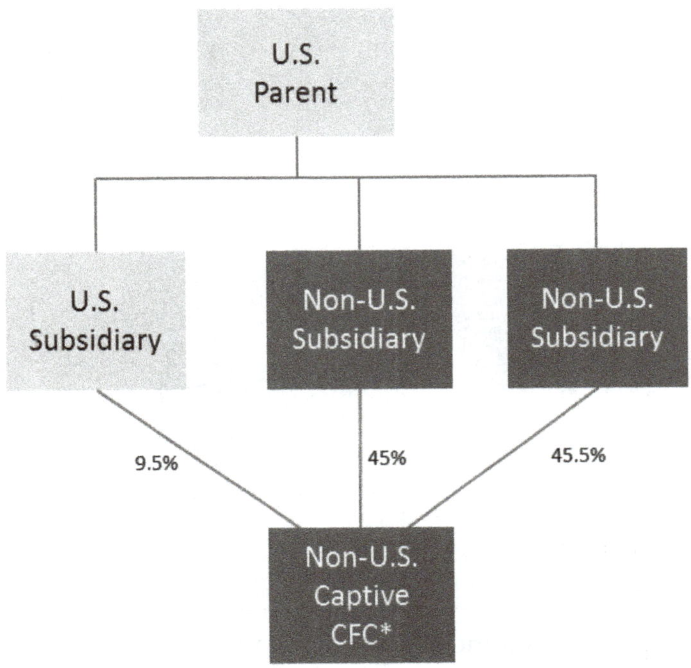

* Is an Insurance CFC if earns insurance income; is also a general CFC.

Figure 4.4 Example of Insurance CFC Status

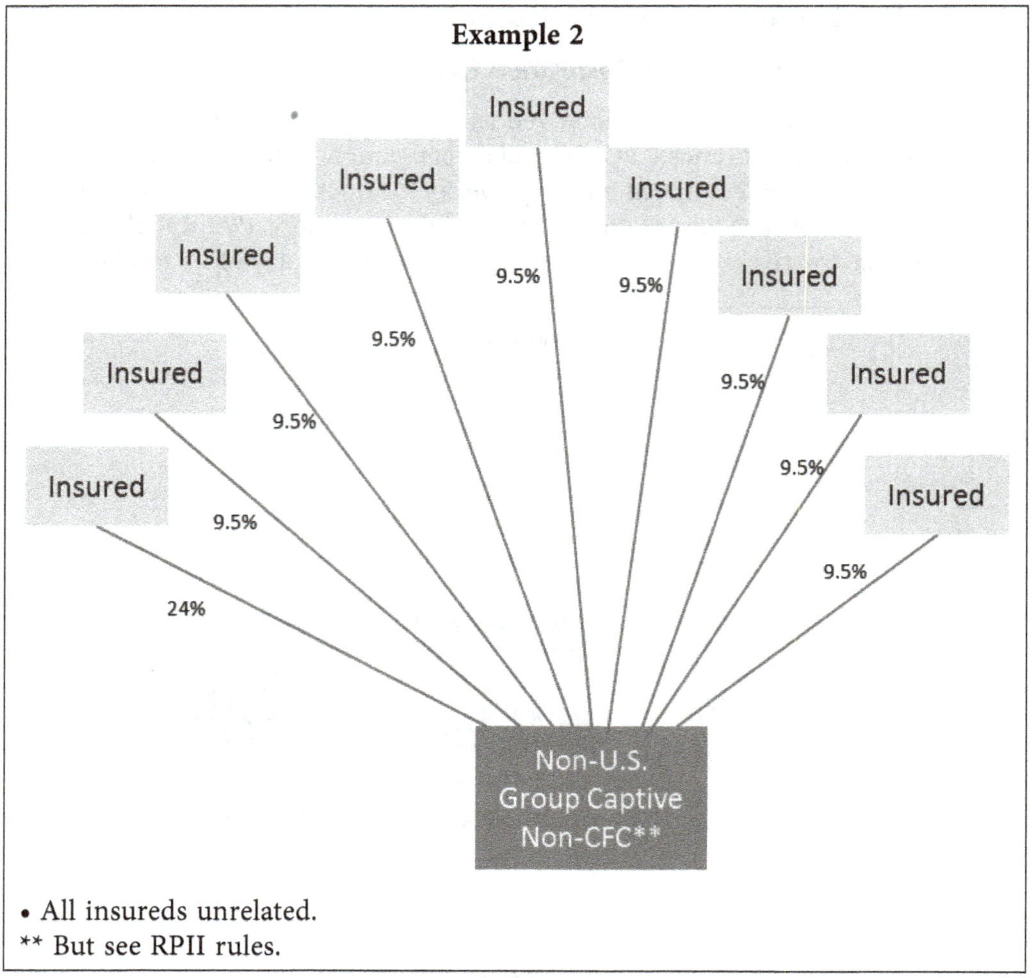

Figure 4.5 Example of Insurance Non-CFC Status

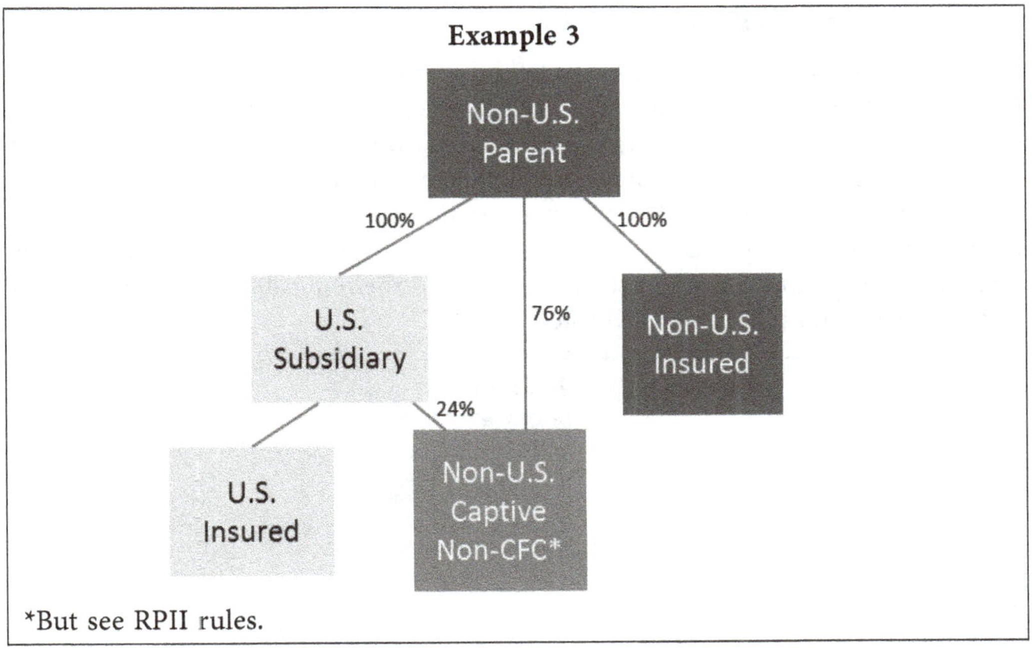

Figure 4.6 Example of Insurance Non-CFC Status‡

2. *Income Inclusions by Insurance CFC Owners*

Under the insurance CFC rules, each 10% U.S. Shareholder of an insurance CFC would include, in the same manner as described earlier under the general CFC rules, only the "subpart F insurance income"[16] of the CFC in its gross income for U.S. federal income tax purposes.[17] Insurance income for these purposes will include both underwriting and investment income. It is important to keep in mind that the income inclusion rules will apply to any income characterized as insurance income, even if the non-U.S. captive is not characterized as an insurance company for federal tax purposes.[18]

C. The RPII CFC Rules

The RPII rules were added to the Code specifically to address group captive situations where the owners of a non-U.S. captive each had less than 10 percent of the voting power of the captive so that the other CFC rules did not apply.[19] As noted below, RPII refers to insurance income of related persons and is technically defined as any insurance income attributable to policies of insurance or reinsurance with respect to which the person insured (directly or indirectly) is a U.S. person who owns (directly or indirectly through non-U.S. entities) any amount of the non-U.S. captive's equity[20] (i.e., a RPII shareholder), or a related person to such RPII shareholder.[21]

A person is a "related person" for this purpose if such person controls[22] or is controlled by the RPII shareholder, or if such person is controlled by the same person or persons who control the RPII shareholder.[23]

‡ Under the provisions of the Act the Captive is a CFC.

1. *What Is a RPII CFC?*

A non-U.S. corporation is considered a CFC under the RPII rules if U.S. persons own (directly, indirectly through non-U.S. entities or constructively) 25 percent or more of the total voting power or value of all classes of voting stock of such non-U.S. corporation on any day of the taxable year of such corporation.[24] The RPII rules differ significantly from the other CFC rules because they take into account all U.S. persons holding shares (directly, indirectly through non-U.S. entities or constructively) of the non-U.S. corporation and not just those who hold the requisite 10 percent required by the general and insurance CFC rules.

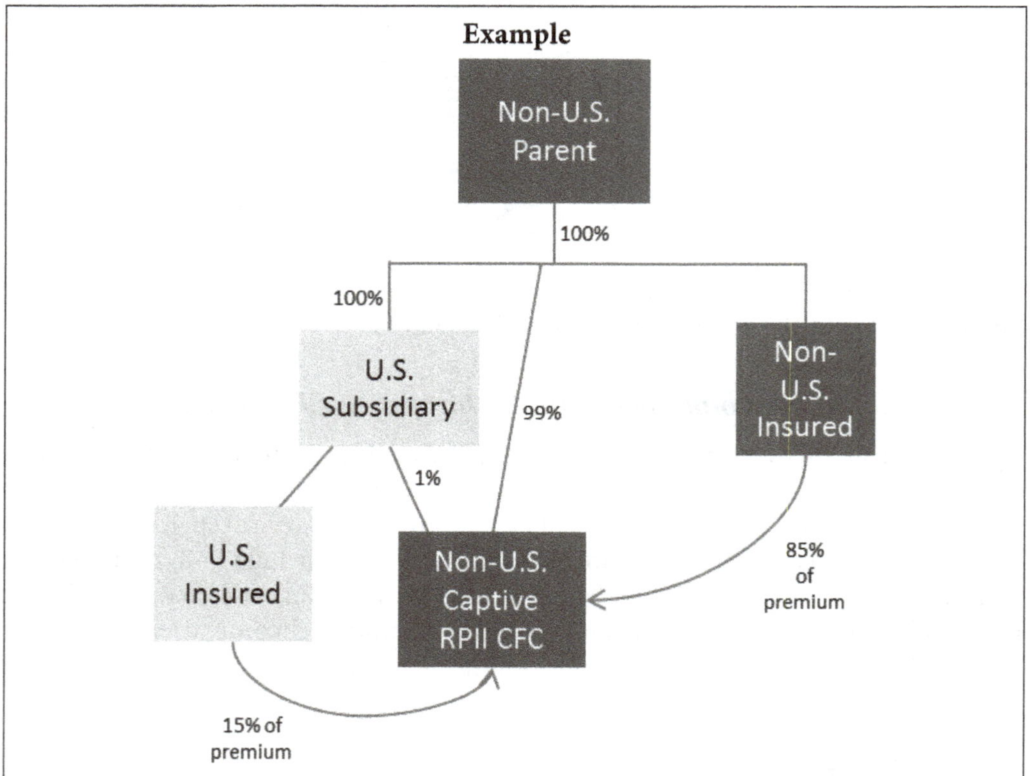

Figure 4.7 Example of RPII CFC Status§

2. *Income Inclusions by RPII CFC Owners*

Under the RPII rules, unless certain exceptions are met (discussed in the following paragraphs), if a non-U.S. corporation is a CFC under the RPII rules for an uninterrupted period of 30 days or more during a taxable year, U.S. persons that own any amount of shares (directly or indirectly through non-U.S. entities) on the last day of the non-U.S. corporation's taxable year on which it is a RPII CFC will be required to include in their gross income for U.S. federal income tax purposes their pro rata

§ Under the Act the Captive is also a regular and insurance CFC.

share of the RPII of the non-U.S. corporation, determined as if all such RPII were distributed proportionately only to such U.S. persons at that date.[25]

There are three exceptions to these RPII income inclusion rules: one is based on the quantum of RPII income (the "income exception"); one is based on the percentage of shareholders that are insureds or related to insureds (the "ownership exception"); and one is based on an affirmative election that the non-U.S. captive can make. If one of the exceptions applies for a taxable year, the U.S. shareholders of the non-U.S. captive do not have to include any amounts in their U.S. federal gross income as a result of the RPII rules for that year. In the captive context, it is often unlikely that either the ownership exception or income exception would apply.[26]

The ownership exception requires that at all times during the taxable year direct and indirect insureds and persons related to such insureds (whether or not U.S. persons) are treated as owning (directly or indirectly through entities) less than 20 percent of the voting power and less than 20 percent of the value of the non-U.S. captive's equity. The income exception requires that the gross RPII of the non-U.S. captive is less than 20 percent of the non-U.S. captive's gross insurance income for the taxable year.

The election referred to above is an election under section 953(c)(3)(C) made by the non-U.S. captive to treat its RPII as income effectively connected with the conduct of a trade or business in the United States and thereby to be subject to U.S. federal income tax under section 11 and the subchapter L provisions of the Code on such RPII as if the non-U.S. captive had a branch in the United States.[27] Such an electing captive would be required to annually file a U.S. federal income tax return on Internal Revenue Service (IRS) Form 1120-PC.[28] The RPII income subject to tax in this manner, although deemed to be income effectively connected with a U.S. trade or business, will not be subject to the branch profits tax (see the discussion that follows in Section VI about U.S. trade or business considerations). In addition, the federal insurance excise tax (FET) (see the discussion that follows in Section VII) would not apply to premiums for coverage subject to U.S. federal income tax under this regime.

D. Special Rules for Tax-Exempt Owners of Insurance and RPII CFCs

In general, although an organization that qualifies for an exemption from U.S. federal income tax under section 501(a) of the Code is exempt from U.S. federal income taxation, it is nevertheless required to pay tax on its unrelated business taxable income (UBTI). Historically, the IRS has generally concluded that subpart F income inclusions of a tax-exempt 10% U.S. Shareholder of a CFC should be treated as dividends for purposes of computing UBTI and, as a general rule, UBTI does not include dividends received by a tax-exempt shareholder.[29] Accordingly, historically, subpart F income was generally treated as a non-taxable dividend.[30]

Section 512(b)(17), added to the Code in 1996, modifies this general dividend characterization rule for subpart F income inclusions by U.S. tax-exempt entities. If the subpart F income is insurance income, a U.S. tax-exempt entity characterized as a 10% U.S. Shareholder or a RPII shareholder of a CFC, must include such income as UBTI (which is generally taxable income to a tax-exempt entity) rather than as a dividend (which is generally not taxable income to a tax-exempt entity) when such income is included in gross income under the CFC rules by the tax-exempt entity.[31] There are exceptions to this characterization, including that if the insurance income is derived from the insurance of risks of (1) the tax-exempt organization itself, (2) certain tax-exempt affiliates of the tax-exempt organization, or (3) risks of directors, officers, or service providers to the tax-exempt organization, it will not be re-characterized as UBTI under section 512(b)(17).[32]

E. Distributions Received from CFCs

When a shareholder receives a distribution of cash or other property from a CFC, the amount will not again be subject to U.S. federal income tax if it has been subject to such tax as described earlier under the general, insurance or RPII CFC regimes.[33]

F. Sales, Exchanges, or Redemptions of CFC Stock

When certain U.S. persons sell, exchange, or redeem their stock in a captive that is a CFC, the section 1248 rules apply to re-characterize any gain from the sale, exchange, or redemption of the shares as a dividend[34] (rather than as capital gain) to the extent of the CFC's earnings and profits[35] during the period that the shareholder held the shares and while the corporation was a CFC. These re-characterization rules apply to U.S. persons that were characterized as 10% U.S. Shareholders of the CFC during the five-year period ending on the date of disposition and to any U.S. person holding shares during such five-year period in a non-U.S. corporation that is characterized as an insurance company for U.S. federal tax purposes in which U.S. persons own 25 percent or more of the shares.[36]

G. U.S. Corporate Taxation as an Alternative to CFC Status

If a non-U.S. captive would be characterized as a CFC, it may be prudent to consider whether taxation of the captive as a U.S. domestic company is preferable to taxation under the CFC regime. See the discussion that follows under Section V, 953(d) Election.

H. CFC Information Reporting

U.S. persons that own shares (directly or indirectly) in a CFC are required to file IRS Form 5471 (Information Return of U.S. Persons With Respect To Certain Foreign Corporations) with their U.S. federal income tax returns in certain circumstances. In general, the reporting requirement applies to a person that has acquired stock (directly or indirectly) that accounts for 10 percent or more of the total vote or value of the non-U.S. corporation's stock or is a 953(c) shareholder[37] or a 10% U.S. Shareholder. Failure to file the Form 5471 when required to do so generally results in a $10,000 annual penalty[38] and will hold open the period of limitations for the relevant year.[39]

III. NON-CFC STATUS

Shareholders of a non-U.S. captive that does not fall within the definition of a CFC or RPII CFC and is not characterized as a passive foreign investment company (a PFIC) (discussed in Section IV) will not be subject to the CFC current income inclusion regime, or either the PFIC penalty tax or current earnings inclusion regime. Such shareholders will generally only be subject to U.S. federal income tax with respect to such captive when the shareholder receives a distribution from the captive or redeems, sells, or exchanges its shares in the captive.[40]

Distributions paid by the captive to a U.S. shareholder are characterized as a dividend to the extent of the captive's earnings and profits.[41] In general, if the captive is domiciled in a jurisdiction that is characterized as having a comprehensive income tax treaty with the United States or is a U.S. possession, such dividends would be characterized as qualified dividend income and subject to tax at capital gains rates for non-corporate shareholders.[42] Distributions in excess of the captive's earnings and profits are characterized as a return of basis to the extent thereof and then as capital gain. For corporate shareholders, the dividends received deduction may not be allowed.[43]

Sales, exchanges, or redemptions of the captive's shares are characterized as a return of basis to the extent thereof and then as capital gain, assuming in the case of a redemption that it is not "essentially equivalent to a dividend."

IV. PASSIVE FOREIGN INVESTMENT COMPANY (PFIC) RULES

The application of the PFIC rules described herein generally only needs to be considered in the context of captives that are not characterized as insurance companies for U.S. federal tax purposes, are not CFCs, or have U.S. owners that are not characterized as 10% U.S. Shareholders. This is the case because the PFIC rules do not apply to 10% U.S. Shareholders of a CFC[44] and, thus, do not apply to single parent captives as well as many other captives. Although there is not a specific exception to the PFIC rules for RPII shareholders, and technically both the PFIC rules and RPII rules could apply, because of the overlap of the consequences of the rules, income inclusions under the RPII rules generally are expected to mitigate the application of the PFIC rules in the circumstances in which the insurance company exception to the PFIC rules (discussed in the following paragraphs) is not applicable.

In general, a non-U.S. corporation will be a PFIC during a given year if (1) 75 percent or more of its gross income constitutes "passive income" or (2) 50 percent or more of its assets produce (or are held for the production of) passive income.[45] For these purposes, passive income generally includes interest, dividends, annuities, certain royalties, rents, and other investment income, such as gain from the sale or exchange of property that gives rise to the types of income noted earlier.[46] Because without an exception most insurance companies would be characterized as PFICs, there is an exception applicable to insurance companies.[47]

Specifically, the exception provides that that income "derived in the *active* conduct of an insurance business by a corporation which is predominantly engaged in an insurance business and which would be subject to tax under subchapter L if it were a domestic corporation" is not treated as passive income.[48] A U.S. domestic corporation will be subject to tax under subchapter L if it is an insurance company. For U.S. federal tax purposes, a property/casualty insurance company is defined as a company more than half of whose business during each taxable year is the issuing of insurance or annuity contracts or the reinsuring of risks underwritten by insurance companies.[49] Although these rules were enacted as part of the major revisions to the Code in 1986, the IRS first issued proposed regulations on what it means to be engaged in the *active* conduct of an insurance business in 2015 in reaction to a perceived abuse by what have been called "hedge fund reinsurers." These proposed regulations have been the subject of much discussion, and many comments were submitted to the IRS in reaction to the proposed regulations. A comprehensive discussion of the proposed regulations is beyond the scope of this chapter, but they did include a provision that would require a non-U.S. insurance company to have its own employees in order to be characterized as *active*. Many captives do not have their own employees and are run by insurance management companies; as such, if the proposed regulations are finalized without amending this provision, captives that are not CFCs exempted from the PFIC rules will be impacted.[50]

In general, if a non-U.S. captive is characterized as a PFIC, each U.S. shareholder would be subject to a penalty tax at the time of the sale at a gain of, or receipt of an "excess distribution"[51] with respect to, their shares. The penalty tax is equivalent to an interest charge on taxes that are deemed due during the period the shareholder owned the shares, computed by assuming that the excess distribution or gain (in the case of a sale) with respect to the shares was taken in equal portion at the highest applicable tax rate on ordinary income throughout the shareholder's period of ownership.[52] For example, if a U.S. shareholder held their shares for ten years and sold the shares at a gain of $100, $10 of income would be allocated to each of the ten years in the shareholder's holding period and U.S federal income tax (at the highest applicable rate), plus interest, would be due for each of the ten years.

If U.S. owners of a non-U.S. captive are concerned about the application of the PFIC rules they can consider making a qualified electing fund (QEF) election[53] to be currently subject to tax on their pro rata share of the ordinary earnings and net capital gain of the captive on an annual basis,[54] instead of being subject to the regular PFIC regime discussed earlier. If the captive were to experience a loss year, neither the captive nor a QEF electing shareholder would be able to use these losses to offset income of a past or future year for purposes of determining the amount of earnings includible by a QEF electing shareholder on its U.S. federal income tax return. When a U.S. shareholder receives a distribution from a PFIC with respect to income the shareholder has already included in income under the QEF regime, the shareholder will not again be subject to tax on this income.[55] A sale, redemption, or exchange of shares in a PFIC by a QEF electing shareholder is generally treated the same as is discussed above in Section III about non-CFCs.

A U.S. QEF electing shareholder's basis in its shares is increased to reflect the tax paid by the shareholder on the undistributed earnings of the non-U.S. corporation; and when a distribution of such previously taxed earnings is made to the U.S. shareholder that is not again subject to tax, a corresponding reduction of basis in the shares occurs. A U.S. person wishing to make a QEF election must make such election on a timely filed IRS Form 8621 for the first taxable year for which the U.S. person held its shares and the captive is treated as a PFIC. In general, a U.S. person must annually file with its U.S. federal income tax return a separate IRS Form 8621 for each PFIC in which the person is a direct or indirect owner during the year.

V. 953(d) ELECTION

As noted above, in Section II discussing the CFC rules, a non-U.S. captive may want to consider being subject to U.S. federal income tax as if it were a U.S. domestic company by making an election under section 953(d) (a 953(d) election). By making the election, the non-U.S. captive will also avoid the application of (1) the CFC rules, and, if relevant, the PFIC rules; (2) withholding tax on certain investment income; and (3) the FET on premiums received, as well as any concern about being engaged in a U.S. trade or business (discussed in the section immediately following).[56] If a non-U.S. captive makes this election, the captive's shareholders would be subject to shareholder level U.S. federal income taxation in the same manner as if they held shares in a U.S. corporation and the captive would be subject to tax as if it were a U.S. company. Generally the calculation of such company's income would be determined in the same manner as for an insurance CFC[57] and the company would file IRS Form 1120-PC or 1120-L.

In order for a non-U.S. company to make a 953(d) election, it must (1) be subject to tax under subchapter L for the taxable year if it was a domestic entity (i.e., be characterized as an insurance company for U.S. federal income tax purposes), and (2) be more than 25 percent owned (directly, indirectly through non-U.S. entities or constructively pursuant to certain attribution rules) by vote or value by U.S. persons that have direct or indirect (through non-U.S. entities) ownership.

The procedural requirements for making a 953(d) election are set forth in Revenue Procedure 2003-47.[58] The requirements include that the captive must enter into a closing agreement with the IRS and must either meet an office and assets test or post a letter of credit to the IRS equal to 10 percent of annual net premium plus investment income. The minimum amount for the letter of credit is $75,000 and the maximum amount required is $10,000,000. The office and assets test may be met by an affiliated company in the same consolidated group as the captive.

If a non-U.S. captive makes the 953(d) election for a year other than its first taxable year, it is characterized as undergoing an inbound transfer pursuant to a reorganization (generally under section 368(a)(1)(F)) for purposes of section 367. These rules require 10% U.S. Shareholders of the electing entity to include in income as a dividend their "all earnings and profits amount"[59] and other U.S. shareholders to either include such amount or recognize gain on the transaction.[60] If the election is made for the captive's first taxable year, it will be characterized as always being a U.S. company for U.S. federal tax purposes.[61] Because one of the requirements for the election includes that the electing company pays all its U.S. federal tax liability, the IRS may take the position that the election cannot be made for a year in which the captive has not paid its estimated taxes. This may be the case even though an electing company need not make the election until the extended due date for the U.S. federal income tax return that would be due for the first electing year,[62] which may be over a year after the first estimated tax payment would have been due.

A 953(d) election is effective until revoked with the consent of the IRS, or until the beginning of the next taxable year after the requirements for the election are not, or are no longer, met.[63] When a 953(d) election terminates, the electing entity will be characterized as undergoing an outbound transfer pursuant to a reorganization (generally under section 368(a)(1)(F)) for purposes of section 367.[64]

Losses of a 953(d) electing company are characterized as dual consolidated losses under the consolidated return rules and, as such, cannot be used to offset the income of any other member of the consolidated group, although they may be carried backward or forward to offset the income of the 953(d) electing company in the same manner that a stand-alone U.S. company would be able to utilize its losses.[65]

VI. U.S. TRADE OR BUSINESS CONSIDERATIONS

One of the most important operational aspects of a non-U.S. captive that does not make a 953(d) election is the conduct of its activities in a manner so that it is not characterized as engaged in a U.S. trade or business. Such determination must be made annually, so it is important that a non-U.S. captive continuously operates so that it is not so characterized. See the discussion at the end of this section for practical considerations in this regard.

A. Imposition of U.S. Federal Tax

If a non-U.S. captive does not operate so that it avoids such characterization, it will be subject to U.S. federal income taxation under section 11, as well as the branch profits tax under section 884 at a 30 percent rate (unless reduced by a U.S. income tax treaty), for a total rate of approximately 54 percent. If a captive is resident in a country that has entered into an income tax treaty with the United States and the captive is entitled to the benefits of the treaty,[66] such taxation will not be applicable unless the captive is engaged in a U.S. trade or business through a permanent establishment in the United States.

The quantum of income that is subject to tax under these rules will depend on which standard is applicable, the general U.S. trade or business standard or the treaty permanent establishment standard. Under the treaty standard, the rule is generally that the income attributable to the permanent establishment in the United States will be subject to U.S. federal income tax. Under the general standard, all income that is characterized as "effectively connected" (ECI) with the trade or business in the United States will be subject to U.S. federal income tax.[67] In addition, the branch profits tax is generally imposed on a corporation's "dividend equivalent amount," which generally means the ECI of the non-U.S. captive that is repatriated from the U.S. business of that captive.[68]

The determination of whether income is ECI of a trade or business in the United States is generally governed under the rules of section 864(c) based on the source and type of income. ECI of a trade or business in the United States includes but is not limited to interest, dividends, rents, salaries, wages, premiums, annuities, compensations, other fixed or determinable annual or periodical income, and certain capital gains from sources within the United States that (1) are either derived from assets used in or held for use in the conduct of such trade or business in the United States (the Asset-Use Test), or (2) with respect to which the activities of such trade or business in the United States are a material factor (the Material Factor Test).[69] Additionally, other U.S. source income is treated as ECI of the trade or business in the United States.[70] Accordingly, ECI would include the underwriting results from U.S. situs risks[71] as well as U.S.-source investment income attributable to the premiums therefrom. A non-U.S. captive engaged in the conduct of a trade or business in the United States may be required to include in income effectively connected with such business (and, consequently, subject to U.S. federal income tax) additional amounts of net investment income under the rules of section 842(b).[72] Moreover, foreign source underwriting income attributable to a U.S. trade or business of a non-U.S. insurance company and certain foreign source investment income of a non-U.S. insurance company that maintains a U.S. office or fixed place of business may be treated as ECI.[73] In determining the taxable income of a non-U.S. insurance company engaged in the conduct of a U.S. trade or business, the rules generally applicable to insurance companies must be used; for example, the reserve deduction must be discounted.[74] If a non-U.S. company is found to be engaged in the conduct of a U.S. trade or business and has not filed U.S. federal income tax returns within the prescribed time period, the IRS has the discretion to impose U.S. federal income tax on the gross income of the company.[75]

B. Definition of a U.S. Trade or Business and a Permanent Establishment

1. U.S. Trade or Business

Neither the Code nor the applicable Treasury Regulations provide a general definition of what constitutes being engaged in a trade or business in the United States. The limited case law that exists generally provides that a non-U.S. company will be considered to be engaged in a trade or business in the United States if it regularly and continuously transacts a substantial portion of its ordinary business in the United States.[76] The test is generally a factual one and, therefore, all facts and circumstances must be examined *annually* in determining whether a non-U.S. corporation is engaged in a trade or business in the United States for a taxable year.

Under certain circumstances, the activities of a taxpayer's dependent or independent agent in the United States may cause the taxpayer to be treated as engaged in a trade or business in the United States (i.e., if the U.S. agent's activities in the United States on the taxpayer's behalf are "considerable, continuous and regular").[77] For U.S. federal income tax purposes, "agency" generally is defined by reference to common law principles. In general, a finding of agency generally requires a finding of an express or implied contract between the principal and its agent pursuant to which (1) the agent has the power to commit its principal to business relationships with third parties, (2) a fiduciary relationship between the principal and the agent is created, and (3) the principal retains the right to direct the agent in the performance of its duties.[78]

Although the ability of an agent to bind its principal has been described in some cases as an "essential" characteristic of an agency relationship, existing case law also indicates the power "to bring about" business relationships may create an agency relationship.[79] Consequently, the ability to bind a principal should not be considered determinative in analyzing whether an agency relationship has been created.

If a substantial part of the activities that produce a non-U.S. company's income occurs in the United States, the company would be deemed engaged in a trade or business in the United States and subject to U.S. federal income taxation.[80] However, the maintenance of a U.S. office by a non-U.S. corporation should not cause the non-U.S. corporation to be treated as engaged in a trade or business in the United States if such office performs only clerical or ministerial acts within the United States and business judgment is exercised offshore.[81] In *Linen Thread Co. v. Commissioner*,[82] a U.K. corporation sold thread in the United States and maintained an office for handling paperwork, collecting payments, and facilitating delivery. The Tax Court held that the U.K. corporation was not engaged in a U.S. trade or business because, except for a single isolated sale, all solicitation and sales activity was conducted outside the United States.[83] By contrast, the IRS ruled that a Swiss company without any office in the United States that conducted demonstrations in the United States of its logging equipment to solicit orders was held to be engaged in a U.S. trade or business.[84] In *Scottish American*, a non-U.S. investment corporation established a U.S. office that maintained records, collected dividends, sent reports to the non-U.S. home office, voted proxies in some instances, and performed other extensive clerical or routine duties. All decisions on the trading of securities and investment policies, however, were made by the non-U.S. home office. The Tax Court concluded that, despite the volume of activity conducted by the U.S. office, the non-U.S. investment corporation was not engaged in a trade or business in the United States.[85]

In PLR 7942078, the IRS determined that a non-U.S. insurance company was not engaged in a trade or business in the United States where (1) it had not qualified to do business in any state; (2) it conducted all of its day-to-day operations through personnel located outside the United States; (3) its management decisions were conducted by a board of directors that met outside the United States or by other personnel located offshore; (4) it did not intend to engage in business in the United States; (5) it maintained no office or fixed place of business in the United States; and (6) claims work performed in the United States was performed by independent service organizations on a fee basis, although some services were procured through a wholly owned U.S. subsidiary of the non-U.S. insurance company.[86]

On the other hand, in Revenue Ruling 80-225,[87] a non-U.S. insurance company that provided surplus lines coverage to U.S. insureds through a managing general agency arrangement was found to be engaged in a U.S. trade or business. In the arrangement described in the ruling, pursuant to authority granted by the insurance company, the U.S. broker signed and countersigned policies on behalf of the insurance company, and also settled claims in the United States on its behalf.[88]

2. *Trading Safe Harbors to Engaged in U.S. Trade or Business Test and Investing Activity*

The Code contains a safe harbor for trading in stocks and securities and provides, in general, that the term engaged in a trade or business in the United States does not include (1) trading in stocks and securities through an independent agent or (2) trading in stocks and securities for the taxpayer's own account provided that the taxpayer is not a dealer in stocks or securities.[89] Trading in stocks and securities for the taxpayer's own account is defined in the relevant Treasury Regulations as the effecting of transactions in the United States in stocks or securities for the taxpayer's own account; the effecting of transactions in stocks and securities includes buying, selling (whether or not by entering into short sales) or trading in stocks, securities, or options to buy or sell stocks or securities, on margin or otherwise, for the account and risk of the taxpayer, and any other activity closely related thereto (such as obtaining credit for the purpose of effectuating such buying, selling, or trading).[90] The IRS has also issued proposed regulations for trading in derivatives.[91]

The stocks and securities trading safe harbor and the derivatives trading safe harbor with respect to trading for the taxpayer's own account is available only to a taxpayer that is a "trader" and not a "dealer" or mere "investor" in stocks and securities or derivatives, respectively.[92] The determination of whether a taxpayer is an investor, trader, or dealer requires consideration of case law, statutory law, and all the facts and circumstances.

For purposes of the stocks and securities trading safe harbor, a dealer in stocks and securities is defined as a merchant of stocks or securities with an established place of business who is regularly engaged as a merchant in purchasing stocks or securities and selling them to customers with a view to the gains and profits that may be derived therefrom.[93] Persons who buy and sell or hold stocks or securities for investment or speculation are not dealers in stocks or securities for these purposes by reason of that activity. Further, a taxpayer's worldwide activities shall be considered in determining dealer status.[94] Generally speaking, a dealer is a market maker that enters into transactions with "customers" as opposed to simply counterparties.[95]

3. *Permanent Establishment*

As noted earlier, most U.S. tax treaties provide that in order for a resident in a treaty partner country to be subject to U.S. federal income tax on its business profits (assuming the resident is entitled to the benefits of the treaty), such person must be engaged in the conduct of a U.S. trade or business through a permanent establishment in the United States. Although the definition of permanent establishment is treaty specific, there are some commonalities, and a generic description follows.

A permanent establishment generally includes (1) an office or other regular place of business through which the business of a non-U.S. company is wholly or partly carried on, and (2) an agent (other than an independent agent[96] acting in the ordinary course of its business) that has and habitually exercises in the United States the authority to conclude contracts on behalf of the non-U.S. company; however, it does not include the maintenance of a regular place of business solely for the purpose of collecting information, advertising, supplying information, or similar activities having a preparatory or auxiliary character.

For this purpose, an independent agent includes a broker, a general commission agent, or any other agent of independent status, provided that such person is acting in the ordinary course of its business. An agent will not be considered independent, however, if substantially all of its activities are performed on behalf of the non-U.S. captive, and the transactions between the agent and the non-U.S. captive are not made under arm's length conditions. The treatment of a dependent agent with authority to conclude contracts on behalf of a non-U.S. captive as a U.S. permanent establishment of the non-U.S. captive may not be avoided simply by having a contract executed by personnel located outside of the United States if the agent in the United States has the authority to negotiate all elements and details of a contract in a way binding on the enterprise.

C. Customary Practical Operational Considerations[97]

Typically, non-U.S. captives that do not make 953(d) elections to be characterized as U.S. domestic companies for all U.S. federal tax purposes adopt procedures or operating guidelines with respect to activities that should be conducted outside the United States to mitigate the risk that they will be characterized as engaged in a U.S. trade or business. Such procedures generally include, among other things, holding board and shareholder meetings outside the United States and ensuring that claims review, contracting, price negotiation, and reserve setting occur outside the United States.

VII. FEDERAL INSURANCE EXCISE TAX (FET)

Premiums paid to non-U.S. captives for U.S. situs risks are subject to the FET if the underlying transactions are characterized as insurance for U.S. federal tax purposes.[98] The rate depends on the type of business and whether it is insurance or reinsurance and the tax is payable by any of the insured/reinsured, broker or captive.[99]

Under section 4371 et seq., the FET is imposed on direct premiums paid under insurance policies issued by any non-U.S. insurer[100] at a 4 percent rate on policies covering risks of an "Insured."[101] An Insured is defined as (1) a U.S. entity or individual with respect to risks located wholly or partly within the United States or (2) a non-U.S. entity or individual engaged in a trade or business in the United States with respect to risks that are located within the United States.[102] It is also imposed at a 1 percent rate for "life insurance, sickness and accident policies and annuity contracts."[103] For this purpose, a "policy of life, sickness or accident insurance or annuity contract" means an insurance or annuity contract with respect to the life or hazards to the person of a U.S. citizen or resident.[104]

The FET is imposed at the rate of 1 percent of the premium paid on reinsurance policies that cover (1) contracts that insure risks of Insureds or (2) insurance or annuity contracts with respect to the life or hazards to the person of a U.S. citizen or resident.[105]

An exemption from the FET is provided in certain U.S. income tax treaties. In order to benefit from the exemption, it is usually required that the risk not be retroceded to a reinsurer that is not either in the United States or entitled to a treaty-based FET exemption. In general, in order for a resident in a country that has a tax treaty with the United States to benefit from the exemption to the FET, the resident must meet the requirements for treaty eligibility.

In the case of direct insurance, because the FET can be imposed on the insured or the insurer, it is possible to choose to have the administrative task of paying the tax and filing returns be done by either the various insureds in the program or by the non-U.S. captive. Payments generally must be made by semi-monthly deposit that relate to the periods in which premium is paid and returns (IRS Form 720) are filed quarterly. In the case of reinsurance, the U.S. insurance company usually pays the tax to the IRS and files the IRS Form 720. The charts set forth in Tables 4.1 and 4.2 illustrate the deposit and form due dates.[106]

Table 4.1 Deposit Periods and Due Dates

Period	Deposit Due	Period	Deposit Due
January 1–15	January 29	July 16–31	August 14
January 16–31	February 14	August 1–15	August 29
February 1–15	February 29	August 16–31	September 14
February 16–29	March 14	September 1–15	September 29
March 1–15	March 29	September 16–26	September 29
March 16–31	April 14	September 27–30	October 14
April 1–15	April 29	October 1–15	October 29
April 16–30	May 14	October 16–31	November 14
May 1–15	May 29	November 1–15	November 29
May 16–31	June 14	November 16–30	December 14
June 1–15	June 29	December 1–15	December 29
June 16–30	July 14	December 16–31	January 14
July 1–15	July 29		

Table 4.2 Form Filing Due Dates

Quarter	Due Date
1st (January, February, March)	April 30
2nd (April, May, June)	July 31
3rd (July, August, September)	October 31
4th (October, November, December)	January 31

VIII. WITHHOLDING TAX

A non-U.S. captive that has not made a 953(d) election and that is not characterized as engaged in a U.S. trade or business will be subject to a 30 percent gross basis U.S. federal income tax imposed by withholding at source on its U.S. source "fixed or determinable annual or periodical" (FDAP) income under chapter 3 of the Code,[107] unless this "withholding tax" is eliminated under the Code[108] or reduced or eliminated by an applicable U.S. income tax treaty. The withholding tax generally does not apply to capital gains because such gains of non-U.S. persons are generally not characterized as U.S. source.[109]

Such a captive is also potentially subject to a 30 percent withholding tax under chapter 4 of the Code if the FATCA information reporting rules are not complied with. The chapter 4 rules are generally referred to as the FATCA[110] rules. Under these rules, payments characterized as "withholdable payments" are potentially subject to the FATCA withholding tax. A "withholdable payment" is defined as any payment of U.S. source FDAP as described in Treasury Regulation sections 1.1441-2(b)(1) and (c) (with certain modifications),[111] which includes income such as interest, dividends, rents, and royalties from U.S. sources, and insurance and reinsurance premiums for coverage of U.S. risks.[112] After December 31, 2017, the term "withholdable payment" also includes gross proceeds from the sale or disposition of any property of a type that can produce U.S. source FDAP interest or dividends.[113]

IX. INFORMATION REPORTING

There are a number of information reporting rules that may be applicable to a non-U.S. captive or its shareholders.

As discussed immediately in the preceding section, in order to avoid withholding under the FATCA provisions, a non-U.S. captive must comply with the FATCA information reporting rules.[114] In general, this means that such a captive characterized as a passive "non-financial foreign entity" (an NFFE) (which is the characterization expected to apply to most captives) has to provide an IRS Form W-8BEN-E to each of its "withholding agents,"[115] including its insureds.[116] The form generally requires certain identifying information with respect to the captive as well as the disclosure of certain identifying information of each "substantial U.S. owner"[117] of the captive or an indication that the captive does not have any "substantial U.S. owners."[118] If a captive is alternatively characterized as a "foreign financial institution" (FFI) which would be the case if it *directly* issues cash value insurance or annuity contracts (cash value contracts),[119] resulting in its characterization as a "specified insurance company,"[120] it would be subject to requirements in addition to providing the IRS Form W-8BEN-E to its "withholding agents."[121]

As noted earlier, under the discussion of the CFC rules, certain U.S. direct or indirect (through non-U.S. entities) shareholders of a non-U.S. captive must annually file IRS Form 5471. In general, the reporting requirement applies to a person that has acquired stock directly or indirectly that accounts for 10 percent or more of the total vote or value of the non-U.S. corporation's stock or is a 953(c) shareholder[122] or a 10% U.S. Shareholder. In addition, a U.S. citizen or resident who is an officer or director of a non-U.S. corporation in which a U.S. shareholder has the requisite amount of stock is required to file IRS Form 5471. Failure to file the form results in penalties, unless waived by the IRS, and will hold the period of limitations open for the year the form was required to be filed.[123]

Also as noted earlier, a U.S. person must annually file with its U.S. federal income tax return a separate IRS Form 8621 for each PFIC in which the person is a direct or indirect owner during the year, including in the circumstance in which the U.S. person has made a QEF election.

IRS Form 926 must be filed by a U.S. person transferring funds to a non-U.S. captive if (1) such person owns immediately after the transfer at least 10 percent by vote or value of the captive (taking into account certain attribution rules) or (2) the transfer, when aggregated with all related transfers under applicable regulations, exceeds $100,000. Failure to file the form may result in a penalty equal to 10 percent of the funds transferred (not to exceed $100,000 unless such failure is intentional).[124]

U.S. individuals that own stock in a non-U.S. captive generally must report this information on Schedule B attached to their IRS Form 1040 as well as on IRS Form 8938 (Statement of Specified Foreign Financial Assets).[125]

Other information reporting that may apply to a U.S. shareholder includes a FinCEN Report 114 (Report of Foreign Bank and Financial Accounts) and Form BE-10 (Bureau of Economic Analysis—Benchmark Survey of U.S. Direct Investment Abroad). In addition, the non-U.S. company would have to file IRS Form 1120-PC or 1120-L if it makes a 953(d) election and would be required to file IRS Form 1120 (for non-insurance companies) or IRS Form 1120-PC/1120-L (for insurance companies) if it is characterized as engaged in a U.S. trade or business.[126]

X. COMPARISON OF NON-CFC, CFC, AND 953(d) ELECTION[127]

Table 4.3 compares non-CFC, CFC, and 953(d) election status.

Table 4.3 Non-CFC, CFC, and 953(d) election comparison.

	Non-CFC	CFC[128]	953(d) Electing Company[129]
Income	Current year income is not subject to U.S. federal income tax, provided the captive is not engaged in a U.S. trade or business.	Current year income of the CFC is included in the U.S. federal gross income of the CFC's 10% U.S. Shareholders.	Current year income is included in the captive's U.S. federal corporate tax return.
Losses	Not applicable.	Prior year losses (i.e., deficits in E&P) of the CFC may be used by a 10% U.S. Shareholder to reduce the shareholder's current year income inclusions from the CFC, provided the shareholder was a shareholder for the year in which the losses were generated.	Losses and E&P generated in a year prior to the effective date of the 953(d) election are not taken into account, unless the company was characterized as engaged in a U.S. trade or business in such prior years. Losses generated after the effective date of the 953(d) election are characterized as dual consolidated losses.
FET	Applies to direct business at a 4 percent rate for P&C and at a 1 percent rate on life and accident and health business. Applies to assumed reinsurance at a 1 percent rate.	Applies to direct business at a 4 percent rate for P&C and at a 1 percent rate on life and accident and health business. Applies to assumed reinsurance at a 1 percent rate.	Does not apply to assumed business; applies to outward reinsurance at a 1 percent rate.

	Non-CFC	CFC[128]	953(d) Electing Company[129]
U.S. Income/ Branch Profits Tax	Applies if characterized as engaged in a U.S. trade or business.	Applies if characterized as engaged in a U.S. trade or business; however, amounts characterized as ECI reduce subpart F income.	Does not apply.
Distributions	Distributions to the extent of E&P are characterized as dividends.	Distributions of previously taxed income are not subject to tax when received by a U.S. shareholder.	Distributions to the extent of E&P are characterized as dividends. The qualified dividend income rate is applicable and corporate holders are entitled to the dividends received deduction.
Sale of Shares	Generally, gain on a sale should be characterized as capital gain.	Gain realized by 10% U.S. Shareholders will be characterized as a dividend to the extent of the captive's E&P allocable to the shareholder. Gain in excess of this amount should be characterized as capital gain.	Generally, gain on a sale should be characterized as capital gain.
Withholding Tax	Applies.	Applies.	Does not apply.

Chapter 5

Employee Benefits

Karin Landry

I. INTRODUCTION

For most companies, employee benefits represent a significant financial investment. As every human resources director knows, the cost of employee benefits, health insurance in particular, has dramatically increased over the last decade.

Employee benefit costs can comprise as much as 31.5 percent[1] of a company's total payroll. Captives can provide effective, long-term solutions to the rising costs of funding a variety of employee benefits, as well as pension and retiree medical obligations.

This chapter will explain the reasons, benefits, and processes for including Employee Retirement Income Security Act (ERISA) and non-ERISA benefits into a captive.

II. USING A CAPTIVE TO FUND EMPLOYEE BENEFITS

Alternative market mechanisms (captives) account for about 30 percent ($98 billion) of the total annual commercial risk-protection market ($326.9 billion).[2]

Twenty years ago, captives were not commonly used for financing employee benefits, as regulatory obstacles and reinsurance restrictions limited eligibility to only the largest of captives. The U.S. Department of Labor (DOL) must approve the placement of ERISA-covered benefits into pure-parent captives. Benefits covered by ERISA include retirement, health, life, and disability insurance.

Many well-known organizations have obtained ERISA-covered benefit captive funding approval, including Archer Daniels Midland (ADM), Alcon Labs, Alcoa, AGL Resources, Astra Zeneca, Banner Health, International Paper, Memorial Sloan-Kettering Cancer Center, Sun Microsystems, and United Technologies. Many more companies have used captives to fund other non-ERISA employee benefits that do not require DOL approval, such as medical stop-loss insurance and voluntary benefits. Moreover, employer groups and associations are establishing captives to fund employee benefits, thus offering an alternative to the commercial insurance markets and providing an incentive for membership growth.

For companies with property and casualty captives, certain employee benefits may be "unrelated business," that is, insurance business unrelated to the captive's parent. Adding unrelated business to a single-parent captive can improve the captive's overall financial efficiency, satisfy the need for third-party business allowing the parent to deduct its captive premiums from its U.S. federal income taxes, and create additional cost savings.

Regulatory changes have led to increased employee benefit captive funding. Some of these changes include the following:

- Internal Revenue Service clarifies risk shifting/distribution and unrelated business requirements. In 1993, the IRS ruled[3] that certain employee benefits insurance written in a pure captive is unrelated business (to the captive's parent) since it benefits the employee and not the employer. In 2002, the IRS issued three revenue rulings clarifying the qualification of captives as insurance companies for federal income tax purposes, including discussions of third-party business, brother-sister arrangements, and group captives.[4]
- The DOL review process provides a roadmap to funding. If the proposed transaction is subject to ERISA, the DOL has a streamlined process for approval through its EXPRO process.
- GASB 45 and FASB 158 requirements raise awareness of post-retirement liabilities. Accounting rules such as GASB 45 and ASC 715 (formerly FAS 87/106 and amended by FAS 158) require that organizations account for retiree medical and pension obligations. These requirements encourage employers to not only account for the liabilities, but also to seek efficient funding methodologies. In addition, GASB statements 74 and 75 are increasing the required disclosures for public retiree medical obligations.
- Court rulings clarify the parameters for funding retiree medical programs. In *Wells Fargo & Co. v. Commissioner*,[5] the Tax Court clarified the amount that can be set aside to fund retiree medical benefits, expanding the potential funding allowed to employers.
- Revenue Ruling 2014-15 clarifies funding opportunities for retiree medical programs. In 2014, the IRS ruled in Revenue Ruling 2014-15 that non-cancellable accident and health insurance policies will receive life insurance tax treatment as long as the following facts and circumstances are met:
  - o The company maintains a VEBA trust that satisfies the requirements of 501(c)(9);
  - o The company purchases a non-cancellable accident and health policy from an insurance company and reinsures the policy through the captive; and
  - o Both the company and the VEBA retain the right to cancel the retiree health coverage at any time.

As a result, insuring non-collectively bargained retiree medical benefits through a captive allows for tax-free growth of reserves without the need for a private letter ruling.

III. ADVANTAGES OF PLACING EMPLOYEE BENEFITS IN CAPTIVES

There are several advantages to funding employee benefits in a captive. These include improved cost savings, increased administrative control, improved risk management, and enhancing a previously established captive, summarized in the following outline:

- Improved cost savings
  - o Control employee benefit premium costs. Estimated potential savings for employee benefits in captives versus commercial insurance[6] are as follows:
    - ▪ Long-term disability (5 to 20 percent)
    - ▪ Group term life insurance (15 to 20 percent)
    - ▪ Accidental death and dismemberment (up to 30 percent)
    - ▪ Active medical stop-loss (5 to 15 percent)
    - ▪ Retiree medical (5 to 15 percent of the accumulated post-retirement benefit obligation)
    - ▪ Multinational pooling (10 to 20 percent)
  - o Reduce frictional costs (commissions, taxes, risk charges, insurer profit, administration) and underwriting savings
  - o Capture investment returns
  - o Improve cash flow and centralize investment of reserves
  - o Improve management reporting and understanding of risks

- Increase administrative control
  - o Design coverage and provisions of benefits
  - o Improve data management and loss cost management

- Improve risk management
  - o Manage a centralized risk pool
  - o Purchase stop-loss reinsurance to manage exposure to catastrophic loss
  - o Quantify the financial benefits of wellness initiatives and specific loss prevention programs

- Enhance a property and casualty captive
  - o Increase reserves and reduce dependence on commercial markets
  - o Improve spread of risk; portfolio diversity
  - o Add third-party insurance business potentially creating tax-deductible captive premiums

IV. EMPLOYEE BENEFIT FUNDING OPPORTUNITIES

A wide range of employee benefits may be funded through a captive. Benefits that pay out over multiple years (e.g., long-term disability and retiree medical) provide cash flow stability, loss predictably, and the ability to accumulate reserves. Lines such as group life insurance, which can be very profitable for commercial insurers, offer the captive the same profit potential. Figure 5.1 shows all employee benefit options, and gives an example of those that a typical employer may wish to fund through a captive.

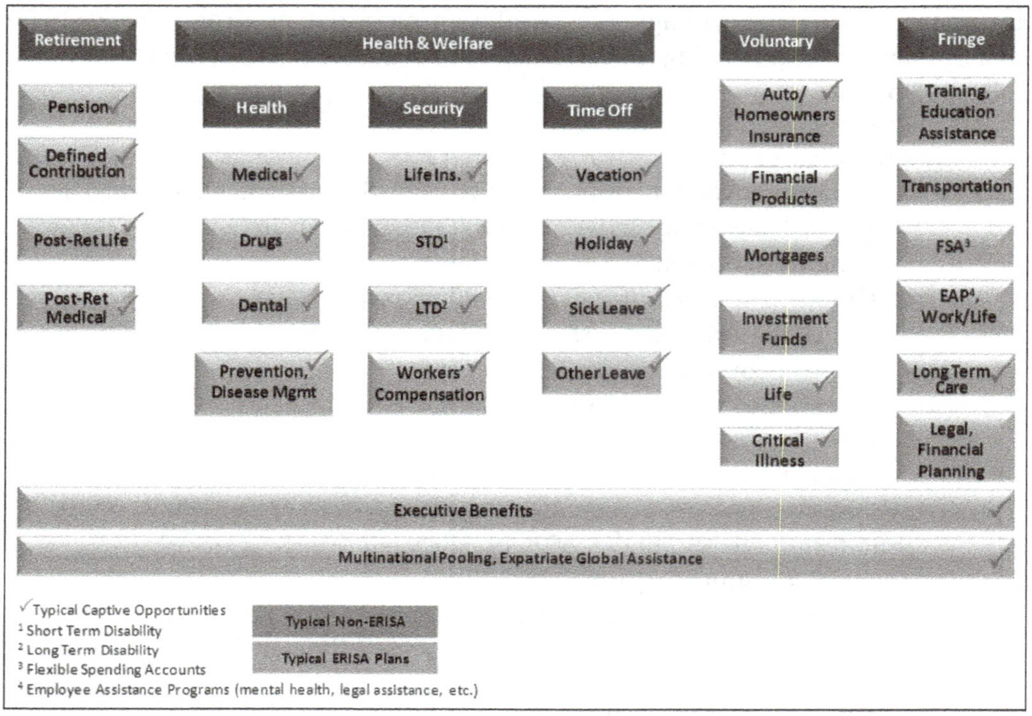

Figure 5.1 Employee Benefits Funded through a Captive

Captive solutions can be used to fund benefits covered by ERISA federal law, or those not covered by ERISA. ERISA benefits are primarily the benefit plans sponsored by and contributed to by employers, such as retirement, group life insurance, health, and welfare plans. These plans are subject to federal oversight, under the auspices of the DOL.

Non-ERISA benefits are often benefit plans targeted to a specific population, such as supplemental retirement plans for executives. These plans may not receive the tax benefits granted to plans covered by ERISA, nor do they require DOL approval for captive funding.

Funding employee benefits in a captive has no direct impact on the plans' beneficiaries with the exception of a Notice to Interested Persons letter explaining the transaction and the benefit enhancements that may be required by the DOL. Once implemented, human resources staff need not worry about significant additional administrative responsibilities, or the possibility that the plans' benefits will be changed other than the positive effect of the benefit enhancements.

Typically, if it is an ERISA benefit, the employer can continue to work with its existing insurer. As a result of this process, the insurer's role is changed. In a captive arrangement, the insurer continues to insure the employer's and employees' risks, but it immediately reinsures the risks into the employer's captive. In this role, the insurer becomes a fronting insurer. This arrangement allows the fronting insurer to continue to administer the program. The employer pays the fronting insurer an annual fee, allowing the captive to retain investment income and underwriting profit (if any).

Figure 5.2 illustrates the typical ERISA transaction between the captive owner, the captive, the fronting insurer, and the captive owner's employees.

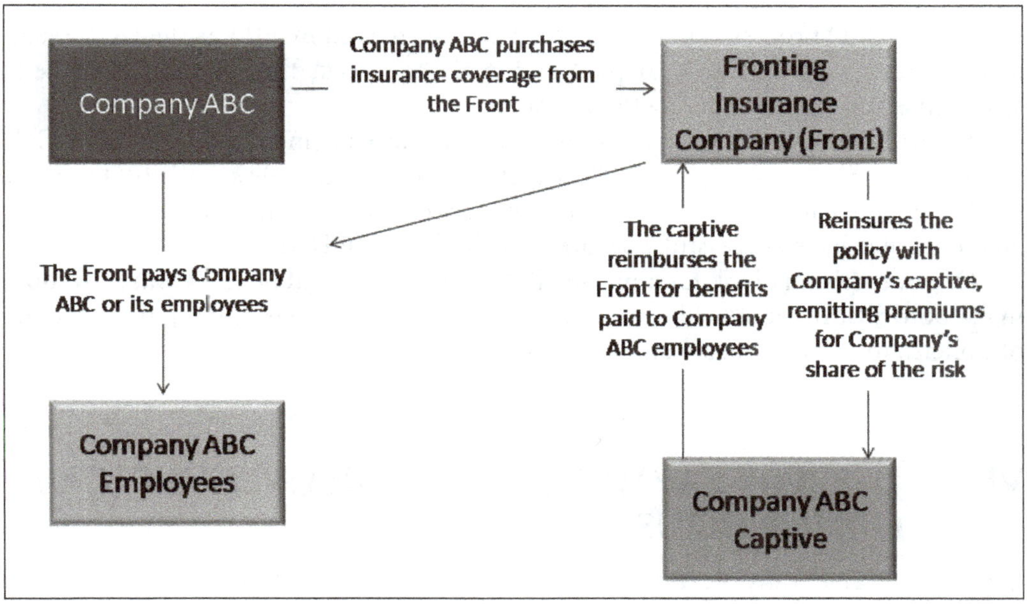

Figure 5.2 Typical ERISA Transaction

Long-tail benefits such as group universal life insurance and long-term disability are ideal captive candidates. Often, medical stop-loss insurance may be placed into a captive.

Funding first-dollar medical benefits does not usually make economic sense, as the captive may add expenses not found in a traditional self-insured approach. Since the Patient Protection and Affordable Care Act (PPACA) prohibits insurers and self-insurers from placing limits on employee benefits, many self-insured employers find themselves assuming additional liabilities because medical coverage is now an unlimited liability. A captive is an ideal vehicle in which an employer creates stop-loss coverage, and purchases excess (unlimited) coverage from the commercial markets above the captive's aggregate retention.

V. A BRIEF HISTORY OF ERISA BENEFIT CAPTIVE FUNDING

Back in 2000 and 2003, Columbia Energy (Columbia) and Archers Daniels Midland (ADM), respectively, became true risk pioneers as they became the first companies to gain a prohibited transaction exemption (PTE) from the U.S. DOL to write employee benefits into their captives. Since then, a number of companies have followed suit and created captive-funded employee benefits programs.

Companies that followed Columbia and ADM on a similar funding path had the luxury of utilizing an expedited process (EXPRO) to gain their PTEs. The Columbia and ADM cases were used by the DOL as model cases by which future companies could mirror and qualify for EXPRO.

The EXPRO process sunsetted in 2012 and reemerged in 2013 as the DOL evaluated the success of the ten-year pilot and explored tweaks that they could make to streamline and improve the EXPRO process.

In 2014–15, EXPRO was re-instated with approvals being granted to Coca-Cola and Intel Corp. These companies' PTEs are the genesis of the new age EXPRO process, reinforcing the pathway for writing employee benefits in a captive. To date, more than 30 companies have successfully secured a PTE from the DOL.

Often, employers look for a non-ERISA approach to fund benefits either by looking at non-ERISA benefits like multinational pooling or by reexamining the structure of policies to use a property and casualty policy.

VI. USING A CAPTIVE TO FUND RETIREE MEDICAL OBLIGATIONS

U.S. GAAP (Generally Accepted Accounting Principles) requires all employers to accrue the estimated amount of total retiree medical and other benefits like life payable to current employees throughout their lifetimes on their balance sheets. This requirement forces employers not to fund these obligations, just to recognize them. Recognition, of course, creates a liability without an offsetting asset, and always raises the question, "how are we going to pay for these benefits?"

Employers that offer retiree medical benefits often respond to this question by restricting eligibility requirements, closing the plan to employees who retire after a certain date, increasing the retirees' portion of the premiums, increasing co-insurance payments and deductibles, transitioning to a defined contribution arrangement, or modifying or reducing plan benefits.

Employers that choose to fund a portion (or all) of their retiree medical obligations are able to offset the liability, but traditional funding options can be problematic. One of the most common funding options, a VEBA (Voluntary Employee Beneficial Association) trust, is subject to Unrelated Business Income Tax (UBIT) on investment earnings on funds supporting non-collectively bargained benefits.

An alternative is to have the VEBA purchase an insurance policy, such as Trust Owned Life Insurance (TOLI) or Trust Owned Health Insurance (TOHI), which is then reinsured into the employer's captive. This arrangement creates a degree of flexibility, well-matched payments for the cash flow requirements of the trust, as well as potential tax efficiencies. Other benefits include, but are not limited to:

- Potential tax deductible premiums;
- Tax-free asset accumulation;
- Tax-free distribution for medical expenses;
- Improved balance sheet performance;
- Long-term cost savings as compared with most pay-as-you-go methods;
- Increased operating income through reduction of retiree life insurance and medical costs;
- Enhanced employee/retiree security; and
- Positive impact on public relations—prefunding demonstrates financial commitment to retirees' welfare.

VII. USING A CAPTIVE TO FUND PENSIONS

IRS regulations require that a plan sponsor fund up to 100 percent of its pension obligations over several years. Today's low interest rates and wildly fluctuating portfolio values make 100 percent funding difficult to achieve. Moreover, once a plan is fully funded, excess funds returned to the sponsor are taxed at the sponsor's ordinary income tax rate, plus a 50 percent excise tax, creating an effective tax rate on excess funding of 85 percent. Thus, if the sponsor can achieve full funding, the market can drop, requiring additional contributions, or the market can rise, without a cash benefit to the plan sponsor, creating a "heads you lose, tails you don't win" situation.

Plan sponsors consider many options for dealing with the volatility inherent in a pension plan. These include asset liability matching (choosing plan assets intended to go up in value when the pension liabilities go up and vice versa) and terminating the pension plan entirely, which can be an expensive and difficult process.

A solution that reduces pension plan risk while retaining assets within the corporate family is a pension buy-in solution. A pension plan buys an annuity matching all or part of its liabilities. The annuity is held as a plan asset. The annuity can be structured to match all or part of the payment stream from the plan, so that movements in the value of the pension obligation are matched by movements in the annuity asset. This approach reduces the plan's cash flow volatility. The annuity can then be reinsured to a captive owned by or otherwise affiliated with the plan sponsor. The sponsor could then avoid paying the high fees associated with purchasing annuities from commercial carriers, and provide stability to the pension plan and the plan participants.

VIII. CRITICAL STEPS IN THE CAPTIVE DEVELOPMENT PROCESS

A. Establishing a Captive for Employee Benefits

Whereas companies with existing captives may use them to cover employee benefits, companies without captives cannot establish new pure captives specifically for funding ERISA employee benefits. The DOL requires that the employer include its captive's latest audited financial statement in the application filing. This means, of course, that the employer must already have a captive to satisfy this requirement. Most employers initially form property and casualty captives, and after a year or so they petition the DOL to permit the placement of certain employee benefits, although they can set up a captive to fund benefits alone.

The decision to form a new captive involves a range of considerations. The employer must contribute capital equal to the minimum solvency ratio of the chosen domicile (based on expected first-year premiums). Like most captive initiatives, the employer must be prepared to make a multi-year commitment to the program. Although some benefits may be received year one, full benefits will only accrue once the captive has been operational for a few years and the risks are stabilized.

A well-established benefits captive can provide ongoing cost savings as compared to purchasing insurance in the commercial markets, and provide cost transparency as the captive's financial performance is audited each year by law. Captives may not be right for some organizations, thus a feasibility study enables potential owners to evaluate the economic impact before deciding to proceed.

Figure 5.3 illustrates the stages and timing of a typical captive development process. At the conclusion of each phase, employers have an opportunity to make a decision whether to proceed to the next phase.

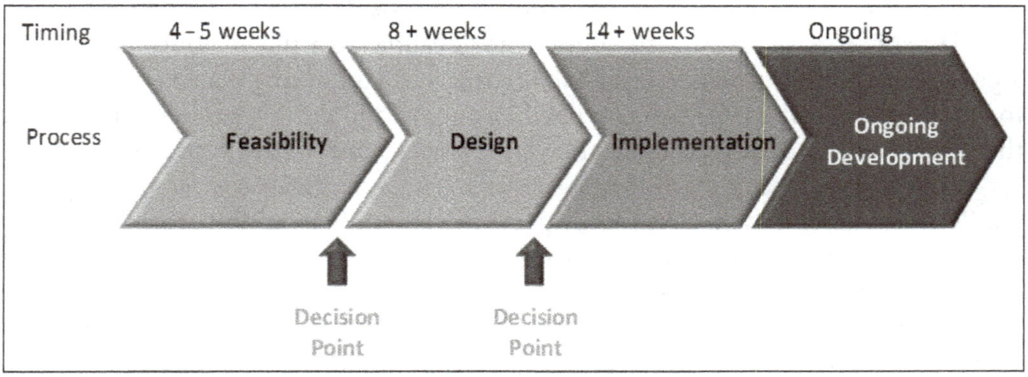

Figure 5.3 Typical Captive Development Process

B. Feasibility

As discussed in Chapter 2, a comprehensive feasibility study provides the rationale upon which the decision to form a captive (or place employee benefits into a captive) is based. The first part of the feasibility study process is dedicated to information gathering. Typically, information regarding plan designs and historical loss experience for the appropriate lines of insurance and financial information about the parent company is gathered.

This data is used to identify the best captive structure for each organization and its particular accounting policies and employee benefits risks. There are several viable captive structures, including participating in a cell captive, which is owned by a third party.

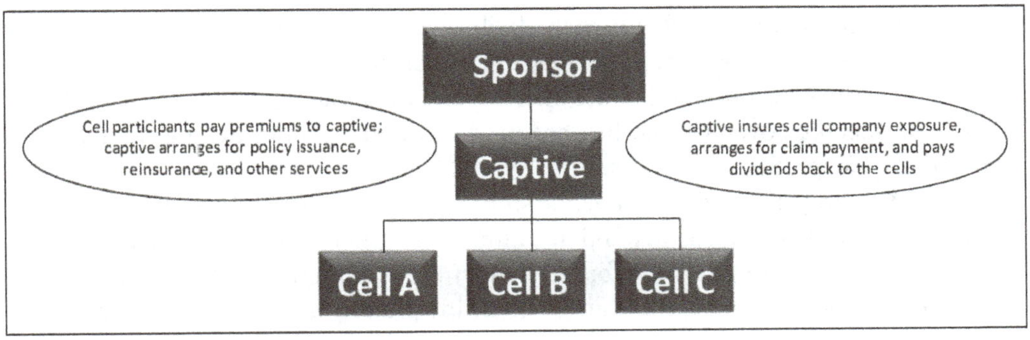

Figure 5.4 Typical Cell Captive Structure

Alternatively, a single-parent (owned) captive provides greater control and flexibility than cell captives (see Figure 5.5).

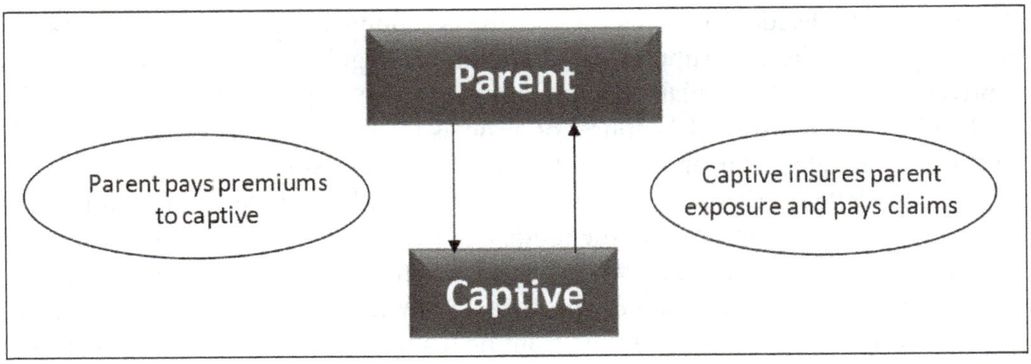

Figure 5.5 Pure Captive Structure

The chosen captive structure is the basis upon which cost savings can be determined for each employee benefits plan. Some benefit plans cannot produce savings sufficient to warrant placement in a captive. Often companies look at cell captives if this is the case.

The captive feasibility study also provides an analysis of captive domiciles and a recommendation that meets the employer's requirements. There are over 30 captive domiciles in the United States, and regulations change periodically, so careful evaluation of domicile options is important. The insurance tests, including risk shifting, risk distribution, business purpose, and so on, must be reviewed.

The DOL requires that ERISA benefits be funded in a captive subject to the U.S. courts. In order to follow the DOL-expedited process (discussed in subsection D, Implementation) most companies use a U.S.-based captive, or form a branch of a foreign domiciled captive. The feasibility analysis provides the information to make an informed decision as to whether to form the captive, as well as providing the basis for the domicile regulator's approval. Briefly, the feasibility study typically covers the following:

- Captive legal structure;
- Optimal retention levels for each eligible line of insurance;
- A review of appropriate domiciles and a preferred option;
- The captive's economic impact on the parent company;
- The specific coverage that belongs (and those that do not belong) in a captive;
- Five-year proformas;
- Cost savings through improved cash flows and expense reductions;
- The impact of various tax and accounting treatments, and an in-depth discussion of the IRS tests for tax deductible premiums and loss reserves;
- Discussion on plan options and benefit integration that may create further savings; and
- Timetable and costs for implementing the captive solution.

C. Design

If the employer decides to form a captive, the feasibility study becomes part of a detailed captive application submitted to the domicile regulator. For employee benefits captives covering ERISA plans, DOL approval is also required. If appropriate, the DOL's EXPRO or "fast track" application process typically requires between 78 to 90 days from the date of the application to the ultimate decision.

The domicile regulator requires a business plan with a detailed description of the captive structure, its owners, and the funded benefit plans. The application also must include information on the captive's board of directors and key committee members. The captive's premium rates are often calculated by the employer's actuarial consultants working in conjunction with the fronting insurer. Five-year financial statements are required to demonstrate that the risks are sufficiently protected by loss reserves, capital and surplus, and reinsurance.

The business plan must include the captive's service providers. These include

- Third-party benefit administration, often provided by the fronting insurer;
- Stop-loss insurance and, if appropriate, reinsurance provider;
- Legal services;
- Tax and accounting services;
- Auditing and banking;
- Captive consulting and actuarial services; and
- Captive management.

D. Implementation

There are a few steps involved in the process to implement employee benefit plans in a captive.

1. Domicile Approval

A well-conceived and executed application covers all the domicile regulator's requirements and should generate few queries. However, it is not uncommon for the regulator to require clarifications or additional information. Most domiciles utilize the services of a third party actuary to review the captive's actuarial calculations and financial projections. As the captive matures and generates excess surplus, the board may decide to declare a dividend or employ the excess surplus in the form of reduced premium rates.

2. Department of Labor Approval

Once the domicile regulator approves the business plan, if the benefits are subject to ERISA, the DOL filing must be created and submitted to the DOL. Like the domicile regulators, the DOL may ask questions regarding the application. These questions will need to be answered as part of the process. If the application has been submitted as part of the EXPRO process, the DOL has 45 days to tentatively approve or reject the application. After tentative authorization is issued, notices are sent to participating employees. Within 78 days or more, the final authorization is issued for the captive.

3. Underwriting the Employee Benefits in the Captive

Once the DOL issues final authorization, the captive begins the implementation process. Vendor contracts are finalized, the new employee benefit plans are communicated to employees, and enrollment can take place.

E. Ongoing Development

Establishing a captive to fund employee benefits risks creates a long-term financial solution that manages employee benefit costs and stabilizes this element of a company's balance sheet. On the other hand, the employees now own an insurance company that requires prudent governance and formal reporting to the captive regulator to remain in compliance, as discussed in Chapter 7.

Governance. As with P&C captives, captive boards and shareholders meet annually and usually within the domicile. The finance committee tracks the captive's financial performance through the services of accounting and captive management advisors. The underwriting committee manages the insurance placements advised by the captive's outside actuaries and consultants.

Re-pricing and new member additions. The actuary will calculate the ongoing impact of cost, utilization trends, changing demographics, and participation levels in the various insurance programs, and will make rate adjustments on an annual basis to ensure that the captive can continue to fulfill its financial obligations in conjunction with the fronting insurer. These changes may necessitate going back to the market to consider alternative vendors where necessary. The captive structure allows a great deal of flexibility to build customized programs and adjust plan designs on employee contribution levels, to reflect the changing needs of the employer over time.

Additional insurance lines. Having invested in the captive structure, it is relatively easy to agree on adjustment in the business plan with the domicile regulator and to add additional insurance lines to a well-established program. Those employers who may start off covering group life and disability coverage through their captive may consider adding retiree medical or medical stop-loss lines at a later date.

Benefit integration. The captive enables employee benefit plans and property and casualty plans to be funded through essentially the same captive program. This provides spread of risk and overall stability. The potential to coordinate and consolidate data also allows for benefit integration that can generate additional savings, as benefit overlaps are eliminated and administrative and risk efficiencies are introduced. This often results in a better employee experience along with continued savings. Workers' compensation, disability, and medical plans particularly lend themselves to integration.

IX. USING A CAPTIVE TO FUND MEDICAL STOP-LOSS

Healthcare reform, increasing costs, lasered coverage, and leveraged trends are causing many employers to reconsider their stop-loss options. These include employers whom are fully insured considering a move to self-insurance and current self-insured employers.

Healthcare reform mandates have led many employers to review the cost of their medical insurance programs including funding alternatives and the need for additional stop-loss coverage. Deciding to insure medical stop-loss and fund it in a captive has proven to be a great way for employers who self-fund their health coverage to add a layer of protection from excessively high individual or aggregate health claims and meet ACA requirements.

Medical stop-loss is not normally considered an ERISA benefit and thus stop-loss captives are not subject to DOL approval in the United States like many benefits are. Also, by funding stop-loss in a captive, an employer gains access to lower-cost reinsurance they might otherwise not be eligible for as a direct purchaser.

A. How Medical Stop-Loss Captive Funding Works

Figure 5.6 depicts a typical medical stop-loss captive funding approach.

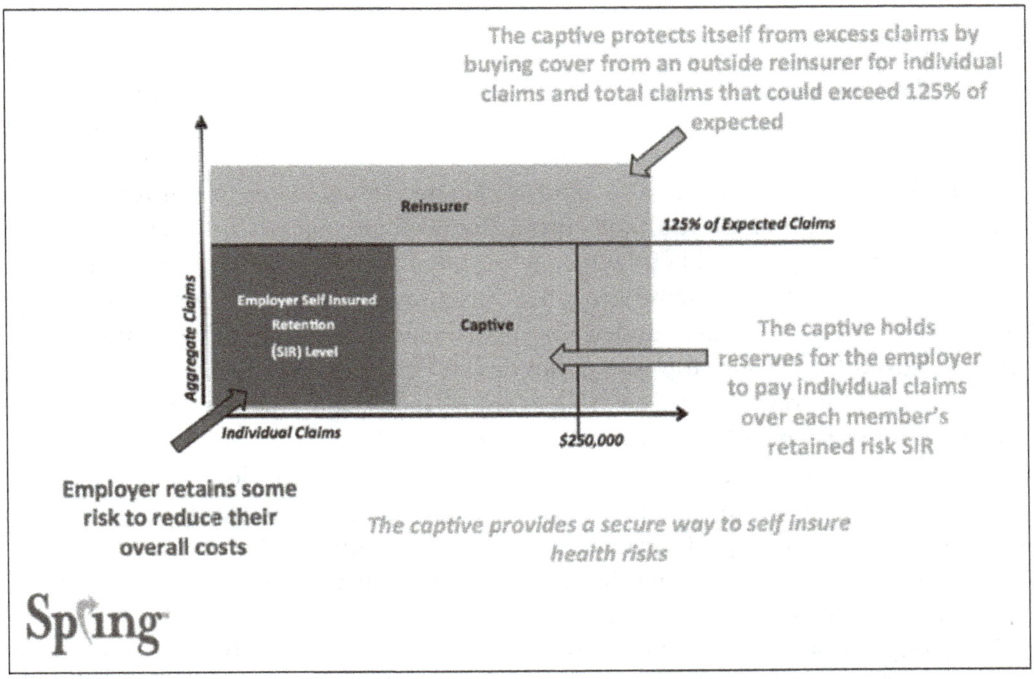

Figure 5.6 Typical Medical Stop-Loss Funding Approach

Self-insurance with stop-loss saves money through elimination of carrier profit, premium taxes, improved cash flow as the employer holds on to the claim lag between date of service and date of payment, exemption from state mandates (though not from ACA mandates), and reduced administration fees as these are bifurcated from the claims costs.

As claim costs are not completely predictable, self-insured employers are usually able to budget fairly closely to actual costs through the purchase of a well-designed stop-loss program.

Claims unpredictability generally arises from variance in the number of large claims for any one claimant and the cost per large claim.

The purchase of specific stop-loss insurance coverage protects from claims on any one individual exceeding a threshold amount, say $200,000, in a given year. Larger employers choose specific stop-loss attachment points as high as $350,000 to $750,000 while smaller employers may choose stop-loss levels of $30,000 to $100,000. An actuary can best recommend an appropriate attachment level to ensure a small likelihood of claims exceeding a tolerable risk level, such as 110 percent or 125 percent of expected.

Stop-loss rates typically increase well in excess of normal medical trend. So if your underlying program costs have gone up 8 percent, your stop-loss costs are likely to go up well in excess (e.g., 13 percent). The reason for this is the leveraging impact of the stop-loss coverage and attachment point. This results from the fact that claims that were just under the attachment point in 2012 with regular medical trend will be over the attachment point in 2013 and these will be added to all the trended claims already over the attachment point. To counteract this, employers often regularly increase their attachment levels. Captive funding minimizes these changes.

The most common stop-loss terms cover claims on a paid basis. For self-insured first timers, moving from a fully insured program is typically "12/12"—incurred in 12 months and paid in 12 months. This first year is referred to as "immature" as there are fewer expected claims paid due to the claim lag. The second year "mature" terms might be "24/12" to cover the incurred claims run out from the first year. For an increased price, a terminal liability option may be offered, where upon termination, the employer can purchase additional protection to cover the remaining claim run out.

In the past, stop-loss policies typically included a lifetime limit of $1 to 2 million. Amounts above this layer can be reinsured or funded through the captive. As employers can no longer limit their underlying plans, it is important to have this lifetime limit removed from your stop-loss policy if you have not already done so. Stop-loss carriers may still look to impose annual limits. It is important that you make sure any annual limits coordinate with your underlying plan.

A crucial coverage for smaller employers is aggregate stop-loss protection. The typical cost is $5 per employee per month (or less) and protects against actual claims on amounts below the specific attachment point exceeding 125 percent of expected. Though the likelihood of hitting the aggregate attachment point is small, the cost for this "sleep-well protection" is cheap.

Aggregate stop-loss should not be confused with another offering to lower price—an aggregating specific deductible. By way of example, see Table 5.1.

Table 5.1 Aggregating Specific Deductible

Claim	Specific Assumption	Net
$225,000	$75,000	$50,000
$150,000	$75,000	$75,000
		$225,000
Aggregating Specific		$100,000
Reimbursement		$125,000

Often the reinsurer will reduce premium one for one, or $100,000 in this example.

At time of purchase and annual renewal, most stop-loss carriers ask for disclosure statements requiring the employer to disclose an adverse developing claims bid submission to the carrier. Typically they would like this about 30 to 45 days prior to the effective date. The disclosure statement asks for individual detail for potential large claimants based on past claim history, certain diagnosis, and so on. If something adversely material shows up, the stop-loss carrier may want to discuss options such as raising the price, putting in aggregating specific deductible or "lasering" (excluding certain individuals or using a higher deductible for certain individuals). Carriers willing to provide final rates earlier may build additional margin into their rates.

Typically, employers purchase stop-loss on a single plan basis, and most coverage is purchased in the commercial market. Some employers purchase coverage from their owned captive reinsurer already providing insurance protections to other risks of the employer. This allows the captive to retain pricing risk margins. Further, as medical stop-loss risk is generally uncorrelated to the remaining captive risks, the overall employer risk profile is reduced through this approach. Finally, the stop-loss program can be geared toward the needs of the employer including, for example, various risk-sharing arrangements. The captive will typically purchase reinsurance protection to cover catastrophic claims and perhaps share in the claims risk. Generally, carriers writing captive reinsurance protection are experts in this area and are not the usual direct stop-loss writers.

B. Common Types of Stop-Loss Captives

Stop-loss captives are very similar in structure and nature as their property and casualty (P&C) counterparts. Like P&C captives, the two most common stop-loss structures are single-parent (pure) captives and group captives, discussed in more detail next.

1. Single-Parent Captives

Single-parent stop-loss captives are generally a subsidiary of a parent organization and are established to insure the parent's risk. Single-parent captives are generally not set up specifically to insure stop-loss risk; rather stop-loss is added into existing captives as an additional line of coverage. This is usually the case due to the size of the premiums and the difficulty a company would have to financially justify a stand-alone medical stop-loss captive.

Adding stop-loss to an existing single-parent captive is one of the common options in the captive industry and one that countless companies are realizing real savings with. With so many employers self-funding their health insurance today and also insuring elements of their casualty risk in captives, this trend is sure to continue single-parent captive funding's share of the medical stop-loss market will continue to increase.

2. Group Captives

Often, employers will form a group captive to fund their medical stop-loss. Such an arrangement provides individual members with the financial benefits of captive funding while sharing the overall administrative burden associated with forming an insurance company; thereby retaining stop-loss pricing risk margins. The employer-owned stop-loss insurer purchases reinsurance protection as necessary.

Group medical stop-loss captives are a great way for small and mid-size businesses to get an extra layer of coverage by banding together with other companies. These group captives can be heterogeneous or homogeneous and, assuming enough companies participate to make it financially feasible, can be set up as their own stand-alone captives. Each member of the group has its own self-funded plans and administration and just buys into the group captive for stop-loss. Typically, these groups can save 5 to 20 percent.

C. Who Should Consider Medical Stop-Loss Captive Funding?

While every circumstance is different and anyone considering captive funding should seek the advice of a professional consultant, generally, $1 million in premiums is the threshold for single parent stop-loss captive funding. For group captives, a total of 1,000 covered employee lives and $2.5 million in premium is the starting point. There are, of course, a number of variable, which may dictate a higher or lower entry point for a particular company or group.

D. Cell Captives: The Right Fit for Many Businesses for Medical Stop-Loss Funding

For companies that don't have an existing captive, aren't large enough for a stand-alone medical stop-loss captive to make sense, and/or aren't interested in forming or joining a group captive, there is an alternative option. Using a cell captive for medical stop-loss coverage is an option that has been exploding of late among the mid-market. By renting space in an existing captive, covering medical stop-loss, and adding an extra layer of security to a self-funded plan, becomes a much more financially viable option.

1. *What Is a Cell Captive?*

A protected cell company (PCC) is a legal entity, set up by a sponsor, which is divided up into individually protected cells that are rented out by the sponsor to companies or groups who want to use a captive cell to fund various risks. The sponsor establishes the core of a PCC and the overall PCC structure. Once established, the sponsor also manages the PCC's day-to-day activities, allowing cell owners to avoid a lot of the corporate and administrative resources typically required for a captive insurance or reinsurance company.

With a PCC, you essentially benefit from pooled administration, but not pooled risk. Each cell in a PCC is independent of and insulated from the others and the core in terms of assets and liabilities. Often, PCCs will allow companies to own more than one cell, and typically each cell is still treated individually.

2. *What Are the Benefits to a Cell Captive?*

There are a number of benefits to insuring your risk using a protected cell company:

- Easy entry into funding risk. While you still have to clear the typical regulatory hurdles of setting up a captive, which vary greatly depending on the risk in question, a great deal of the administrative time and money that you would typically spend is eliminated since we have already set up the shell entity for you.
- Economies of scale. With a protected cell company, you enjoy continued administrative savings due to economies of scale from potentially pooled administrative costs.

- Professional captive management. As an owner of a cell, you generally can expect day-to-day management services from professional captive managers.

3. *Is a PCC Right for You?*

Participation in a protected cell captive is attractive, but not for everyone. Generally speaking, mid-size companies that are dipping their toes in captive funding are the likeliest participants given the lower barriers to entry and management assistance a PCC offers. That said, there are a number of other reasons why companies of all sizes would strategically use a cell captive to address their risk portfolio. A feasibility study will go a long way in identifying if a company is a good fit for participation in a PCC.

Chapter 6

The Role of Corporate Counsel

Michael T. Scott

I. INTRODUCTION

According to my friends at Spring Consulting[1] there are almost 7,000 captive insurers globally and over 90 percent of the Fortune 500 companies have a captive insurance company. Suffice it to say, if you are corporate counsel for a medium or large firm, it is likely that you will find yourself dealing with a captive insurance company and the issues that arise out of them.

In this chapter we are going to explore the roles of corporate counsel within the world of captive insurance companies and discuss how corporate counsel should manage the conflicts of interest that arise within these different roles. Before delving into these topics, it is important to understand the business reasons that your company may have to participate in the world of captives.

II. BUSINESS REASONS TO HAVE A CAPTIVE INSURANCE COMPANY[2]

Prior to exploring the various reasons to form a captive insurance company, I want to make an important point. A company should only establish a captive insurance company if there is a valid non-tax business reason to do so. While there are tax advantages to forming a captive, they should not be the sole reason a company forms a captive. Also, if your company is not comfortable with assuming risk of loss and taking some volatility with respect to loss, don't form a captive. Moreover, when forming a captive, or making any risk-management decision for that matter, you should never risk more than your company can afford to lose. Finally, your company has, or will form, a captive because of the benefits that it can achieve through captive insurance. As such, always keep in mind that the sole purpose of the captive is to help your company achieve its business goals.

When deciding to form a captive, a company should also be of the mind-set that captive insurance is a long-term commitment. It is well known in the captive industry that captives are easy to get into but hard to get out of. Finally, if your company doesn't spend enough on insurance premiums or have a good loss experience, it's probably not a good candidate for a captive insurance company.[3]

If your company doesn't already have a captive insurance company, it will need to form one. The first step in forming a captive is to commission a feasibility study, discussed more fully in Chapter 2. Most captive managers can provide this service, but corporate counsel should be involved. A feasibility study will help determine if the benefits of a captive insurance company outweigh the additional costs. The study will look at items such as potential domiciles, costs, coverages that might be included, premiums, the capital needed, and so on.

A. Reduce the Reliance on Commercial Insurance

The main business reason that your company may have a captive is to reduce the reliance on commercial insurance when the corporation or captive can retain the risks for the business. By reducing the risk on commercial insurance the company can also reduce cost of risk by eliminating frictional costs of commercial insurance.

When determining how much retention a company should take in the captive, corporate counsel should play a big role, especially with regard to third-party liability retentions. It is important to analyze past losses, past exposures, and future expected losses. In general, companies should retain expected losses and only transfer losses that are considered catastrophic. Risk transfer decisions, though, should also take into consideration the cost of outside risk transfer. Corporate counsel and risk managers should consult with financial and business leaders of the organization when determining corporate retentions. The decision on risk retention is a critical decision. While I encourage companies to retain expected losses, don't risk more than the company can afford to lose. Figure 6.1 demonstrates the appropriate analysis when picking a retention.

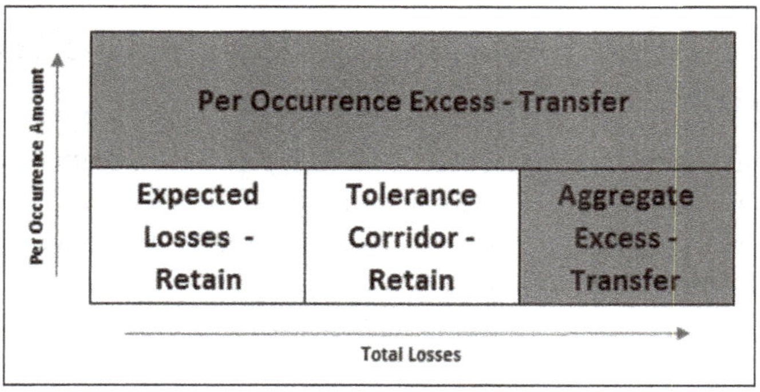

Figure 6.1 Determining Appropriate Retentions

With regard to reducing friction costs, we need to understand how insurers set insurance premiums for larger corporations. Just like when a company estimates expected losses in retention decisions, insurers will also estimate a company's expected losses when setting premiums. Added to expected losses will be expense charges for things like policy issuance and loss adjusting, a charge for catastrophic losses, a charge for overhead and profit, and a charge for the insurer's cost of capital. As such, by transferring expected losses to insurers, a company will end up paying overhead and profit and expense charges on expected losses while, over the long term, will still pay for expected losses. Utilizing a captive means that the company can avoid these frictional costs while also retaining premiums until losses are actually paid.

B. Provide Stability with Respect to Insurance Premiums, and Provide Loss Control Services

The second business reason to utilize a captive is to provide stability with respect to insurance premiums and to provide loss control services. With respect to price stability, this is achieved in two ways. First, by retaining a loss corridor in excess of expected losses, the company avoids premium effects of loss years that are slightly worse than expected. Also, during hard insurance markets increased retentions can be traded in exchange for no premium increases, whereas in soft markets retention can be taken down if needed or the company can take advantage of premium decreases.

In today's world companies are extremely focused on reducing losses. Not only is this important to protect property, but it is even more important to make sure that employees return home safe every day. By taking retentions and paying premiums into a captive, companies can make sure appropriate loss control services are provided. While most insurers will provide loss control services, by taking control over these services, companies can make sure that the services fit the needs of the company and are coordinated with the company's loss control objectives. Moreover, if these loss control efforts result in an actual reduction in losses, then the benefit of this will result in underwriting gains for the captive. If the company bought risk transfer as opposed to retaining losses, the benefit of a reduction in losses inures to the benefit of the insurer.

C. Provide Coverage That Is Not Otherwise Available

A third reason that companies utilize captives is to provide coverage that is not otherwise available from the commercial markets and to provide customized insurance programs. This is especially important if the company has exposures or risks that cannot be addressed in the conventional insurance market. Utilizing a captive can also give a company direct access to reinsurance capacity, which may have costs advantages over commercial coverage or can also help address difficult risks.

D. Allocate the Cost of Risk

A fourth reason to utilize a captive is to help allocate the cost of risk among business units and to provide better loss data and analysis. By helping allocate the cost of risk, the captive can help business units share risk. While a loss may be within the company's overall risk appetite, an individual business unit may not want to absorb the loss within its own profit and loss center. The captive can help smooth losses between business units and allow business units to budget and plan better without the variability of losses. Finally, underwriting profits can fund loss analysis and modeling that can help companies make better business decisions.

E. Provide Improved Claim Handling and Control Over Claims

A fifth reason that companies utilize captives is to provide improved claim handling and provide control over claims. While insurers are experts in claims handling, their services may not be tailored to your company's need. This can be especially important with respect to claims involving important customers or with professional liability claims.

F. Investment Income

A sixth reason that a company may utilize a captive is to gain control over capital and earn investment income. When a company pays premiums to a captive, the parent company can control the investment of those funds until the funds are needed to pay claims. If a company pays premium to a commercial carrier, that carrier earns the investment income on the funds.

G. Opportunities to Write Related Third-Party Business and Tax Advantages

The final two reason that companies may use a captive is that the captive can give companies opportunities to write related third-party business which reduce costs and earn profit, and the captive can provide tax advantages regarding claim reserves. An example of a third-party business that reduces cost would be an owner-controlled insurance program where the captive takes certain risks of the company's contractors. Examples of a third-party business that can earn profit for the company are warranty plans and cargo insurance on CIF sales. Such offerings may also help a company distinguish itself from its competitors (see Chapter 2).

III. CORPORATE COUNSEL'S ROLE WITHIN A CAPTIVE

As corporate counsel for a company with a captive insurer, there may be many roles within the captive that you may have to fill. These roles could be the risk manager/president of the captive, claims manager for the captive, board member on the captive, or legal advisor to the captive. All of these roles are important and we will explore each one in turn. All of these roles also create conflicts that corporate counsel will have to manage. It is important to remember that the captive exists to benefit the parent company and help it meet its goals. While it is important to manage conflicts of interest in order to maximize the value of the captive to the parent company, always keep in mind that if conflicts between the captive and the parent can't be managed properly, the parent company may not continue to support the captive.

A. Risk Manager/President of the Captive

The first role we explore is the role of risk manager/president of the captive. In most companies, the risk manager position either reports to the general counsel or to the chief financial officer (or treasurer who reports to the CFO). Risk managers reporting through the CFO is the most common. But regardless of where risk managers report, this role can be performed by corporate counsel.

When corporate counsel is appointed as the risk manager, he or she may have many duties, including developing and implementing risk management and insurance programs that support the company's business strategies while cost-effectively reducing and managing risk, managing risks through various risk control and risk financing methods, administering the company's claims, and managing the company's captive insurance operations. A big part of a risk manager's responsibility involves negotiating reinsurance contracts for the captive, buying insurance on behalf of the company, and managing relationships with brokers, loss control engineers, third-party administrators, lawyers, and captive managers. A risk manager is also responsible for the financial results of the captive and making sure programs in the captive are underwritten properly and that the programs help the parent company achieve its goals.

Responsibility for the financial results of the captive insurance operations also requires that corporate counsel should be familiar with both statutory accounting principles (SAP) and generally accepted accounting principles (GAAP). SAP are accounting principles used in the insurance industry. Model laws developed by the National Association of Insurance Commissioners (NAIC) and passed by all states require that insurance companies follow SAP. While captives may not have to follow SAP based on the domicile chosen, your captive may have to if it is rated by a rating agency such as AM Best or it participates in a certain third-party business. GAAP, on the other hand, the accounting method used for all other business, is required by the Securities Exchange Commission, and will be the method used by the parent company. It will also be the method used by the parent company when consolidating the results of the captive into the overall results of the parent company. Corporate counsel must understand the difference and develop policies and procedures for the management of the captive that makes it easy to consolidate the results of the captive with the parent company.

The main difference between SAP and GAAP is that under SAP the financial statements will indicate its value as if it were in liquidation rather than an ongoing concern. This helps users of the financial statements determine whether the captive is in a position to pay insurance claims. Under GAAP, financial statements are prepared on a going-concern basis. This allows users of the financial statements to measure the profitability of the business and to assess its future value.

GAAP financial statements follow the matching principle, whereas under SAP no matching principle is followed. The matching principle means that a company can record expenses related to revenue only when the revenue is also recognized. For example, if an insurer sells an insurance policy, under SAP it must recognize all the costs associated with selling that policy while it can only recognize revenue as it is earned. Under GAAP, the expenses and revenue will be matched.

Finally, being responsible for the financial results of the captive may also mean that the corporate counsel may have to sign various financial statements and regulatory filings as the president of the captive. Corporate counsel should be aware of the responsibilities and liabilities associated with signing financial statements and must fully understand the contents of such statements before signing off on them.

B. Claims Manager

At some companies, the claims function reports to the risk manager while at other companies the claims function and the risk management is split. In those companies where the functions are split, the claims function tends to reside in the legal department. Sometimes casualty claim responsibility and property claim responsibility is separated into two functions with corporate counsel managing the casualty claims function. The claims function entails such duties as managing third-party administrators (TPAs), managing carrier claims relationships, managing litigation, and setting proper reserves for the captive.

At companies where the risk management and claims function do not reside in the legal department, corporate counsel still has a role in the operation of the captive. At these companies, corporate counsel will still serve as the legal advisor to the risk manager and/or the claims manager. In this role, corporate counsel must understand many aspects of the law that relate to captives. The first area of law that corporate counsel must understand is the basic regulatory law in the jurisdiction where the captive is located. There are over 70 global captive insurance domiciles, with Bermuda and Cayman Islands being the largest, and over 35 U.S. states that support captives, with Vermont being the largest. While there are similarities in most captive laws, there are nuances from domicile to domicile. Moreover, corporate counsel must also understand the law relating to reinsurance and policy coverage as well as the tax aspects of owning and operating a captive.

C. Board of Directors

The final role that corporate counsel may fulfill with regard to a captive is that he or she may be asked to serve on the board of directors of the captive. Of course, as with any board, corporate counsel must be aware of the fiduciary duties associated with serving on a board. The basic fiduciary duties of board members are the duty of loyalty, the duty of care, and the duty to act in good faith. While these concepts are beyond the scope of this chapter, corporate counsel should seek advice on their obligations and duties. For the most part, the business judgment rule will protect directors as long as they meet their fiduciary obligations while making decisions for the captive.

With a vast majority of these roles, corporate counsel must be diligent to manage the conflict of interest that exists in each role. As you can see, there are many roles that corporate counsel can fulfill within a captive insurance company.

IV. MANAGING CONFLICTS OF INTEREST

A conflict of interest is a situation whereby a person has a duty to more than one person or entity and the interest of those multiple parties may not be aligned. As discussed earlier, corporate counsel can have multiple interests when it comes to captive insurance. Examples of multiple interests in the world of captives include (1) conflict of interests between the parent company and the captive in setting up an insurance program (this could include coverages written in the captive and premium charged by the captive to the parent company's business units); (2) conflict of interest in claims situations (this could include conflict between the parent company and the captive itself, the parent company and a reinsurer, or the captive and a reinsurer and the captive as a primary insurer and excess insurers); and (3) conflict of interest when corporate counsel represents both the captive and the parent company as legal advisor. It is very important to manage the various conflict of interest that arise with regards to captive insurers. In this section of this chapter, we will explore each type of conflict and give thoughts on how to manage those conflicts. Again, I will remind corporate counsel that the reason the parent company forms a captive insurer is to help the parent company meet its strategic goals. Thus, you should sure that when managing conflicts that you do so in a manner to make sure that the captive is meeting this goal. Again, if the captive is not helping the parent company in achieving its goals, management may lose interest in captive insurance.

A. Conflict of Interest in Setting Up Insurance Programs

As discussed earlier, one of the main reasons to have a captive is to reduce the overall cost of risk to the parent company. When corporate counsel serves as both the risk manager for the parent company as well as a legal advisor to, or president of, the captive insurer, conflicts will arise where the cost savings resulting from the use of the captive will reside within the company. While on a consolidated basis it should not make any difference where the cost savings reside, in most companies operational managers will want to share in the cost savings created by using the captive. While utilizing a captive insurer does give a risk manager the ability to share cost savings with the parent company's business units, it must make sure it does so in a structured, well thought-out manner. If programs in the captive are not underwritten properly and risk premium is not adequately determined, it can cause problems with tax authorities, regulators, and with fronting companies. To avoid these issues, the best approach is to remove the conflict of interest by developing written underwriting guidelines for the captive. For example, most commercial insurers will target a 60 to 65 percent loss ratio. Captive insurers can target a higher loss ratio, 85 percent for example. This is because frictional costs are less in a captive insurer than a commercial insurer. By establishing premiums based on this higher loss ratio, business units can share in the cost savings a captive creates. But even though a captive can operate at a higher loss ratio than a commercial insurer, written underwriting guidelines must be developed and followed. Also, by developing written underwriting guidelines, the way that the captive shares costs savings with business units can be spelled out in advance.

Conflicts can also arise when the captive allocates premium to business units. Usually these types of conflicts arise when one or more business units of the parent company takes issue with the premium allocation that they are receiving from the captive insurance company. Just like underwriting guidelines, captive insurers who allocate premium must have a thought-out and logical method to do the allocation. Fair allocation methods can be based on exposures, such as insured values, sales, payroll, number of vehicles, and so on, or based on loss experience of business units. Allocation decisions should be based on written criteria that are easily explained to business unit managers at the parent company. Cost allocations are a good way to motivate business units to reduce losses and focus on loss control and safety.

Finally, as stated earlier, one of the reasons to form a captive is to write coverage that is not otherwise available in the commercial markets. Corporate counsel and risk managers need to be careful when writing such programs into a captive insurer. While some coverages may not be available because of the risk profile of the parent company, for example risky products liability or professional liability exposure, the coverage can still be written in a captive. But coverages that are not commercially available because they do not represent risk transfer should be avoided. Corporate counsel should become familiar with FAS 113 and the requirements of risk transfer for insurance and reinsurance transactions to avoid problems.[4]

B. Conflict of Interest in Claims Situation

We previously discussed the many factors that enter into the decision of a company to form a captive insurance company. While some or all of the reasons to form a captive may have been taken into consideration when forming a captive, it seems that many captives over the years were formed due to dislocations in the insurance market and a company's desire to reduce costs. But more and more it seems like one of the main reasons that companies form a captive is to give them more control over the claims process. This is because claims are the largest portion of the cost of risk and difficult claims typically become very visible to upper management. While forming a captive insurance company to gain more control over the claims process can provide a large benefit to your company, it can also create conflicts of interest that need to be managed. The most important thing to remember to avoid conflict of interests in the claims management process is that while the captive should tailor claims handling to meet the needs of the parent company, the captive must always act in a good faith manner and handle claims in a similar manner that a commercial insurer would.

The first way that a captive can make sure it acts like a true insurance company is to make sure that there is a formal claim notification process. Regardless of whether the parent company buys coverage from a captive or a commercial insurer, it has a contractual obligation to notify its insurance carriers when a claim occurs. Likewise, if the captive buys reinsurance, or the parent company buys excess insurance, there will be a contractual obligation to notify reinsurers or excess carriers of a claim. To ensure that these obligations are met and to avoid the allegation that a conflict of interest exists, the captive should have a formal claims notification process that follows the claims notification clause in the insurance policies that it issues. This is particularly important when the risk manager of the parent is also the president of the captive. Do not fall into the trap of thinking that knowledge by the risk manager will also serve as notification of the claim to the captive. If formal notification is not given, it can lead to issues of "which hat" the risk manager was wearing in the claims process and allegations by reinsurers and excess carriers that the captive is not operated as a true insurer. This process can be further complicated if the captive program is a "fronted" program. In these cases a third party issues an admitted policy and reinsures the risk 100 percent to the captive. In these cases, best practice is for the parent company to give formal notification to both the fronting company as well as the captive. Captives should also make sure that fronting companies are providing notices of claims and cession statements to the captive.

When a claim occurs, the actual handling of the claim can also give rise to allegations of conflicts of interest. This is especially true when the claim is large enough to breach the captive's retention or when there is a coverage issue.

The first issue that the captive needs to address is who will actually handle claims. There are several options and they can vary depending on the type of claim. For example, the captive can develop an internal claims program, use a third-party administrator (TPA), or allow a fronting carrier to handle the claims. While all of these options can work for a captive, the best practice is to have all parties, including fronting carriers, the parent company, the captive, reinsurers, and excess carriers, expressly sign off on how the claims will be handled. This should be done in claims-handling instructions and in insurance and reinsurance agreements. Also, excess carriers and reinsurers may want to participate in claims handling of large claims, and this option should also be spelled out and agreed by all parties in advance.

If your company is new to the captive insurance world, you will most likely be looking at an outside service provider to handle claims. This is because it is difficult and costly to try to establish an in-house claims solution early on. By relying on an outside claims expert, it will free up resources to focus on other issues, such as program development. Once a captive is more mature, captive owners should revisit the issue of who will adjust losses. Also, mature captive programs have more data on the number and size of losses that helps in deciding if an in-house solution to managing losses makes sense.

To avoid conflicts, the relationship with the TPA should be documented in a written contract. The contract should clearly state the expectations the captive has of the TPA. This should be accomplished by having detailed, measurable results that the TPA will be held accountable for meeting. The contract should be reviewed with fronting carriers and reinsurers.

Regardless of who is chosen to adjust losses, the loss adjuster must adjust the claim in a good faith manner and in a manner similar to that which a commercial insurer would. The loss adjuster should not deal with the claims investigation in a summary manner simply because the claim is made by the captive's parent company. Basically, the loss adjuster should handle the claim as if the captive were a commercial insurer and the parent company was a policyholder of that commercial insurer. This is especially important when the parent's business units have strong feelings on settlement of claims, whether first party or third party claims. The adjuster should issue both interim reports as well as a final report. In first party claims, the parent should fill out a formal notice of loss. Best practice is to have someone in the risk management function review the reports to make sure there are no issues between what the business unit is claiming and the value of the claim, as determined in the discretion of the loss adjuster. If there are significant differences that could affect reinsurers or excess carriers, best practice is to invite those carriers to become involved in the claims handling.

When using a captive, care should also be taken in setting out a procedure for approving claim settlements. Specifically, written procedures should be developed on how claims payments will be approved. With some liability claims, the parent company will want to have the ability to settle claims. This is particularly important on certain lines of coverage such as products liability claims with important customers, medical professional liability coverage, and so on. This is acceptable as long as safeguards are in place before the captive pays the loss. Best practice is that while the parent company can settle such claims on its own, the parent company will have to provide evidence supporting both liability to the third party and the quantum to a third-party adjuster. The third-party adjuster will then make a recommendation of payment of the claim to the captive. Of course, allowing the parent company to settle losses may mean that the amount paid to settle the loss may be more than the amount recovered from the captive.

Also, recognize that corporate counsel, whether serving on the board of directors of the captive, in the role as risk manager, or a legal advisor to the captive and parent company, will have a fiduciary duty to both the captive and to the parent company. This creates a conflict of interest in some circumstances. Best practice is to appoint independent legal advice to the captive when there is a coverage issue or when the amount claimed by the parent company for settlement of a loss is different than the amount the independent adjuster is recommending for the claim.

Some captives have gone as far as to appoint a claims subcommittee of the board of directors that doesn't involve employees of the parent company or hiring an independent claims consultant to sign off on claim settlements. Of course, when a captive utilizes a claims subcommittee or an independent claims consultant to authorize settlement of claims, it will still have to employ loss adjusters as described earlier or hire independent legal counsel if coverage issues arise. Another option to avoid conflicts of interest would be to have separate corporate counsel who represents the captive. This corporate counsel should be different than the corporate counsel used to manage litigation for the parent company or who represents the parent company's business unit making the claim. Again, regardless of the solution chosen, it should be signed off by all parties in advance of claims.

There may be claims control and/or claims cooperation clauses in reinsurance contracts that the captive enters into. These clauses can also cause conflicts of interest in the claims-handling process. Captives can have reinsurance contracts with both fronting companies and with reinsurers. These clauses can give insurers or reinsurers the right to take over the handling of a claim or at least give them the right to associate in the handling of the claim. When these clauses exist, best practice is to have the carrier sign off on the claims process as noted previously prior to claims occurring. Also, the captive needs to be diligent in giving the carrier notice of losses. Failure to follow these clauses can lead to a denial of a claim. In general, these clauses should not provide a problem for captives as best practice is to include reinsurers and fronting companies in claims. Captives should develop long-term relationships with fronting carriers, reinsurers, and excess carriers and in order to build such long-term relationships, cooperation on claims is important.

In conclusion, effective claims handling will be critical to the ongoing success of the captive. Corporate counsel should be cognizant of the various conflicts that can arise in the handling of claims and take steps to avoid and minimize the conflicts. The best approach will always be to deal with conflicts before they exist. Also, all parties involved must keep in mind whose money is at stake when establishing claims-handling guidelines and processes; by understanding whose money is at stake, conflicts can be avoided. Finally, remember that the purpose of the captive is to help the parent company meet its goals and to make sure that conflicts in claims situations are managed in a way to ensure that the parent company can meet its goals.

C. Conflicts of Interest When Corporate Counsel Represents Both the Captive and the Parent Company as Legal Advisor

While most conflicts of interest related to captive insurers arise in the claims process, conflicts can also arise when corporate counsel represents both the captive and the parent company. In most companies with captives, there will be only one legal department for the entire corporate entity. In smaller and middle-size firms the entire legal department may be made up of just one attorney, the general counsel. In the vast majority of situations, the interests of the captive insurance company and the parent company are aligned, as they should be. As such, if the guidelines spelled out earlier regarding avoiding conflict of interest in claims situations are followed, there generally is not an issue with having one counsel for both the parent company and the captive insurance company. But there could be instances where conflicts of interest do arise and they need to be managed in a manner to maximize the benefits of having a captive insurance company.

The most obvious instance where a conflict of interest arises is when there is a dispute regarding a claim. Claim disputes are interesting because if the loss falls wholly within the captive insurer's retention, whether or not the loss is paid by the captive will make no difference in the overall consolidated results of the parent. This fact alone probably eliminates any potential conflict of interest for corporate counsel. But if the loss is in excess of the captive's retention, or the captive has aggregate loss protection, then how the loss is handled will affect reinsurers or excess carriers. In these situations, corporate counsel should be careful to avoid conflicts of interest to maximize the insurance or reinsurance claim for the captive and the parent company.

There generally will be two types of disputes that give rise to conflicts. The first is when the captive denies the claim based on coverage. The second is when the captive accepts liability, but its valuation of the claim differs from what the parent company is claiming. These situations should be handled differently.

When the captive denies coverage and the parent company disagrees, the first question becomes should the captive issue a reservation of rights letter and/or denial of coverage letter. In practical terms this is rarely done. Best practice requires the captive to go ahead and issue such letters to the parent. If the claim involves a fronting carrier, then the captive's job becomes easy, as the fronting carrier can deal with such matters.

Generally, when a conflict exists because an insurer issues a reservation of rights letter, the issue becomes whether the policyholder is entitled to appoint its own counsel. But in the captive context, corporate counsel usually represents the policyholder that is the parent company. Thus, the issue becomes whether or not the captive should retain independent counsel. In most cases, corporate counsel should be able to be independent, but if the parent company wants to challenge the coverage decision, then independent counsel should be hired for the captive.

The conflict gets even more complex if reinsurers or excess carriers also take the same coverage opinion that the captive takes. In these circumstances, the best practice is to have the reinsurer or excess carrier take over the claim and agree that the captive will follow the outcome of the dispute between the reinsurer/excess carrier and the parent company. By doing this, the conflict that exists between the captive and the parent company can be avoided.

When a conflict exists because of a dispute in the quantum of the claim, the best practice is to appoint independent accountants for the parent company and the captive. Generally if an agreement or compromise cannot be made on the claim and the claim is wholly within the captive's retention, a simple arbitration-like process can generally settle the claim. When excess carriers or reinsurers are involved and also dispute the quantum of the claim, a more advanced arbitration might need to be conducted to resolve the claim. If a full arbitration is to be conducted, independent counsel should be appointed for the captive.

V. CONCLUSION[5]

As you can see, a captive insurance company has a major influence on the parent company's risk-management strategy. Moreover, captives can provide many benefits to their parent if managed properly. Corporate counsel can play many roles within the captive and is a crucial component in making sure that the captive is successful. Regardless of the role corporate counsel takes in the captive, he or she must understand the reasons to form a captive and how to manage the conflicts that can arise in the operation of the captive.

Corporate counsel should be front and center when a company is considering forming a captive and should help the company answer the critical business, legal, and tax issues that must be addressed. This includes being heavily involved in the feasibility study and answering the questions of what programs should be placed in the captive, what the ownership structure should be, what domicile should be chosen, and how claims are to be managed.

My final word to corporate counsel is to focus on the four points discussed earlier in this chapter. First, remember that there must be a compelling non-tax reason to form a captive. Second, when making any risk management decision do not risk more than your company can afford to lose. Third, identify potential conflicts of interest in a claims-handling situation and address them with all involved parties before the conflict arises. Finally, the reason that your company formed a captive is to achieve benefits from it and to help your company meet its strategic needs. As such, you must manage your captive in a manner that helps your company meet its strategic goals.

Chapter 7

The Role of the Domicile Regulator

David F. Provost

I. INTRODUCTION

One of my favorite quotes that I have clipped to my PC monitor—I can't recall where I clipped it from for attribution—is "insurance departments should be concerned with creating a reasonable regulatory environment focusing on solvency and protecting the consumer and should not be the focus of economic development." That's a laudable ideal, but legislatures that pass captive laws have certain expectations that captive insurance will be a boon to their economy, so regulators often find themselves acting in the capacity of promoters of their domicile, while simultaneously serving as the gatekeepers of the domicile's business, and guardians of the domiciles' reputation. If promotion focuses on the benefits of captive insurance to prospective captive owners, and if no one sets a target for numbers of licenses issued, the regulator can avoid creating a "come one, come all" environment and prudently license and effectively regulate the captives under his or her domain. The consumer protection focus of the traditional regulator can be relaxed in most captive situations, since the consumer owns the insurance company. Captive insurance companies rarely get complaints from their policyholders!

II. MISSION OF THE VERMONT DEPARTMENT OF FINANCIAL REGULATION

The mission of the Captive Insurance Division OF THE Vermont Department of Financial Regulation is to maintain a regulatory system that attracts quality business to Vermont, promotes our reputation in the industry, and ensures the solvency of captive insurers while recognizing the special purpose for which they were created. The division pursues this mission by:

- Attracting and licensing quality programs whose primary purpose is risk management or risk financing;
- Performing ongoing financial surveillance;

- Performing periodic financial examinations;
- Implementing and enforcing laws and regulations;
- Developing effective and reasonable policies and procedures; and
- Advancing the growth of Vermont's captive industry.

III. REGULATORY APPROVAL PROCESS

We attract and license quality programs whose primary purpose is risk management or risk financing with a rigorous application process.

A. Meeting with a Regulator

It starts with an in-person meeting with the regulator, the prospective captive owner, and in most cases includes the selected captive manager. Other key service providers such as auditors and actuaries may also be invited. The meeting is a chance for the regulator to learn about the parent company operations, and to ask questions about the parent company's need for a captive insurance company. The prospective captive owner should be able to detail the issues facing the business that lead to the need for its own insurance company. Discussions will address the particular concerns facing the parent company such as cost, availability, or capacity of the traditional market, or an opportunity for the captive to operate as a profit center (or conversely as a major cost saving), or both. There's no need to avoid discussion of taxes, but if it appears the chief driver of the captive is a tax benefit, the regulator will be on high alert. Regulators will be expecting to see either a history of losses or a clear potential for losses that would be threating to the business. Lacking such a history or demonstrated risk, a regulator should be questioning the need for a business to form its own insurance company, and frankly, so should the prospective captive owner, who really must ask if the captive would make good business sense without the promised tax savings.

Usually, the result of the meeting is a green light to file an application, but there are occasions when we decline to accept an application, or insist on significant changes to the plan before we will accept it. Declinations are usually due to a poor fit with the domicile's ideals or statutes, and occasionally the regulator's preferences.

B. Feasibility Study

Each application must include a supporting feasibility study (discussed in Chapter 2). The submission of thorough and complete information in the study is vital to this process, as it forms the foundation of the application and demonstrates the economic viability of the captive. All financial discussions in the application must reference and closely correlate to the study findings. The application and other supporting documents form the business plan of the captive that regulators will use to track the captive's operations in the future. Broadly speaking, the study should address/include

- An actuarial evaluation of the exposure to claims;
- The proposed premiums to finance the expected value of claims and expenses;
- The proposed capital to support the exposures to be underwritten. Generally speaking, the premiums will support the expected losses and operations of the captive, while capital will help it absorb shock losses or other adverse scenarios;
- A pro forma financial statement showing an expected and adverse scenario;
- A summary of coverages, policy forms, lines of business, limits, deductibles, reinsurance, and retentions;
- Summary of the source and nature of resources for premiums and capital (i.e., cash, debt, loans, LOCs, assessable polices, etc.); and
- Discussion of marketing and sales plans if applicable (mostly applicable to group captives).

The actuarial study should discuss the methods used to project the value of claims. Also, the actuarial study should discuss adjustments for trend, loss development, benefit level, relevance of benchmarks, discounting for the time value of money, retention for the projection, and risk margins. We expect these discussions to be documented in a report.

Since this is the bulk of the application, you can imagine that it's also the focus of our review. We spend a great deal of time cross-referencing the study and other components of the application for consistency (no Hobgoblins here, Mr. Thoreau!). Vermont has made it standard practice for many years to hire a consulting actuary to assist in the review of the application. The consulting actuary provides a second pair of eyes for the regulator, challenges the assumptions and judgments used, and ensures that the feasibility study has been conducted and reported in accordance with accepted actuarial standards of practice. Increasingly, particularly with small captives, the consulting actuary may challenge whether or not the captive business constitutes risk transfer, due to the paucity of historical loss information.

Insurance companies are regulated entities, so the potential captive owner must understand the regulatory environment of the selected domicile, and if there does not appear to be any regulation, all of the necessary alarm bells should be ringing. An entity that is about to receive a license to conduct the business of insurance, even if only with affiliated organizations, must expect a degree of scrutiny, skepticism, and due diligence from the regulator. Licenses should not receive a rubber stamp handed out through a drive-up window!

IV. PERFORMING ONGOING FINANCIAL SURVEILLANCE

Once the company is licensed, it is expected to operate as an insurance company would by issuing policies of insurance, prudently investing the premiums, timely paying claims, and keeping accurate books and records.

A. Required Filings

There are certain standard filings to be made. Here are Vermont's basic reporting requirements; many domiciles will be similar:

- File an annual statement, using prescribed and permitted accounting principles, on the prescribed forms;
- File an audited financial statement each year, including a reconciliation to the annual statement, a report of evaluation of internal controls, accountant's letter of qualifications, and certification of review of audit work papers;
- Submit a statement of actuarial opinion on reserves;
- Pay required premium taxes, and
- Submit to a regulatory examination every three to five years.

B. Annual Meeting

Most domiciles also require the board of directors of the captive to hold a meeting annually in the domicile. This is more than just a tourism generator or a chance to visit a nice place for pleasure trip at the business' expense; it is a dedicated time each year to devote full attention to the captive and to sit down with the people that have been hired to help operate it. Captive owners should take this obligation seriously, and conduct detailed board meetings, and use the visit as a time for some checking up on their service providers. A critical legal consideration, often overlooked, for the annual domicile meeting is to demonstrate that the captive is conducting insurance business only where it is licensed. The annual meeting is an opportunity to review all of the captive's insurance operations, policies, and procedures. It can also be a time to refresh connections with the local regulator—our department is frequently invited to attend board meetings to speak and to listen, and we accept as many of those invitations as we possibly can.

C. Monitoring and Surveillance

It might sound like a spy novel, but "surveillance" is the accepted term for the regulator's job of keeping a watchful eye on the companies under his or her purview. For single-parent captives, that entails a detailed review of the annual filings, and a regular monitoring of the parent company. We have adapted many of our surveillance procedures from standards developed by the National Association of Insurance Commissioners (NAIC). For certain types of captives, we follow NAIC rules to the letter, but for most pure (single-parent) captives, we modify the requirements to suit what we find to be sufficient. Regulators use a variety of tools, including ratio analysis or risk-based capital reports to effectively triage the annual filings so that attention can be directed first to those companies who might be exhibiting signs of difficulty.

Annual monitoring and surveillance activities include review of annual CPA-audited financials for both the parent company and the captive; review of the actuarial certification of loss and loss expense reserves for the captive; certification that a qualified, approved CPA has reviewed the audit work papers for the audit submitted; and, opinion and internal control letters.

Monitoring of the captive parent company level is conducted through review of SEC filings, daily financial newspapers, trade papers, and other resources.

V. EXAMINATIONS

"Trust but verify" is the mantra of many regulators, and it applies equally to the captive insurance world. Every domicile should have some method for checking up on the insurance companies under their supervision. Some domiciles achieve this by direct regulation and auditing of the captive managers, but most U.S. domiciles conduct periodic examinations of the captive itself. Vermont examines each of its captives every three to five years, depending on our assessment of the company. The scope of the exam will vary with the type of captive. In the United States, risk retention groups are subject to the same examination rules as any traditional insurance company, and will undergo a risk-focused exam that follows the NAIC Financial Condition Examiners Handbook. At the other end of the spectrum, a single-parent captive will likely be subject to a much simpler exam, but still based on the best practices in the aforementioned handbook, proportionally applied.

VI. IAIS GUIDANCE

The United States has the NAIC to help develop high standards for the regulation of insurance companies. While the NAIC's work is rarely applied directly to captives, it is useful as a starting point for adapting to captive-specific regulation. The rest of the world has a similar guiding body in the International Association of Insurance Supervisors (IAIS). Like the NAIC, the IAIS is a voluntary organization of insurance regulators, and includes members from more than 200 jurisdictions. Its mission, as stated on the IAIS webpage, in part, is to "promote effective and globally consistent supervision of the insurance industry." The IAIS published its application paper on the regulation and supervision of captive insurers in November 2015. This document discusses the application of 18 insurance core principles (ICPs) to the regulation of captives. Included in those ICPs are many of the same things already discussed: licensing procedures, suitability of persons, corporate governance, risk management and internal controls, supervisory review and reporting, off-site monitoring and on-site inspections, and capital adequacy. Taxes are not mentioned in the paper. Any domicile regulator should be familiar with this document, and there should be corresponding similar provisions in the domicile's statutes and regulations.

VII. CAVEAT EMPTOR

A captive insurance company can be a very effective way to help manage and finance risk of parent companies of any size. Smaller organizations are less likely to have professional risk-management staff, and thus are more likely to rely heavily on outside advisors. Business owners should still use their own judgment when deciding how to accept that advice, and keep in mind all of the old adages that warn you that if it sounds too good to be true, it's probably trouble. Here are some specific questions for prospective captive owners to consider:

Was the captive presented as a tax savings, or as an insurance problem-solver? It's the American Way to avoid paying unnecessary taxes, but there must be a demonstrable insurance purpose to the captive—it needs to make good business sense without tax considerations.

Does the advisor do business in multiple domiciles, both onshore and offshore? Is the selected domicile chosen because it suits your business . . . or his? Most captive managers operate in many jurisdictions to suit the best interests of their clients, and can provide a detailed side-by-side analysis of recommended domiciles for the client to choose from.

How many captives are in the domicile? What is the total premium volume? If you do the math, you will find that in some domiciles, total premium divided by number of captives miraculously (suspiciously?) yields $1.2 million. That sounds more like a tax haven than a captive domicile. You might also find their premium volume doubling overnight when the 831(b) election limit increases from $1.2 million to $2.2 million!

Is pooling being pushed? Pooling can help insurance companies stabilize losses, but if none of the pool members have losses, pooling may be just a ruse to achieve risk distribution for income tax purposes. Will the pool actually pay up, without strings, if you have a loss? Why spend thousands each year on consultants and captive managers, and add on the possibility of sharing someone else's loss, if you expect no losses to share in turn?

What capital levels are being suggested? Each domicile has a statutory minimum capital requirement for all types of insurers, captive or traditional, but that is a solvency "floor," and is rarely appropriate. The feasibility study should provide a documented recommendation for the captive's initial capital needs, and that capital should support an adverse loss scenario.

Does the investment in a captive make sense? But for a tax benefit, would the allocation of capital and the premium volume be justified? The Risk & Insurance Management Society Inc. together with Advisen Ltd. conducts an annual survey of risk management professionals. The benchmark report defines "total cost of risk" as the cost of insurance plus the costs of the losses that are retained and the administrative costs of the risk management department. The average total cost of risk in 2014 was $10.80 per $1,000 of revenue, or 1.08 percent of revenue. Smaller businesses are likely to have a higher relative cost, but real questions should arise from both the potential captive owner and the regulator if the premiums to the captive alone are more than a few percentage points of revenue.

The captive should be an integral part of the business' insurance program, and (usually) augments, not replaces, traditional insurance coverage. How has the potential captive owner's consultants "fit" the captive into the rest of the insurance program? What changes are recommended to the purchase of traditional insurance as a result of forming a captive insurer?

If potential captive owners ask enough questions, they may help themselves avoid an untenable situation with the IRS. Does a family jewelry store really need its own insurance company? I'm skeptical.

Note: While Mr. Provost is employed by the State of Vermont as the chief regulator of captive insurance companies, this discussion does not necessarily reflect the view of his office, the Department of Financial Regulation, or the State of Vermont.

Chapter 8

Closing the Captive

Andrew Rothseid

I. INTRODUCTION

Captives are efficient risk-management and capital tools for corporations. As addressed in previous chapters, captive structures allow corporations to maximize their use of capital, retain more control over their risk-management activities, and reduce the cost of third-party insurance. Yet, what happens when a captive ceases to operate or is no longer needed?

The captive owners may decide to handle the captive in various ways, from keeping the captive in existence, but not write any more business (also known as "run off"), to completely terminating the captive (the tax consequences of termination are briefly discussed in Chapter 3). The various options and associated consequences of closing a captive are addressed in this chapter.

II. DORMANCY

Certain states, including Delaware, Montana, and Vermont, allow captive insurers to enter a "dormancy" status. Criteria for dormancy include (1) minimal retained capital requirements, (2) the absence of insurance liabilities in the captive, and (3) a representation that the captive no longer transacts business as an insurer. This process allows a captive owner to maintain a minimally capitalized shell entity (often without premium tax obligations) for future use. The utility of the process may be measured by the captive owner's ability to rid itself of its insurance exposures (particularly IBNR for liability exposures); the need for the residual captive tied up in the captive; and its prospective desire for future use of a captive in its risk and capital management strategies. Consequently, it is likely that dormancy may not be suited best for many types of long tail run off liabilities, such as workers' compensation or complex general liability claims.

III. RUN OFF: DEADWEIGHT ON THE BUSINESS

The most straightforward definition of a captive in "run off" is an entity that no longer accepts new business and administers its liabilities from its existing pool of assets. Various circumstances may require opting for run off status versus the use of other closing options. In some cases, a captive might go into run off because it has become insolvent, in which case the state would step in to protect eligible claimants. Yet, there are nearly as many cases in which the captive being put into run off is perfectly solvent (i.e., has sufficient assets to cover its obligations to policyholders and creditors).

The parent might choose to put the solvent captive in run off because the reasons for its establishment no longer apply (e.g., premium prices have changed) or it wants to withdraw from a business line that has become unprofitable or excessively risky. Other common reasons why a captive might be put into run off include the takeover of a parent or merger with another entity, which creates duplication of captives and means that one or some are no longer necessary.

The big difference between closing down a captive and winding up most other types of businesses is that the captive still has remaining "legacy" liabilities and the possibility that claims could emerge for many years into the future. While some captives can wind up relatively quickly based on the volume of business and types of coverages involved, others may not.

As a result of these legacy liabilities, running the captive through to closure can take many years, maybe even decades. For example, quite a few of the captives in run off were set up in the 1970s and 1980s to allow companies to reinsure their own risks rather than relying on expensive "hard" market cover, but were subsequently closed when prices fell. More than 30 years on, they are still going. Other captives formed at the same time insured or, more commonly, reinsured third-party risks in addition to the owner-related exposures. The third-party reinsurance obligations that these captives assumed often consisted of long tail asbestos, pollution, or workers compensation risks.

Captive insurance and reinsurance companies in run off tie up a huge amount of corporate capital, staff time, and management attention, all of which could be more productively redeployed within "live" business. What are the options for accelerating final closure and freeing up these resources? How do these options work and what are the pros and cons? Where do the untapped opportunities lie? A captive in run off is therefore a deadweight on the premium generating live business. A substantial portion of assets are locked into the captive to back the liabilities. During this period, the captive needs to be managed and claims administered.

IV. OPTIONS FOR SPEEDING UP CLOSURE

Fortunately, there are options to speed up the closure process. So what are the available options and how useful are they in reducing or eliminating risk, cost, and exposure and releasing trapped capital residing within the captive? How are the options affected by the jurisdiction and captive liability profile? How does the captive owner evaluate the benefits and pitfalls associated with the various options?

In this chapter, we review the application and efficacy of each of the main options and provide examples of traditional and non-traditional solutions to close a captive insurer or reinsurer in ways that enable it to honor its obligations to the relevant stakeholders and repatriate capital to its parent for more productive purposes.

A. Putting Run Off into Perspective

Although there is no definitive figure for the amount of reserves tied up in run off entities in the United States, it is considered widely that entities in run off make up a substantial segment of the U.S. and wider global insurance markets. The lack of *absolute* quantification stems in large part from the manner by which insurers are required to report the extent and segmentation of their exposures. Additionally, many companies are reluctant to reveal too much about run off business as it can be seen as a sign of corporate failure or weakness. However, in 2018, the consultancy, PwC, estimated that global run off reserves for non-life business total approximately $730 billion—comprising approximately $350 billion emanating from the U.S. and $380 billion from the rest of the world.[1] Regardless of any uncertainty that may surround these figures, what is certain is that there is a lot of capital tied up with these exposures.

1. *Market Context*

At a time when U.S. insurers and reinsurers are grappling with soft market rates, subdued asset returns, and pressure to invest in new technological capabilities, they cannot afford to tie up financial and human resources needlessly. A key source of trapped value is the billions of dollars held in captives and portfolios in run off. As a result, captives in run off can no longer be tucked away in a corner and allowed to edge gradually toward final closure. The spotlight on capital efficiency is intensifying and boards, regulators, rating agencies, and shareholders are increasing the pressure on insurers and reinsurers to clear away legacy liabilities and release trapped funds as quickly as possible.

2. *Time Is Money*

The longer a captive takes to run off, the greater the cost. Run off to expiry could take decades, which means (1) continuing management distraction, (2) lost opportunity costs of the inability to take advantage of trapped capital, (3) erosion of that capital as a result of increased management expenses and reserve deterioration, and (4) a continuing drain on administrative resources.

So if time is money, then accelerating closure creates value. However, to release the capital from discontinued business, the company needs to address a myriad of client obligations, regulatory stipulations, and reputational sensitivities. The key considerations come down to five main questions:

- How do I maximize and extract the value associated with the run off business?
- How do I reduce my risk of future loss?
- How do I bring this run off to a close in the least amount of time, with the least amount of management distraction, and at the most reasonable cost?
- How do I preserve—and even enhance—my business reputation in the process?
- How can I find third-party capital to monetize my exposure to distressed insurance/reinsurance assets?

At the same time, the closure needs to assure claimants and regulators that proper safeguards are in place. Successful run off is therefore a careful balance between the interests and perspectives of policyholders, insurers, and regulators. The path to effective resolution therefore has five main priorities:

- Valid policyholder obligations are honored;
- Liabilities are adjusted fairly and correctly;
- Assets, capital, industry rating and, in the case of public companies, shareholder value are preserved;
- Expenses are controlled and reduced; and
- A path toward finality is planned and achieved.

B. Closure Options Available to Solvent Insurers and Reinsurers in Run Off

So what are the options for accelerating the freeing up of resources, while honoring all the obligations?

1. *Running Off to Expiration*

The default option is to allow the captive to run off its liabilities until they are eventually resolved. Yet while some might assume that liabilities and losses will gradually recede over time, in fact the longer the captive is in run off before being finally terminated, the more the costs are likely to increase. Property, auto liability, and other types of shorter tail claims can be resolved, generally, in a reasonable period of time. Worker's compensation liability provides one example of the types of claims that require perseverance in run off. As people live longer and medical fees grow more expensive, the liabilities rise. This "adverse claims development" can be hard to predict (as it often occurs that certain types of claims may only emerge many years after the policy was taken out) and reserving levels are often highly volatile. Asbestosis is a clear example of these "unknown liabilities" as asbestos-related illnesses, such as mesothelioma, can develop many decades after exposure,[2] though similar uncertainties can apply to many other types of property and casualty business.

2. *Speeding Up Conventional Closure: Y-Mutual Case Study*

The closure of Y-Mutual Insurance Company Ltd demonstrates that it is possible to significantly accelerate conventional run off to final closure.

Y-Mutual was incorporated in Bermuda in 1986 as a non-assessable captive mutual reinsurer "owned" by member YMCAs throughout the United States.

The Y-Mutual captive was formed when the high premium prices of a "hard" underwriting market made it difficult for YMCAs to secure affordable cover for workers compensation and general liability. Y-Mutual did not issue direct policies; rather it reinsured a series of "fronting carriers" that issued the direct coverage to the individual YMCA members. Underlying policies were for $1 million. Y-Mutual retained the first $500,000 for most claims. At the company's height, it operated on behalf of over 450 separate members. Yet as premium prices came down in a softening market, the company faced declining "membership" participation. It went into run off in February 2007 with over 1,000 pending claims.

The Y-Mutual story highlights the complex and challenging issues faced by captives that have become surplus to their owner's requirements and moved into run off. In this case, the non-assessable status meant that the company was unable to ask members for further capital contributions and therefore faced limited financial resources for managing run off. In turn, the potentially volatile exposures deterred fronting carriers from coming to an agreement that would allow all future obligations to be discharged (commutation).

Given the nature of the risks covered (e.g., workers' compensation), Y-Mutual would need to run off to expiration. Yet options were available to reduce administration costs, accelerate claims settlement, and hence alleviate the financial challenges. In particular, proactive oversight of third-party service providers administering the underlying claims, combined with an accelerated effort to commute the relevant fronting agreements reduced claim counts, released trapped collateral posted for the benefit of the fronting carriers, and enabled the company to honor its reinsurance obligations to the front carriers in less than five years, which was half the originally anticipated time to close the run off. Y-Mutual deregistered as a licensed Bermudian reinsurer and closed through a solvent members' liquidation process.

3. *Sale*

Many insurers and reinsurers might look to sell their run off captives. On the surface, sale looks like a quick and easy, "clean" solution, providing the seller with the certainty of closure, revenue from the sale, and reduction in ongoing operating costs. Yet quick sale can often be at a cost—in the form of reduced net asset value. Acquisition prices need to take account of the risk of adverse claims development, continued administrative expense, and the profit the seller needs to generate. Moreover, once sold, the entity ceases to be a captive and, if domiciled in the United States, is thus subject to regulatory filing and statutory risk-based capital requirements.

4. *Reinsurance*

Owners of captive companies can transfer the losses through standard reinsurance arrangements, loss portfolio transfers or assumption agreements. However, once again value is lost as the transfer price (i.e., the reinsurance premium) needs to be high enough to protect the buyers from adverse claims development and therefore the amount of funds that are left to be extracted can be limited.

In addition, whether selling a discontinued portfolio or transferring losses via reinsurance, the transactions may not be without complication and cost.

5. *Merging Captive Companies*

Rationalizing the number of captive entities through merger eliminates duplication, allows for more orderly deployment of funds, and reduces ongoing operating costs. Consolidating the capital may allow some of it to be released for dividend payments and investment in business development. However, companies need to take account of the transactional costs and the concentration of risks into fewer entities. There may also be resistance from fronting carriers, though this could be eliminated through discussions with the fronting carriers regarding the type, amount, and adequacy of collateral posted to secure the captive's obligations to the front company.

6. *New York Regulation 141*

New York regulation 141 allows for commutation of reinsurance liabilities as an alternative to voidance, but only applies to impaired or insolvent entities domiciled in New York.

7. *Solvent Scheme of Arrangement (Bermuda and United Kingdom) and Part VII Transfer (United Kingdom)*

A "solvent scheme of arrangement" is an agreement between the insurer and its creditors that would pave the way for the final closure of the entity. The insurer pays 100 percent of the net present value of the agreed claim amount. The advantages include orderly and equitable distribution of liabilities, and the elimination of prospective liabilities. The sequence of steps toward agreement has the further benefit of encouraging cedents and policyholders to actively participate in the process. In the United States, the Rhode Island Commutation Plan is the closest available option to the United Kingdom's solvent scheme of arrangement.[3]

A Part VII Transfer of Liabilities allows for court approval of the transfer of legal obligation for the risk based upon an actuarial assessment of the liabilities.

8. *Rhode Island Commutation Plan*

A commutation plan allows insurers and reinsurers to accelerate closure of an eligible business in run off. The closure is final and complete and the capital release is accelerated and maximized. Although there may be frictional cost and execution risk, full discharge of liabilities can be achieved more quickly than through run off to expiration.

The benefits include

- Preserve industry reputation by honoring all policy claims in full;
- Avoid prospective adverse reserve development on posted reserves;

- Avoid prospective rehabilitation or insolvency of financially impaired entities;
- Realize value from reserve redundancy and ceded reinsurance collections;
- Eliminate management distraction and expense from legacy liabilities; and
- Release trapped capital for productive purposes.

Unlike the solvent schemes of arrangement or Part VII transfers available in the United Kingdom, the openings for U.S. commutation plans are limited to those brought under the Rhode Island Commutation Plan Statute. Originally enacted in 2002, the statute allows eligible insurers domiciled in Rhode Island to terminate liabilities and close down a business for good.

The Rhode Island Commutation Plan has proved contentious, with detractors arguing that it puts claimants' rights at risk. A closer reading can allay many of these concerns. The Rhode Island Commutation Plan process is a highly regulated and scrutinized, court-monitored process. To provide full protection for policyholders, the process is subject to rigorous eligibility criteria and close scrutiny by both courts and regulators. The statute only applies to commercial business and, hence, knowledgeable parties (rather than personal lines or workers' compensation business.) Crucially, the company and the book of business in run off need to be entirely solvent (this has been reinforced by subsequent amendments on the transfer of business to be discussed). The process does not apply to troubled companies, putting it beyond the situations in which the National Association of Insurance Commissioners (NAIC) will permit some form of alternative closure mechanism to stave off the risk of insolvency.[4] Commutation must be approved by (1) 50 percent or more of the creditors by number, and (2) 75 percent or more of the creditors by value, who vote in person or by proxy. The process also requires review by the Rhode Island Department of Business Regulation (DBR) and approval by the court overseeing the process, in order to ensure that the plan does not adversely affect the rights of the policyholders in a material way.

9. *Rhode Island Commutation Process: GTE REinsurance Company Case Study*

The accelerated closure of GTE RE in 2011, a former Bermuda-domiciled captive insurer and reinsurer, which went into run off in 1990, demonstrates the potential of the Rhode Island Commutation Plan Process and its application to eligible U.S. domiciled captives.

GTE RE was formed as a captive in Bermuda in 1976. It underwrote owner-related and non-related assumed reinsurance. The company went into run off in 1990 when the owner-related business was adversely affected by developments in the non-related book. The company moved to Vermont in 1994, and then moved to Rhode Island in June 2010 following the novation of owner-related risks to another group captive. The company was no longer a true "captive" for regulatory filing purposes when it moved to Rhode Island.

In order to discharge its exposures, GTE RE filed a Petition to Implement Commutation Plan in June 2010. The process covered 440 non-commuted cedents and applied to assumed reinsurance rather than direct insurance exposures. The company held reserves for 125 cedents, while another 227 were covered by short tail property or catastrophe covers. A further 88 cedents with no reported reserves were covered by casualty contracts. More than 90 percent of these 88 have had zero reserve balances and no activity for 11 or more years.

Through the subsequent commutation plan, GTE RE paid all valid claims and was discharged from all obligations to creditors. This enabled the company to extract capital and avoid the cost and distraction of a prolonged, perhaps 25-year, run off operation.

To win approval, GTE RE needed to develop a clear justification focused closely on the protection of policyholder interests. It also needed to develop effective structures for the plan, which reflected the demands of the Rhode Island Commutation Plan Statute and the particular characteristics of each block of business. Figure 8.1 outlines the stages of the process and what they entail.

Figure 8.1 Commutation Plan in Action—Key Steps

Developing a viable plan, passing through the legal hoops, and assuring policyholders, cedents, and creditors required considerable care, structuring expertise, and knowledge of the statute. The GTE RE case highlighted the potential for legal challenges, though in this case, the legal challenges were soundly rejected by the courts and have provided strong precedents for future commutations.[5]

V. THE CASE FOR COMMUTATION

The GTE RE commutation plan has spurred many insurers and reinsurers to consider similar options. But for now, at least, it has not been repeated. Why is this? First, the scope for commutation is effectively limited to assumed reinsurance and insurance coverage for large commercial enterprises. Second, a sale or extended run off are more familiar options. Staff and outsourced providers administering the run off may also have a vested interest in continuing, rather than terminating, the process. It remains to be seen, however, how much longer companies can justify the loss of value to analysts and investors. Finally, and arguably, however, the biggest barrier has been the legal terms of the statute and their implementation, which only allow whole companies to use the commutation plan process.

Recent developments to the Rhode Island Commutation Plan Statute have sought to overcome the hurdles created by the legal terms by providing a path for the creation of new Rhode Island companies that house only liabilities eligible for closure under the statute.

So, what has changed? In 2007, the Rhode Island legislature amended the statute to allow insurers and reinsurers to transfer a block of business eligible for closure under the statute into a newly created or existing shell company in Rhode Island "for the sole purpose of entering into a voluntary restructuring under this chapter." As before, only whole companies are eligible for closure under the statute, rather than portfolios of business within a Rhode Island-domiciled company.

However, in an important new development, amendments to the statute's implementing regulations (Regulation 68)[6] provide a regulatory, procedural, and judicial process that allows an insurer to separate books of run off business eligible for closure under the statute into separate legal entities. By being able to separate blocks of business, transfer them to Rhode Island, and bring them to accelerated final closure, the new Regulation 68 greatly increases the opportunities to (1) discharge liabilities fully and (2) release trapped capital.

In August 2015, the Rhode Island DBR amended what was known as Regulation 68, which set out the terms and conditions for how the transfer process could be achieved. These include

- Full review and approval by the transferring company home-state regulator and the DBR;
- Demonstration of solvency, including assurance that backing assets must exceed the liabilities;
- Policyholders, cedents, and creditors must be informed and allowed time to review the transfer process, though their explicit approval is not required; and

- Extensive transparency provisions to support the review and approval process, including audited financial statements, expert witness reports, and demonstrations of solvency within the assuming company.

1. Who Benefits from the Insurance Business Transfer Plan?

- Domestic and foreign owners of active insurers and reinsurers that have legacy liabilities, eligible for closure under the commutation plan process within the active underwriting entity;
- Domestic owners of insurers or reinsurers in run off with discreet lines of business that are eligible for closure under a commutation plan;
- Regulators who are looking to improve the financial condition of active and discontinued business; and
- Shareholders, reinsurers, and counterparties to insurers with run off liabilities.

2. Insurance Business Transfer (IBT) Plan Process Safeguards

The steps along the journey to transfer highlight the levels of court- and regulatory-imposed scrutiny, transparency, and checks and balances in the process:

- Transferring company receives approval from home-state regulator to move eligible business
- Assuming company submits IBT to DBR
- Notice given to DBR "Interested Persons" list
- DBR approval of the IBT
- Petition for implementation of IBT
- Formal notice to all policyholders
- Hearing
- Approval/Denial

The limitations further highlight the safeguards built into the process. Only a business in run off for at least five years qualifies and any cherry picking of liabilities will not be allowed. The first hurdle is the home-state regulator. If it approves, the application moves to the DBR, where it needs to be approved after review by the regulator and its independent expert.

If the DBR gives the go-ahead, the transfer plan goes before the court for final approval. All interested parties, including policyholders, have the opportunity to comment. The court needs to be satisfied that there is no materially adverse impact to the policyholders from the transfer. If the court approves, the specified obligations of the transferring company are taken on by the assuming company. Following an approved transfer, the assuming company may petition for implementation of a commutation plan, but that petition may occur at some time after the transfer has been completed.

3. Addressing the Objections

The amendments to Regulation 68 have been hailed as a landmark by many service companies, opening the way for what they see as a surge in accelerated closure. At the other end of the spectrum, opponents believe the updated provisions are legally flawed, which could put policyholder rights at risk and potentially open up a legal and reputational minefield. Neither of these polarized viewpoints tells the real story, however.

So, what are the objections and are they really justified?

Objection 1: Insurance business transfer plans may raise public policy and constitutional concerns. In fact, the transfer process strengthens rather than lessens policyholder safeguards and should therefore be welcomed from a public policy perspective. The policyholders in the eligible blocks of business are all knowledgeable parties—they are insurers themselves or large commercial enterprises; they are not individual policyholders.

Transfer is subject to full review and approval by the home-state regulator. The DBR provides a further tier of scrutiny and evaluation, both by its own officials and by independent experts. The assuming company must be in sound financial condition rather than troubled. Indeed, the protection within the company assuming the block of business should be as strong, if not stronger, than within the transferring company. In addition to prevailing solvency requirements, the value of assets transferred to the assuming company must be higher than the liabilities.

While the assuming company cannot be a "troubled company," which is an important distinction, the 2009 NAIC white paper on alternative mechanisms for troubled insurers provides useful reference points for determining public policy and policyholder interests within a run off business.[7] The primary goals of a run off plan, as outlined in the NAIC white paper, are: the inclusion and achievement of consumer protection, satisfaction of all policyholder obligations, and the maintenance of positive surplus and sufficient liquidity. Each of these criteria is inherent, if not specifically referenced, in the statute and updates to the implementing regulation.

Moreover, the issues of public policy concern and statutory constitutionality were raised in the legal challenge filed against the GTE RE commutation plan and addressed by the 2011 court ruling, which found that the process did not adversely affect the interests of creditors or policyholders in any material way.[8]

Objection 2: Federal law preempts transfers involving reinsurance. Objectors claim that Regulation 68 violates the "credit for reinsurance" provisions in the Nonadmitted and Reinsurance Reform Act of 2010, enacted as part of Dodd-Frank. However, these provisions were not intended to apply to insurance companies in run off. Instead, they are meant to apply to the credit for reinsurance requirements in various states' laws.

Moreover, even if these provisions were applicable, they are not affected by the amendment to Regulation 68. The statute was amended in 2013 to address areas in which objectors contend that Dodd-Frank prohibits these types of activities. This includes an amendment assuring that the contractual counterparties' original agreement on the selection of the governing law remains paramount in the claim adjudication process.

Objection 3: The amendments to implementing Regulation 68 are beyond the scope of the statute. In fact, the amendments to Regulation 68 are explicitly required under the terms of the statute. In particular, part of the definition of a commercial insurer in run off is a company "whose liabilities consist of commercial liabilities transferred to said company with the approval of the commissioners and pursuant to the regulations."[9]

Objection 4: An insurance business transfer plan is similar to a solvent scheme of arrangement, which when implemented would materially alter the rights of the affected parties. This was the focus of the legal challenge to the GTE RE commutation plan, which was rejected by the court. Whether a commutation plan preserves or impairs a policyholder's rights is what the court and the DBR reviews are there to determine. That being said, the one commutation plan to go to fruition fully upheld policyholders' interests by paying 100 percent of present value for all agreed claims timely submitted.

Objection 5: Novation could violate an anti-assignment provision in reinsurance contracts or be contrary to state statute or case law prohibiting novation without policyholder consent. First, it is unclear how many contracts have such a provision. In those that do, it is frequently accompanied by a commutation provision. Second, those state statutes that require explicit policyholder consent before an insurance contract can be novated to another carrier are in place to protect individual policyholders rather than sophisticated insurance and commercial counterparties.

Some states empower their insurance departments to judge whether to allow a prospective novation. Similarly, for the benefit of sophisticated insurance and commercial counterparties, the amendments to Regulation 68 require explicit approval by the domiciliary regulator, the DBR, and the court. Moreover, the result from novation is no different from a sale transaction where the reinsurer sells its business, including assumed obligations, to a third party.

In fact, the insurance business transfer under Regulation 68 is a complete novation, rather than a reinsurance arrangement with opt-out provisions. The provisions are therefore quite distinct from those in the Assumption Reinsurance Model Act, which serve different purposes and have different results and requirements. This includes an opt-out provision, which can result in insufficient assets remaining to support the opt-out obligations.

Objection 6: Rhode Island should adopt rules for business transfer more in line with the Vermont Legacy Insurance Management Act. The "Vermont Statute" was intended to facilitate and streamline the process for transfers of commercial insurance policies and reinsurance agreements between solvent insurance companies. The Vermont Statute has many merits, but it does not provide the same level of transparency, review, and policyholder protection as the Rhode Island Statute and its implementing regulations. Moreover, the Vermont Statute applies only to excess and surplus lines carriers and not to admitted companies—thus excluding Vermont domiciled captives. The Rhode Island Statute applies to admitted and non-admitted carriers.

Under the Vermont Statute, that state's insurance commissioner decides whether or not to sanction the transfer. The transferring party's home-state regulator must only submit a letter of "no objection." The Rhode Island Statute allows for much broader scrutiny by requiring review and approval by the home-state regulator, the DBR, and the Rhode Island court. That scrutiny is key to fair consideration of all interests and therefore key to finality.

Under the Vermont Statute, certain policyholders can choose to opt-out of the transfer process. This has the disadvantage, however, of splitting the assets and making it more difficult to ensure that liabilities are covered by sufficient backing assets.

Under the Vermont Statute, the assuming company may be just that—a company—and not necessarily an insurer or reinsurer. Moreover, the Vermont Statute does not require that the assuming company file quarterly or annual statements as prescribed by the National Association of Insurance Commissioners.

Finally, the Vermont Statute does not provide a process for the liabilities to be crystallized and closed. This leaves the policyholders subject to the potential erosion of capital in the newly created Vermont entity.

Objection 7: Policyholders should be informed and consulted when the business transfer plan is first presented to the Rhode Island Department of Business Regulation rather than waiting for the petition to go before the court. In fact, this has been addressed in the amendments to Regulation 68. When a transfer plan is submitted, the DBR notifies all parties of the filing on its interested persons list. Policyholders then have an opportunity to express their concerns to the department before it reviews the plan.

VI. CONCLUSION: FROM PASSIVE TO ACTIVE RUN OFF

The timing, quality of structuring, and efficient management of run off resolution are all critical in determining the amount of value that can be released and realized. Given the amount of value that can be eroded by sale or reinsurance transfer, the Rhode Island Commutation Plan is emerging as an increasingly attractive way to accelerate closure and maximize value release. While a clear understanding of what the statute does and does not allow is important, the real key is to think about what regulators and policyholders expect from the process. If insurers and reinsurers approach the updated Rhode Island process in the right way, it can facilitate even greater transparency, scrutiny, and policyholder protection than before.

Insurers are moving from passive to active run off management and efficient exit strategies are becoming ever more realizable. However, to execute the process in the most efficient way and satisfy all the stakeholders, there remains a balancing act that requires care, patience, and expertise. Ultimately, the decision to close a captive (or enter dormancy) is one that must consider a multitude of factors, and all the various options, in order to determine what makes the best sense for captive owners.

Chapter 9

Captive Insurance Tax Controversy

Steven Miller and Meeren Amin

I. INTRODUCTION

Internal Revenue Code section 831(b) captive insurance companies and their insureds have increasingly become the focus of the Internal Revenue Service (IRS). In 2015, 2016, and 2017, the IRS included abusive captive insurance arrangements on its "Dirty Dozen" list—an annual list of tax "scams" that highlights the IRS's focus for the year and provides notice to tax practitioners of transactions they should be leery of. This inclusion confirmed what many in the captive insurance industry had already noticed or experienced—a significant uptick in the number of IRS audits of IRC section 831(b) captives coupled with hardline stances taken by the IRS.

On November 1, 2016, the IRS went a step further by issuing Notice 2016-66, which makes certain captive insurance arrangements "Transactions of Interest."[1] This notice requires captive insurance companies, insured parties, owners of insureds, intermediary insurance companies, and captive managers to meet certain disclosure requirements. Participants and material advisors in most captive insurance arrangements must file Forms 8886 or 8918, respectively, with each tax return and include detailed information such as how premiums were determined, description of claims, descriptions of assets and investments, and any other details describing their captive program. Given how infrequently the IRS classifies arrangements as "Transactions of Interest," this notice highlights the IRS's growing concern and attention to IRC section 831(b) captive insurance companies.

This chapter will focus not only on IRS examinations of IRC section 831(b) captive insurance companies, but also on all potential stages of a tax controversy. First, this chapter will discuss the audit process and key issues the IRS may examine. Second, this chapter will focus on the appeals and fast-track process and possible pathways to settlement for taxpayers. Third, it will move into litigation, the final possible stage of a controversy, which offers a viable opportunity for settlement when appeals cannot resolve a dispute. Lastly, this chapter will provide pre-controversy strategies that a taxpayer might consider to prepare for an examination.

As those who practice in the field recognize, this is an evolving area of law and while the authors have tried to draft these chapters to survive the passage of time, the reader will have to verify events that occur post-publication. For example, there are several fully tried Tax Court cases pending at the time of this publication.

II. IRS EXAMINATIONS OF CAPTIVE INSURANCE COMPANIES

An IRS examination of a captive insurance company and its insureds[2] can be a long, exhausting, and costly process. IRS examinations vary in duration and intensity based on the number and complexity of the issues. Examinations in which the IRS raises only a small number of simple issues oftentimes can be resolved quickly with minimal disruption to the taxpayer. However, more complex audits, such as those involving captive insurance companies, can be more intense and can drag on for years.

An IRS audit is a review of a company's accounts and financial information[3] and is largely a fact-finding mission by an IRS examiner/agent. The audit process begins with a written notice of an audit being sent to the taxpayer with the name of the IRS examiner assigned to the audit. This examiner will lead the audit and act as the person to contact within the Service. However, there may be others involved in the examination, such as the examiner's manager, territory or area manager, IRS counsel, and technical specialists.

Before discussing the captive insurance audit process, it is important to first consider the issues that the IRS will focus on. These issues shed light on the reasoning behind some of the IRS's practices during an examination of a captive insurance company. These issues have been derived from the authors' experience in numerous client examinations and most recently were outlined by the IRS in Notice 2016-66.

A. Key IRS Issues during a Captive Insurance Audit

Purpose for formation of captive. The IRS will first analyze the facts surrounding the formation of the captive. The Service is looking for the reasons why the captive was formed and the purposes of the arrangement. In the best case, a desire for managing one's own risk and other non-tax business purposes will permeate available documentation, rather than any tax and estate planning purposes. The authors have found in these and other IRS audits that the Service will almost always seek e-mails and that these e-mails often are a window into the transaction. This will be discussed in the last part of this chapter.

Other important considerations in determining intent include prior insurance coverage, loss history of the insured, why the decision was made to choose captive insurance rather than commercial insurance, why the particular captive manager was selected, how captive insurance was marketed by the manager or broker, how the captive was capitalized, and the domicile selected. Again, justification that a captive is needed by the insured and was entered into for reasons other than tax purposes is the gold standard the insured will want to show.

Coverages provided and risks covered. Next, the IRS will focus on the insurance coverages provided to the insured. It will likely analyze each policy to determine the risks that are being covered. The IRS will analyze whether the coverages make sense for the insured party and if they are in fact covering insurable risks, rather than investment or business risks. Note that as of the date of this chapter, the IRS is taking a relatively narrow view of what constitutes insurable risk. It is expected that the courts will ultimately address and possibly refine these definitions.

Pricing of premiums. The IRS will then look at the premiums paid in relation to the policies' risk types and coverages. Specifically, the inquiry will focus on whether these amounts are reasonable and based on sound actuarial principles. The IRS will want to ensure that the premiums have been actuarially determined and are substantively supported by actuarial reports and feasibility studies. The qualifications of the actuary will be a key component, as well as the actuary's process in determining the premiums.

Existence of claims. The IRS will focus on actual claims and the claims process as an indication that actual insurance is being provided rather than a vehicle to deductions and tax-free buildup or underwriting profits. (See Chapter 6 regarding the claims process and the importance of following formal insurance company procedures.) The IRS will want information on the number and severity of claims filed by the insured, as well as the general claims process employed by the captive or captive manager. Also of key importance will be the existence and severity of claims from any risk pool participants. The Service may begin with the idea that the risk pool is designed and operated to yield no claims to a captive other than its own operating company claims.

B. Audit Process

Information document requests. The IRS examiner will gather much of his/her information through Information Document Requests (IDRs). IDRs are document requests that generally ask for copies of documents and records maintained by the taxpayer that relate to the issue being audited. Examiners often ask for documents including, but not limited to, financial records, memoranda, and e-mail correspondence. The definition used for "documents" is often broad and requires the taxpayer to produce any related document in its possession.

IDR procedures vary depending on whether they originate with Large Business and International Division (LB&I) or the Small Business/Self-Employed Division (SB/SE) of the IRS. SB/SE does not have formal procedures in place regarding the issuance of IDRs. However, in 2014, LB&I launched a new audit process that created more issue-focused examinations for LB&I audits. A part of this change requires LB&I examiners to discuss IDRs with the taxpayer before issuance, work with the taxpayer to determine a reasonable response date, and issue separate IDRs for each issue.[4] Note that the entire examination process is once again under discussion at LB&I as of the date of this chapter.

As with other examinations, captive insurance examinations often involve numerous IDRs, in which taxpayers are asked to provide documents related to its captive insurance arrangement. Examples include formation documents, documents submitted to and received by government agencies, bank records, account balances, financial statements, investment information, policy documents, insurance agreements, marketing materials presented to prospective owners, documents showing an insured's loss history, actuarial reports, underwriting documents, and so on.

While potentially all records are important for an examiner's review of a captive insurance arrangement, as indicated, e-mail correspondence in particular has become a major area of focus for the IRS. E-mails can help shine light on a taxpayer's intent in creating a captive insurance company. Specifically, the IRS will be looking for e-mails that indicate that the taxpayer is not operating a captive insurance company as it would a normal company, or that its intent in creating the captive is solely or in large part to obtain tax benefits. For example, the IRS may be interested in an e-mail that highlights the taxpayer's desire to obtain estate-planning benefits from the captive insurance company.[5]

Often times, early in the audit process, the IRS will issue a semi-standard form captive IDR that requests a large amount of information from the taxpayer. This IDR will contain requests such as

- Produce all insurance and reinsurance agreements and binders related to the captive insurance program for all insurance period(s) beginning with the year taxpayer was formed to the present;
- Produce all agreements related to the captive insurance program to which taxpayer was a party;
- Produce documentation of all payments taxpayer made or received under any agreements;
- With regard to the initial capitalization of taxpayer, identify each person who made a capital contribution, the date(s) of the contribution, and the amount(s) of the contribution;
- Provide taxpayer's business plan and other documents related to taxpayer's goals, objectives, and business strategies;
- List all of taxpayer's current and former contractors, including but not limited to actuaries, attorneys, accountants, and other specialists and experts, from the time of taxpayer's formation to the present;
- Provide all financial statements for taxpayer for periods from its formation to the present;
- Provide all documents submitted to any governmental authority after taxpayer became a licensed insurance company or captive insurance company, including but not limited to annual statements, reports, certifications, reserve computations, and applications;
- Provide all documents taxpayer reviewed or relied upon in the underwriting and/or pricing of the reinsurance or insurance agreements and binders, including but not limited to loss runs, historical loss cost data, other historical or loss data, actuarial tables, and industry data;

- Identify each underwriter, actuary, employee, or other person who played a role in the underwriting and or pricing of the insurance policies, reinsurance agreements, and binders;
- Provide all documents reflecting or providing information as to taxpayer's percentage or quota share of liability under reinsurance agreements;
- Provide all documents related to or reflecting taxpayer's investment of premiums, including but not limited to brokerage statements, account records, planning documents, memoranda, notes, and correspondence;
- Identify each person who participated in drafting insurance policies, insurance binders, reinsurance agreements, and/or reinsurance binders for taxpayer;
- Describe the process by which taxpayer determined the percentages and amounts of reserves to maintain for the insurance policies and reinsurance agreements under the captive insurance program;
- Provide documentation of all claims, invoices, or other requests for payment from taxpayer pursuant to insurance policies, reinsurance agreements, and/or binders;
- Provide all documents reflecting or related to determining, communicating, and/or substantiating the amount of taxpayer's quota share of the liability for each claim submitted under the reinsurance agreements and binders;
- For each claim, describe all oral communications related to determining, communicating, and/or substantiating the amount of taxpayer's quota share of the liability and identify all of the persons who were parties to such communications;
- Provide all tax opinions or other documents on which taxpayer relied in excluding from income on its federal income tax returns premiums received under the captive insurance program for the taxable years under examination; and
- Explain how taxpayer distributes risk under the captive insurance program.

Summons. The time to respond to an IDR varies, depending on a number of factors, including the amount and type of information requested and whether the examination originates from the Large or Small Business Division of the IRS. If a taxpayer does not respond in a timely or complete manner to the IDR, the Service may issue a summons to the taxpayer. If the examination is being handled by SB/SE, there are only minimal formal procedures that need to be followed, and the IRS can immediately issue a summons. However, if the examiner is an LB&I agent, there are a specific set of procedures that he/she must follow. Specifically, before a summons can be issued, the IRS must first send a delinquency notice and then a pre-summons letter to the taxpayer, with specific requirements as to timing and approval for each letter.[6]

If the taxpayer does not respond in full to the IDR by the date specified in the pre-summons letter, the examiner and IRS counsel will then issue a summons to the taxpayer, which is an administrative summons issued by the IRS and not a court. Therefore, it is not a self-enforcing summons. The IRS can enforce this summons by having the Department of Justice bring an enforcement action in district court.[7]

If the government establishes a prima facie case for enforcement, the court will enforce the summons unless the taxpayer can disprove the elements of the prima facie case or demonstrate enforcement would be an abuse of the judicial process. A full review of the summons process and summons enforcement actions are beyond the scope of this chapter. However, it is important to note that the IRS ability to compel disclosure is very broad but there are restrictions, such as attorney-client privilege.

Interview process. A large portion of the audit process for captive insurance companies involves interviews of shareholders of the captive or the insured. The purpose of the interviews is similar to that of the document request stage—to determine not only the facts surrounding the captive arrangement, but also the subjective intent of the taxpayer. They are used "to develop information and establish evidence" and the testimony of taxpayers "are major factors in resolving tax cases."[8] In-person interviews allow the IRS to discuss the facts face to face with the taxpayer and ask questions that can't be answered through the simple production of documents.

The interviews can be informal or the IRS can require that testimony be given under oath. Regardless of whether they are under oath or not, or if they are recorded by the IRS, interviews are an important tool for the Service and should not be taken lightly by a taxpayer. Even if no oath is taken at the beginning of the interview, the witness is still under an obligation to be truthful. Often, the examiner will be joined by a manager, technical specialists, and even IRS counsel. It will most likely be a comprehensive interview, and because of the adversarial nature of the proceeding, the taxpayer is strongly recommended to have representation. As captive insurance has become a hot area of focus for the IRS, it will likely ask a number of detailed questions to help it determine the taxpayer's intent.

Initial captive insurance interviews are often recorded and given under oath. This reflects the significance that the IRS has placed on the testimony offered by captive insurance owners. The IRS will likely ask a number of fact intensive questions, including, but not limited to the following topics:

- How the taxpayer discovered captive insurance
- How it was marketed by its captive manager
- The specific reasons for creating a captive insurance company
- How the insurance and reinsurance operates
- How claims were handled
- Purpose for domicile
- Specifics on each policy and which risks are covered or excluded

At the end of the examination, a revenue agent will issue a Form 5701 Notice of Proposed Adjustment, generally giving the taxpayer 15 to 30 days to respond and/or request a conference with the agent's manager. The revenue agent will then issue a Revenue Agent's Report, which includes a Form 886-A Explanation of Items. The Form 886-A provides the IRS's arguments and reasons for the adjustment.

The taxpayer then has 30 days to file a protest letter, which must state that the taxpayer is requesting an appeals conference.[9] The written protest must provide the facts supporting the taxpayer's position on any disagreed issue, and the law or authority on which the taxpayer relies.[10] This protest must also be signed by the taxpayer under penalties of perjury. The protest letter provides the taxpayer a unique opportunity to set the scope and tone of the appeal. As such, the protest should lay out in full detail the taxpayer's arguments, as it will form the basis for the taxpayer's position to the appeals officer. As with a legal brief, the protest should include citations to law to provide a basis for the taxpayer's arguments. All facts the taxpayer wishes to utilize in appeals must be included in the exam file and preferably in the protest. Appeals cannot engage in its own fact-finding.

The rules for a captive insurance focused protest letter are no different than a protest letter for any other issue. A taxpayer should include its full arguments objecting to the IRS's positions. Taxpayers should determine exactly what the IRS is arguing and then draft a protest using the established case law and administrative guidance that defines insurance along with the relevant facts of the case. It is just as important for a taxpayer to provide their analysis and arguments as it is to counter the IRS's arguments with facts and legal authority.

The protest letter will be reviewed by the appeals officer assigned to the case. The appeals officer will review both the protest letter and the Revenue agent's report, and will determine whether or not to send the case back to exam. The appeals officer will send the case back to exam rather than hearing the appeal for a number of reasons, including: if the protest is deficient; the taxpayer provides new information or evidence; raises new issues; or some action must be taken or some event must occur before appeals can adequately consider the case.[11]

III. THE APPEALS PROCESS

As discussed earlier, an unfavorable determination by the examination function is not the end of the road for taxpayers. Rather, there is an administrative appeals process at the Internal Revenue Service. This process is managed by the Office of Appeals, which provides an independent assessment of the litigation hazards the IRS and taxpayers face if they proceed to court.[12] Appeals is the last step for a taxpayer before taking his or her case to court. It is meant to be an independent function of the IRS, and is supposed to be "objective, impartial, and neutral."[13] The mission of appeals is to resolve tax controversies, without litigation, in a fair and impartial manner to "enhance voluntary compliance and public confidence in the integrity and efficiency of the Service."[14] The objectives of the appeals office are to provide a prompt and high quality conference and decision in each case and a satisfactory number of agreed settlements.[15]

A taxpayer who is unhappy with the results of an examination may take two different avenues as part of the appeals process: fast-track settlement/mediation and the regular appeals process. A taxpayer can take advantage of one or both of these options.

In the regular appeals process, the appeals officer will serve as decision maker on the case and determine whether a settlement can be offered by the IRS to the taxpayer. If the taxpayer receives no offer or declines an offer, then they can proceed to court. The fast-track process is slightly different. It is a non-binding mediation that allows the IRS and taxpayers to utilize the mediation skills of an appeals officer to see if a particular issue in exam can be mediated to settlement.

A. Fast-Track

Fast-track is mediation between the taxpayer and the IRS exam team, with an IRS appeals officer acting as mediator. Pursuing mediation must be agreed to by all parties. The taxpayer does not have to opt for fast-track, and similarly, the exam team does not have to agree to a taxpayer's request for mediation. If a taxpayer wishes to apply for fast-track at the end of an exam, it must submit an application at the conclusion of an examination/collection determination.[16] However, taxpayers can request fast-track "at the earliest possible stage in the examination process" if there is a dispute on an issue.[17]

The mediator's role is to facilitate communication between the two parties with the goal of resolving the dispute between the exam team and the taxpayer.[18] Fast-track mediation will generally function as a non-binding mediation in the normal sense, in that the mediator will attempt to facilitate conversation between the two parties with the purpose of coming to an agreement. The appeals officer will have joint conversations with the parties, but will also have individual meetings/sessions with each party to better understand the positions of the exam team and taxpayer. The appeals officer will outline his or her views on the strengths and weaknesses of each side's position almost utilizing "shuttle diplomacy." In this way, the appeals officer can move the parties closer to an agreement.

Fast-track mediation can be a good opportunity for taxpayers who receive an adverse determination in a captive insurance examination. As of the date of this chapter, however, the authors are unaware whether the IRS has agreed to utilize this in any captive case. However, more generally, taxpayers should consider fast-track for the following reasons and under the following circumstances:

- Taxpayers who had a good relationship with the exam team during the examination will have an opportunity to negotiate with the examiner in a way it could not during the audit. The two parties will be able to engage in a straightforward negotiation using dialogue either directly or through a mediator.
- If the parties are unable to reach an agreement, the mediation is non-binding. If a taxpayer does not want to accept exam's offer, then it is not bound to do so and can simply walk away and move to appeals.
- Fast-track is a confidential process. If the parties cannot come to an agreement and the taxpayer wishes to proceed to regular appeals, the IRS appeals officer assigned to hear the taxpayer's appeal is not supposed to have access to the record from mediation.
- Unlike the exam stage or formal appeals, fast-track is a very short process. Once a taxpayer submits an application, the goal of the IRS is to have a resolution within 40 days.[19] Appeals and examination on the other hand, are long processes that take months or years to complete.

- Fast-track mediation may give a taxpayer improved insight into the IRS's arguments. While much of exam's argument will be laid out in the Revenue agent's report, fast-track may offer the taxpayer insight into what the IRS may argue at appeals.
- Fast-track can also help prepare a taxpayer for appeals. In both fast-track and appeals, the taxpayer will need to present its argument; in fast-track this will be to the exam team and mediator, and in appeals, it will present to the appeals officer. Preparing and presenting an argument in fast-track can help prepare the taxpayer for appeals by allowing refinement of his or her argument and determining strengths and weakness in his or her position.

However, fast-track may not always be the best approach, even if agreed to by exam. Taxpayers should be aware of the following considerations:

- Offers made at exam are no longer available at fast-track mediation. At fast-track, exam is not bound to any offers it made during audit. If the exam team makes a reasonable adjustment to a taxpayer's return, the taxpayer waives his right to that adjustment by entering into fast-track. If the exam teams determines during fast-track that its adjustment was too low, it is not bound to make this same offer to the taxpayer. Therefore, fast-track may not be beneficial for a taxpayer who receives a good offer in exam.
- In the spirit of negotiation, the taxpayer may have to concede more than he or she would like to. Because mediation is a negotiation, taxpayers generally never receive 100 percent. Taxpayers must make some concessions, even if they believe that everything about their captive insurance program is valid and should not be subject to any adjustments. In addition, some captive audits are binary in nature, focusing on whether the arrangement is insurance or not. This type of legal issue may not be easily resolved in fast-track.
- Fast-track is only useful when the issues are narrowed. If the exam team raises multiple issues related to captive insurance, it may be too difficult to reach an agreement with exam in mediation. However, if the issues are narrow and more focused, then it may be easier for the parties to build consensus and reach an agreement.

B. The Regular Appeals Process

If fast-track settlement is not utilized or is not successful, then a taxpayer can still take his or her case to appeals. As indicated earlier, the IRS Office of Appeals is "an independent organization within the IRS whose mission is to help taxpayers and the Government resolve tax disagreements."[20]

In 2012, the IRS updated the appeals process by creating the Appeals Judicial Approach and Culture (AJAC). AJAC returns appeals to a quasi-judicial approach, clarifying the distinction between the exam function and appeals. AJAC attempts to ensure that appeals receives cases from exam that are fully developed and well documented. Appeals officers are neither investigators nor examiners, and they are not to analyze new information or, arguably, new issues. Appeals may "consider new theories and/or alternative legal arguments that support the parties' positions when evaluating the hazards of litigation . . . but the officer will not develop evidence that is not in the case file."[21] The protest letter is generally the final place a taxpayer can raise any new issues and these rules underline the need to put all facts necessary into the protest.

The taxpayer has a right to an appeals conference.[22] These conferences are telephone or in-person conversations with the appeals officer, in which the taxpayer presents his or her positions and arguments and is able to discuss settlement of the case.[23] Conferences are meant to be "informal to promote frank discussion and mutual understanding."[24] Appeals officers are supposed to act objectively and favor neither the taxpayer nor the exam team. As the goal of appeals is to reach a settlement with the taxpayer, appeals officers are supposed to have "an open mind and genuine interest in reaching agreement."[25]

Until recently, appeals conferences were usually in-person meetings between the taxpayer, the taxpayer's representative, the appeals officer, and any technical specialist the appeals officer may want present. However, on October 1, 2016, the IRS updated and adopted IRM section 8.6.1.4.1, which states that subject to certain exceptions, appeals officers should "hold conferences by phone."[26] This means that appeals officers may now be holding most appeals conferences by phone, rather than in-person. In-person meetings are a good way for appeals officers and taxpayers to discuss the issues face-to-face and present information in an interactive manner. However, with this new procedure, both taxpayers and the Service could lose a valuable tool during the appeals process. This new measure is a direct result of the tight budget facing the Service.

However, an appeals officer can grant an in-person conference based on the existence of the following factors: (1) substantial books and records to review that cannot be easily referenced with page numbers or indices; (2) the appeals officer cannot judge the credibility of the taxpayer's oral testimony over the phone; (3) the taxpayer has special needs (e.g., disability or hearing impairment); (4) numerous conference participants that create a risk of unauthorized disclosures; (5) alternative conference procedures will be used; or (6) another IRM section calls for an in-person conference.

Regardless of the manner in which they are held, appeals conferences still allow taxpayers with captive insurance issues a good opportunity to settle cases without litigation. The exam team will generally not be present unless it requests a pre-conference meeting, in which it would rebut the arguments from the taxpayer's protest letter. The taxpayer will be notified if exam requests the meeting, and will be given an opportunity to participate. However, if no pre-conference meeting is requested, then exam will have no contact with the appeals officer, allowing the taxpayer to have a frank and open discussion with the appeals officer about the merits of its case.[27]

It is important to recognize that appeals officers and the exam team cannot, in general, communicate without the taxpayer's knowledge or presence. Ex parte communications between appeals and employees of any originating IRS function are prohibited without the taxpayer or their representative being given an opportunity to participate in the communication.[28] The purpose of this prohibition is to preserve the independence and appearance of independence of appeals, providing for a fair and impartial process.[29] However, this does not prevent all communications between appeals officers and the Office of Chief Counsel. If a taxpayer believes that an ex parte communication has occurred, it can submit an FOIA request to assess potential breaches.

If a taxpayer is unable to reach settlement at appeals, there is one final step that can be taken before litigation: Post-Appeals Mediation (PAM). PAM is mediation between the taxpayer and the appeals officer. PAM has to be agreed to by both the taxpayer and the appeals officer. The goal is to have a resolution within 60 to 90 days after a PAM application is accepted.

PAM utilizes either a trained mediator from the appeals office or one paid for and provided by the taxpayer, or both. This mediator is supposed to be "independent of the Appeals employee" with whom the taxpayer has been working.[30] PAM has similar benefits as fast-track, in that it provides the taxpayer with another opportunity to work with the appeals officer to resolve the case. However, one drawback of PAM is that once it is agreed to, any previous offers of settlement made by the appeals officer are now off the table. Therefore, taxpayers should carefully evaluate whether they believe they would get a better offer in PAM than from appeals.

As of the date of this publication, there are many captive insurance cases in the appeals office. Results have varied but few have been resolved entirely favorably to the taxpayer. Results may change as the Tax Court issues opinions on some of the cases described next.

IV. CAPTIVE INSURANCE LITIGATION

Although courts around the country have issued a number of decisions concerning insurance and captive insurance, case law specifically pertaining to IRC section 831(b) captives is sparse. As of September 2017, only a few IRC section 831(b) cases have been tried by the Tax Court, with only one opinion rendered.[31] The facts present in each of these cases are unique, so each decision could provide valuable guidance for the captive insurance industry. Some of the issues at stake in these cases are described herein. The Internal Revenue Code and regulations do not provide a definition of "insurance," so for its analysis, courts and the IRS generally look to case law.[32] It should also be noted that, while section 831(b) decisions are scarce, there is relevant guidance involving general insurance issues and captive insurance companies that did not make an election under section 831(b).[33] However, readers must research cases past the date of this publication, as the pending cases will provide a great deal of context for the future treatment of captive insurance.

A. Definition of Insurance for Tax Purposes

A common issue that the courts focus on in captive insurance cases is whether the captive insurance arrangement constitutes insurance for tax purposes. In making this determination courts must decide whether the arrangement involves insurance in its commonly accepted sense—specifically, that it contains insurable risks, risk shifting, and risk distribution.[34] In this regard, based on IRS examinations and pending litigation, there appears to be a large disparity between the definition used by the government and the captive insurance industry.

The government often compares the operations of electing IRC section 831(b) captives to large commercial insurance companies. Taxpayers, however, have generally argued that captive insurance companies are more appropriately measured against other captives. In general, the determination of whether an insurance company operates like insurance in the commonly accepted sense is based on the particular terms of the arrangement. Some of the factors that are considered include (1) whether the insurer is organized as an insurance company in the states(s) in which it does business; (2) whether the insurer is adequately capitalized; (3) whether the insurance policies are valid and binding; (4) whether the premiums are reasonable; (5) whether premiums are paid; and (6) whether claims for loss are satisfied.[35] A few of the factors that the IRS has focused on specifically in IRC section 831(b) litigation are described next.

Insurance versus business risk. Insurance risk is generally seen by the courts as involving a "fortuitous event" such as a fire or automobile accident.[36] This risk is differentiated from "business or investment risks," such as a greater-than-expected decline in property value.[37] In determining whether a policy insures insurance risk, courts look at the terms of the agreement. Business expenses that are expected to happen—and are therefore "not fortuitous"—are not insurable risks.[38] The government has argued that business and investment risks are not insurable, as these are expected events that are part of the competitive nature of the economy.[39] Losses that result from the affirmative actions of the insured are also not fortuitous or chance events, and, therefore not insurable risks.

Risk shifting. For an arrangement to be considered insurance for tax purposes, it must shift the risk of loss from the insured to the insurer.[40] To determine whether the risk of loss has been transferred to the insurer, courts look at whether the insurance company accepts the risk; whether the insurer is adequately capitalized and able to pay its claims; and whether valid claims are actually paid.[41] An additional consideration likely to be relevant to the government's analysis is whether claims are customarily made for qualifying events. If the losses are not claimed then the risk is not shifted because the operating business keeps the liability on its books, rather than passing it on to the insurer. Lastly, for a transfer of risk to occur, the policy should insure loss that actually has some likelihood of occurring.

Risk distribution. One of the fundamental purposes of insurance is to spread the risk of an event over a multiple individuals in order to take advantage of the "law of large numbers."[42] Risk distribution enables the members of the group to insure against a potentially expensive—albeit unlikely—event for a relatively low cost. It also reduces the probability that a single expensive claim will be greater than the cost of coverage.[43] Further, it generally "entails the pooling of premiums, so that a potential insured is not in significant part paying for its own claims."[44]

While there must be meaningful distribution, complete independence of risks is not required.[45] To determine whether a captive arrangement contains sufficient risk distribution, courts look to a number of items, including the number of related party risks taken on by the insurance company.[46] Revenue Ruling 2002-90[47] provides that risk is sufficiently distributed where a captive insures the risks of 12 entities have liability coverage between 5 percent and 15 percent of total risk insured by the captive.

Revenue Ruling 2002-89 creates an alternative safe harbor that has laid the groundwork for many modern IRC section 831(b) captive insurance programs. This Revenue Ruling provides that an arrangement in which a captive insurance company receives 90 percent of its premiums and risk from a related entity lacks sufficient risk shifting and distribution and would not be treated as insurance.[48] However, this Revenue Ruling also holds that an arrangement in which the captive receives less than 50 percent of its premiums and risk from a related entity has the requisite risk shifting and risk distribution to constitute insurance in the commonly accepted sense.

Notwithstanding this guidance, the line where coverage of related entities becomes unacceptable remains blurred.[49] It is also unclear whether the IRS fully supports its own safe harbor rulings, as it has used litigation to attack risk pools that appear to meet the safe harbors.

Capitalization and liquidity. The IRS looks at liquidity and capitalization to ensure that a captive insurance company is actually capable of paying its claims.[50] In its assessment, the IRS compares the amount of assets available to the captive to the total amount it would pay if claims were made according to policy limits.[51] The government does not seem to find it dispositive that the state regulatory capitalization requirements have been satisfied.[52] An insurance company must, however, generally meet the regulatory requirements of the jurisdiction in which it conducts its business.[53]

Premium setting. The IRS will focus on the amount of premiums paid for each coverage and whether these premiums are actuarially determined at arm's length.[54] The IRS may argue that premiums for certain coverages are unreasonable, attacking not only the actuary's methodology, but also whether the actuary determined the premiums without influence from the captive insurance company, insured, or captive manager.

B. Economic Substance Doctrine and Related Penalty

The economic substance doctrine and its successor, the recently enacted economic substance penalty, form another potential avenue of attack on IRC section 831(b) captive insurance companies. The doctrine enables the government to invalidate a transaction that, despite form or appearance, is entered into solely for tax avoidance purposes.[55] The economic substance provision requires a transaction to be evaluated on its economic reality and whether it serves any "meaningful economic purpose" beyond the satisfaction of "the literal terms of the statute" or the relevant regulations.[56] The purpose of the economic substance doctrine is to distinguish between legitimate business transactions and transactions that are "shaped solely by tax-avoidance features that have meaningless labels attached."[57]

Courts have treated the economic substance doctrine as a means to "prevent taxpayers from subverting the legislative purpose of the tax code" by engaging in fictitious transactions with no economic purpose other than the possibility of reaping a tax benefit.[58] It is therefore critical to identify transactions that do not alter the taxpayer's economic position in any meaningful way apart from their tax consequences, typically entailing no risk and no significant possibility of profit other than as a result of tax considerations. This is to ensure that tax benefits are available only if "there is a genuine multiple-party transaction with economic substance which is compelled or encouraged by business or regulatory realities, is imbued with tax-independent considerations, and is not shaped solely by tax-avoidance features that have meaningless labels."[59]

Whether a transaction has economic substance is a factual determination.[60] If a transaction lacks objective profit potential, the transaction must be disregarded.[61] Some courts apply a rigid two-prong test in determining whether economic substance exists: (1) whether the taxpayer had a non-tax business purpose (subjective prong) and (2) whether the transaction had economic substance beyond the tax benefits (the objective prong).[62] Other courts instead focus on the transaction holistically on whether it has any practical economic effects other than the creation of the tax benefits.[63]

In 2010, Congress codified the economic substance doctrine as 26 U.S.C. section 7701(o). That statute provided that a transaction shall be treated as having economic substance only if "the transaction changes in a meaningful way (apart from Federal income tax effects) the taxpayer's economic position" and "the taxpayer has a substantial purpose (apart from Federal income tax effects) for entering into such transaction." The statute was made applicable only to transactions initiated after 2010; however, courts still rely on judicial doctrine from prior to 2010.

Items that can potentially impact this determination include misuse of insurance company assets, lack of documentation and substantiation of transactions, lack of arm's-length dealings, and failure to adhere to formalities. More specifically, the government will look at loans to related parties, especially if they are not at market rates, use of tax deductible life insurance, failure to have or make claims, failure to keep proper books and records, and failure to use an actuary to reasonably price premiums. The IRS will look to argue that this is not insurance but rather a deferral mechanism for tax deducted dollars.

C. Penalties—IRC Section 6662

The government consistently applies the underpayment penalty to captive insurance transactions. IRC section 6662 imposes a penalty for an underpayment of tax attributable to any disallowance of claimed tax benefits by reason of a transaction lacking economic substance or substantially understating income tax.[64] The normal statutory penalty rate is 20 percent of the portion of the underpayment of tax, but IRC section 6662(h) increases the penalty to 40 percent for gross valuation misstatements[65] and nondisclosed noneconomic substance transactions.[66]

Taxpayers have attempted to avoid the IRC section 6662 penalty by claiming a reasonable basis for their position.[67] This argument is bolstered by the lack of clear guidance on IRC section 831(b). A taxpayer can further strengthen its argument against the assertion of certain penalties acting on the advice of counsel or an advisor.

D. Expert Witnesses

Part of the issue that presents itself in captive insurance litigation is that taxpayers have relied on professionals they believe are experts in the field, while the IRS believes these experts to be interested parties that benefit from helping the taxpayer avoid taxes. Taxpayers must defend the qualifications and methodologies of the experts they rely upon during litigation, while the government utilizes its own expert testimony. The experts used by the taxpayer will either be third-party expert witnesses brought in during litigation to defend the premiums and coverages provided by the captive, and/or the actuaries that determined the premium for the captive itself.

The first issue is experience. This involves three levels of experience: (1) education, (2) work experience, and (3) professional designations. Each of these is then considered with respect to insurance generally, actuarial services, and underwriting. In the cases that have been decided and are pending, taxpayers have emphasized the captive insurance experience of their experts. This allows them to highlight and justify the reasons for any actuarial differences between captive insurance and commercial insurance that the government believes are critical. Meanwhile, the government often uses experts with general experience in the insurance industry.

The difference in the experts being used by taxpayers and the government demonstrates a major disconnect in what the captive insurance industry believes is insurance in the commonly accepted sense and what the government believes this means. How this issue is handled by courts could have a substantial impact on the industry. Practitioners are hoping to get some guidance in this area.

In addition to experience, courts have focused on the methodology used by the taxpayer's experts to determine coverage and premiums. The taxpayer's pricing model is very important in determining the reasonableness of the premiums. With regard to this issue, experts have had to defend pricing for policies that are generally available commercially and for policies that are not.

E. Summons

As discussed in the audit section of this chapter, if the IRS believes that a taxpayer has failed to provide a complete response to an IDR, it can issue a summons and the Department of Justice can bring an enforcement action in district court.

An often-litigated summons issue involves whether the taxpayer has possession, custody, or control of documents that the IRS is requesting. Courts have held that taxpayers are not required to produce documents that are not in their possession, custody, or control.[68] In many of these cases, the IRS has sought documents from captive insurance companies that are actually in the possession of each company's captive insurance manager. For example, the IRS may seek from the captive insurance company e-mails that are internal to the captive insurance manager, a wholly independent entity. However, due to contractual terms or the nature of the relationship between the captive insurance company and captive manager, such e-mails may not be in the possession, custody, or control of the captive insurance company or any insured.

V. PRE-AUDIT STRATEGIES

There is a limit on what a taxpayer can do to prevent its captive insurance company from being selected for audit. With the new disclosure requirements under Notice 2016-66, the IRS will have more information at their disposal to determine which participants should have their returns examined.

However, there are a number of best practices or steps that a captive insurance company can employ before an examination to increase the likelihood of surviving an IRS audit without major adjustments, penalties, or material changes to the captive arrangement.

Before discussing best practices, one must first anticipate what the IRS will be looking for when it comes knocking, when examining a captive insurance company. These examinations have to date been centralized, in that a small group within the IRS has created relatively uniform sets of document requests that are employed nationwide. As indicated earlier, the major topics of the IDRs have been, in no particular order: formation of the captive, insurance coverages and policies, premiums, claims, investments, distributions, risk shifting and distribution, and compliance with the new diversification requirements of IRC section 831(b)(2). Rather than awaiting the IRS knock on the door, it is suggested that the captive engage in some introspection and self-help.

As discussed earlier, these areas of inquiry all relate to the fundamental question of whether the captive is providing insurance and operating as an insurance company in the commonly accepted sense.[69] Specifically, insurance in "the commonly accepted sense" exists when premiums are determined at arm's length; the insurer is organized, operated, and regulated as an insurance company; and the insurance policies are valid and binding.[70] That is not to say that other factors are not important, specifically whether there is adequate risk shifting and risk distribution.

A. Issue: Purpose for Formation of Captive

Best practice: Keep captive insurance information well organized. An IRS examination of a captive insurance company will almost certainly require the taxpayer to respond to a number of information document requests. These requests will require the taxpayer to produce captive insurance related documentation. This will include formation documents, bank statements, wire transfer receipts, copies of policies, e-mail correspondence, and a number of other business records. Deadlines to respond to document requests are often tight, requiring taxpayers to quickly provide documents to the revenue agent. Keeping captive insurance records organized can help speed up the examination process, which can last months, or even years.

Best practice: Document positive facts. Deductions are a matter of legislative grace[71] and the burden of proof during an IRS examination falls on the taxpayer. As a result, the taxpayer in a captive insurance audit must prove that it is entitled to deductions for premium payments and that premiums received by an IRC section 831(b) captive insurance company are not taxable. A strong way to make this case is with well-documented evidence. For example, e-mails or written records of conversations with a captive manager inquiring about specific policies and coverages can help show an intent to use the captive as an actual insurance vehicle. Without a written record of these conversations, it could be difficult for the taxpayer to prove that any such conversations occurred and that they occurred around risk management and not tax savings.

Best practice: Understand structure of captive insurance program. The IRS will pay close attention to the structure of the insurance program—specifically, how reinsurance and risk pooling occurs. It will likely gauge the captive owner's level of understanding of pooled risks and how any reinsurance arrangement works.

B. Issue: Coverages Provided and Risks Covered

Best practice: Understand and document coverages and risks. A key aspect of an insurance arrangement is for an insured to understand which risks they are being insured for. It is important for an insured to the show the IRS that it has coverages in place for actual risks that it faces. An individual who has an auto policy for example, may generally know that he or she is covered in case of an accident, but may not know the specific details of the coverage. The IRS generally will hold an insured business to a higher standard—requiring the business to have a greater understanding of the insurance policies they are covered by and the risks that those policies cover. An operating company acting as an insured in a captive insurance arrangement should know which risks its insurance premiums are covering. During an examination, the IRS will likely ask the insured about individual coverages to gauge the insured's level of knowledge about each policy and to determine if it is insuring real risks that it faces in its business. Not knowing which risks are covered and any large exclusions for any coverage could very well be seen in a negative light by the IRS. Therefore, it is important for an insured to study the policies and coverages and know the major exclusions. Documented conversations with the captive manager discussing coverage details could be strong evidence in an IRS examination.

Best practice: Review premiums annually. Insured parties should review coverages annually with an eye toward changing risk profiles and have them recalculated based on experience. This should occur periodically or at least every couple of years. Note that it is absolutely permissible for the overall level of premiums to vary yearly due to the financial capabilities of the insured. However, it is important that premiums do not fluctuate based on need for tax deductions to offset a particular year's profits.

C. Issue: Pricing of Premiums

Best practice: Ensure premiums are actuarially determined. As discussed earlier, the IRS will look into whether premiums are priced at arm's length and actuarially determined. Insureds and captive owners should first ensure that such actuarial work occurs, and second, review the resulting reports to make sure they are credible and make sense. It is recommended that taxpayers have documented discussions with both the captive managers and actuaries who prepare the report to understand how the premiums were determined and the actuarial process utilized.

D. Issue: Existence of Claims

Best practice: File claims that arise and establish and adhere to formalities of the claims process. There may be no better indicator for the IRS that insurance is present than a robust claims history at all layers of the insurance (i.e., at the primary and reinsurance or other secondary layer). The existence of claims filed by the insured and paid out by the captive can evidence the fact that the captive is engaged in a valid insurance arrangement. As a result, it is a best practice for the insured to file claims as they arise, as would be the case outside the captive context. When a covered event occurs, an insured should file a claim and document conversations with the captive or captive manager regarding the loss. Additionally, it is important to follow the formal claims procedures established by the captive manager when filing claims.

Best practice: Diversify coverages. Many of these insurance programs insure low-frequency catastrophic-type events, and in such cases the paucity of claims is justified. Nonetheless, it seems an IRS axiom that the fewer claims, the harder the exam will be. As a result, it could be beneficial to diversify coverages. Adding coverages for more frequently encountered events will likely increase the number of covered events that occur each year, thereby increasing the number of potential claims. Coverages can be changed yearly depending on a business' risk profile.

E. Issue: Flow of Monies

The IRS at the agent level suspects that many captives are merely piggybanks for the owners of the insured operating company. Thus, the IRS will be interested in the flow of money to and from the captive. The IRS will review the liquidity of investments and whether premiums are truly just a circular return of the tax-favored payments to the owners or operating company. Questions to consider include: Have there been loans back to the insured? Have reserves been used as collateral for other financial transactions? Has life insurance been purchased? Has equipment been purchased directly?

There are no explicit rules limiting these types of activities engaged in by the captive. However, as stated, liquidity and how these practices compare to commercial insurance companies will be reviewed. The amount of any distributions and loans, along with the formalities adhered to, will influence whether the IRS views the arrangement as an arms-length insurance agreement.

Best practice: Establish procedures, adhere to formalities, and ensure transactions occur at arm's length and are for fair market value. Evidence of self-dealing investments, loans, or distributions will certainly complicate any examination. However, if an insured or captive is engaging in any of these activities, it is important to adhere to formalities and establish fair market value terms. For example, if an insured seeks a loan from the captive, the loan should be perfected, secured, and charge interest at a market rate. The terms of the loan should be determined at arm's length between the two parties. Failing to adhere to these principles may point to self-dealing between the parties, causing the IRS to view the entities as piggybanks for the shareholders.

Best practice: Know where premiums are invested. Often times, captive managers direct the investment of premiums paid to a captive insurance company. While this is not necessarily a negative fact, a captive owner should ensure that a sizeable portion of its premiums received are invested in liquid assets. In the event of a covered catastrophic loss by the insured, the captive must have sufficient funds readily available to cover the claim. Therefore, documented conversations with a captive manager and/or investment advisors are necessary to ensure that funds are not tied up in non-liquid assets.

Endnotes

Chapter 2: Captive Insurance Company Feasibility

1. For tax issues related to these options, see Notice 2004-2 C.B. 599 (2004) ("This document modifies Notice 2002-70, 2002-2 C.B. 765, and Notice 2003-76, 2003-49 I.R.B. 1181, to remove certain reinsurance arrangements, which involve producer owned reinsurance companies (PORCs) from those identified as a 'listed transaction,' and notifies taxpayers that the Service will continue to scrutinize such arrangements.").

2. Rent-A-Ctr., Inc. v. C.I.R., 142 T.C. 1 (2014).

3. *Id.* at 11.

4. As discussed in Chapters 3 and 4, business owners should carefully consider the impact of taxes on various levels (e.g., city, state, Federal, foreign country, etc.). Further, recent changes in Federal tax law (e.g., reduction in corporate tax rate, changes to foreign tax regime, etc.) pursuant to the Tax Cuts and Jobs Act, should be considered not only for captive feasibility purposes, but for other purposes as well (e.g., mergers and acquisitions, public offerings, etc.).

5. *See* Rent-A-Ctr., Inc. v. C.I.R., 142 T.C. 1, 13 (2014) ("In addition, [captive owner] established [the captive] for legitimate business reasons, including: increasing the accountability and transparency of its insurance operations, accessing new insurance markets, and reducing risk management costs.").

6. *See* Paul Sullivan, *I.R.S. Is Looking into Captive Insurance Shelters*, N.Y. Times, Apr. 10, 2015, https://www.nytimes.com/2015/04/11/your-money/irs-is-looking-into-captive-insurance-shelters.html.

7. Avrahami v. Comm'r, No. 17594-13, 2017 WL 3610601 (T.C. Aug. 21, 2017).

8. See I.R.S. Notice 2016-66, *available at* https://www.irs.gov/pub/irs-drop/n-16-66.pdf.

9. *See* Chapters 3 and 9 regarding the IRS investigation with respect to captive insurance companies that make a section 831(b) election.

10. *See* Rent-A-Ctr., Inc. v. C.I.R., 142 T.C. 1, 3 (2014) ("Aon representatives informed David Glasgow, petitioner's director of risk management, about the financial and nonfinancial benefits of forming a captive. Aon convincingly explained that a captive could help petitioner reduce its costs, improve efficiency, obtain otherwise unavailable coverage, and provide accountability and transparency. Mr. Glasgow presented the proposal to petitioner's senior management, who concurred with Mr. Glasgow's recommendation to further explore the formation of a captive."). *See also* Gulf Oil Corp., Petitioner v. Comm'r of Internal Revenue, Respondent, 89 T.C. 1010, 1013 (1987), *aff'd, sub nom.* Gulf Oil Corp. v. C.I.R., 914 F.2d 396 (3d Cir. 1990) ("In further response to the changes in the third-party primary insurance and reinsurance markets, Gulf contemplated the formation of a captive insurance subsidiary to provide coverage for Gulf and its subsidiaries and affiliates. In 1968 Gulf conducted a feasibility study in concert with Marsh & McLennan, Inc., an insurance brokerage and consulting firm, with regard to the advisability of establishing an affiliated insurance Insured outside of the United States. This study, which updated a 1964 study, included consideration of the potential tax and financial benefits to be obtained through the operation of such an insurance affiliate.").

11. *See* Avrahami v. Comm'r, No. 17594-13 (T.C. complaint filed July 31, 2013).

12. See Chapter 1 for discussion of various types of captives.

13. See Vt. Stat. Ann. tit. 8, § 6004.

14. See section 9 of the Nevis International Insurance Ordinance.

15. See Chapter 7. ("Each domicile has a statutory minimum capital requirement for all types of insurers, captive or traditional, but that is a solvency 'floor,' and is rarely appropriate. The feasibility study should provide a documented recommendation for the captive's initial capital needs, and that capital should support an adverse loss scenario.").

16. See Jay Adkisson and David Slenn: IRS Noose Starting To Tighten On Sham Captive Risk Pools, LISI Asset Protection Planning Newsletter #242 (Apr. 8, 2014).

Chapter 3: U.S. Taxation of U.S. Captives

1. Carnation Co. v. Comm'r, 71 T.C. 400 (1978), *aff'd*, 640 F.2d 1010 (9th Cir. 1981).

2. Ocean Drilling & Exploration Co. v. United States, 24 Cl. Ct. 714 (1991), *aff'd, per cur.* 988 F.2d 1135 (Fed. Cir. 1993); Kidde Indus. v. United States, 40 Fed. Cl. 42 (1997) and Humana Inc. v. Comm'r, 881 F.2d 247 (6th Cir. 1989); Rent-A-Center v. Comm'r, 142 T.C. 1 (2014), citing Harper Grp. v. Comm'r, 96 T.C. at 57–59. *See also* Avrahami v. Comm'r, 149 T.C. No. 7 (2017).

3. For instance, Rev. Rul. 83-172, 1983-2 C.B. 107 ruled that an arrangement was insurance for Federal income tax purposes, even though there was no insurance license, and it was not regulated by the Department of Insurance. In that ruling, 40 companies that self-insured their respective workers' compensation exposures agreed to enter into a joint and several indemnification arrangement under the state workers' compensation act, and provided a deposit pursuant to a formula prescribed by the state's commerce agency. The state called this self-insurance, but the arrangement was an insurance company for Federal income tax purposes, because it met all the tests. *See also* Rev. Rul. 83-132, 1983-2 C.B. 270 (a non-corporate member of an insurance exchange issues insurance contracts and reinsures risk, so it is an insurance company for Federal income tax purposes). *See also, e.g.*, PLR 201732021 (5/12/17, released 8/11/17), an obligor company is an insurance company for Federal income tax purposes if more than half its business is issuing vehicle service contracts, even though it is not regulated by the domicile's department of insurance; PLR 201314020 and PLR 201229008.

4. Presumably, the captive can perform these tasks directly or contract them to others; *see, e.g.*, Rev. Rul. 2002-89, 2002-2 C.B. 984: "In implementing the arrangement, S may perform all necessary administrative tasks, or it may outsource those tasks at prevailing commercial market rates."

5. JCS-41-85 Sept. 20, 1985. *See also* Rev. Rul. 2002-89 and Rev. Rul. 2009-90.

6. Helvering v. Le Gierse, 312 U.S. 531, 539 (1941).

7. *See* Humana Inc. v. Comm'r, 881 F.2d 247 (6th Cir. 1989), *aff'd*, in part, *rev'd*, in part and remanded, 88 T.C. 197, 206 (1987). See also note 8.

8. More specifically, in Humana, the Sixth Circuit cited Clougherty Packing Co. v. Comm'r, 84 T.C. 948 (1985), *aff'd*, 811 F.2d 1297 (9th Cir. 1987), and stated it would "look solely to the insured's assets, and consider only the effect of a claim on those assets."

9. *See* Rev. Rul. 2002-89, at 2002-2 C.B. 984 (stating risk shifting and risk distribution existed where 50 percent of the wholly owned captive's insured risk was unrelated party risk) and Harper Grp. v. Comm'r, 96 T.C. 45 (1991), *aff'd*, 979 F.2d 1341 (9th Cir. 1992) (holding that risk distribution and shifting are present where a captive insurer's unrelated insurance business was between 29 percent and 33 percent unrelated risk).

10. *See* Rev. Rul. 88-72, 1988-2 C.B. 31, clarified by Rev. Rul. 89-61, 1989-1 C.B. 75, obsoleted by Rev. Rul. 2001-31, 2001-1 C.B. 1348.

11. Rev. Rul. 2002-89, 2002-2 C.B. 984.

12. The significance of homogeneity, if any, is unclear. *See id.* and Rev. Rul. 2002-90, I.R.B. 2002-2 C.B. 985, where the entities are exposed to similar risks, with similar expected outcomes of loss. In

Notice 2005-49, the IRS National Office requested comments on the role of homogeneity in determining the presence of insurance. The IRS has not issued any guidance on homogeneity, and it is not clear that it was a factor in either Rev. Rul. 2002-89 or Rev. Rul. 2002-90. In CCA 200849013, the national office stated: "We have mentioned homogeneity in several revenue rulings without addressing the relevance of homogeneity as a factor in the subsequent insurance analysis. See Rev. Rul. 2002-89, Rev. Rul. 2002-90, Rev. Rul. 2005-40, and Rev. Rul. 2008-8. In 2005, we issued a notice asking for comments regarding the relevance of homogeneity in determining whether risks are adequately distributed for an arrangement to qualify as insurance. Notice 2005-49, 2005-2 C.B. 14. We have not yet published guidance expressing our position on this issue." Compare with non-precedential authorities emanating from the Tax Exempt Organizations group, PLR 201025077 and PLR 200837041, citing FSA 1998-578, 1998 FSA Lexis 167. Also compare, R.V.I. Guaranty Ltd v. Comm'r.

13. See note 11.

14. *Id.*

15. Carnation Co. v. Comm'r, 71 T.C. 400 (1978), *aff'd*, 640 F.2d 1010 (9th Cir. 1981).

16. Clougherty Packing Co. v. Comm'r, 84 T.C. 948 (1985), *aff'd*, 811 F.2d 1297 (9th Cir. 1987).

17. Humana Inc. & Subs. v. Comm'r, 88 T.C. 197, 206. In a Brother-Sister Arrangement, none of the sibling affiliates own any stock in the captive, or vice versa.

18. *Id.* at 206.

19. *Id.* at 206–07.

20. *Carnation*, 71 T.C. 400, *aff'd*, 640 F.2d 1010 (9th Cir. 1981).

21. *Clougherty*, 84 T.C. 948, *aff'd*, 811 F.2d 1297 (9th Cir. 1987).

22. *Humana*, 88 T.C. 197 at 213.

23. Humana, Inc. v. Comm'r, 881 F.2d 247, 251 (6th Cir. 1989).

24. More specifically, the Sixth Circuit cited *Clougherty* and stated it would "look solely to the insured's assets, and consider only the effect of a claim on those assets."

25. 84 T.C. 948 (1985), *aff'd*, 811 F.2d 1297 (9th Cir. 1987) at 253.

26. In Humana Inc. & Subs. v. Comm'r, the Sixth Circuit also relied on the principle from Moline Properties, Inc. v. Comm'r, 319 U.S. 436 (1943). In *Moline* the taxpayer petitioned to have a corporation, of which he was sole shareholder, be ignored as merely fictitious. The Supreme Court affirmed the Court of Appeals decision in treating the taxpaying entity as having an identity distinct from its shareholder. The Tax Court also discussed *Moline* in the *RAC* Case (discussed at note 36) in the context of whether Legacy (the company's captive insurance entity) was a sham entity.

27. Malone & Hyde v. Comm'r, 62 F.3d 835, 841 (6th Cir. 1995).

28. *Id.* at 840.

29. *Id.* at 841.

30. Rent-A-Center, Inc. & Affiliated Subsidiaries v. Comm'r, 142 T.C. 1 (2014).

31. *Id.*

32. *Id.*

33. *Id.*

34. *Id.* The court did not distinguish a $25 million guaranty that was not tied to the deferred tax asset.

35. Securitas Holdings, Inc. and Subsidiaries v. Commissioner T.C. Memo. 2014-225 (2014).

36. JCS-41-85 Sept. 20, 1985. *See also* Rev. Rul. 2002-89 and Rev. Rul. 2009-90.

37. In Malone & Hyde, T.C. Memo 1993-585, the Tax Court followed the Sixth Circuit's opinion in *Humana*, in finding that risk distribution was present in a brother-sister situation: "Respondent interprets the Sixth Circuit's discussion in Humana as suggesting that numerous insureds must be present to achieve risk distribution. The Sixth Circuit concluded that 'we see no reason why there would not be risk distribution in the instant case where the captive insures several separate corporations within an affiliated group and losses can be spread among the several distinct corporate entities.' Humana Inc. v. Commissioner, 881 F.2d at 257. It is clear from the Sixth Circuit's opinion that, when several separate corporations are present, risk distribution ordinarily is present. However, we do not think the Sixth Circuit meant to foreclose the ability of a few insureds with many different insurable risks to demonstrate that they also had achieved risk distribution." The Tax Court mentioned that there were eight insured entities, although the opinion states that in one of the years in issue, there were five insureds, whose premium as a percentage of the total were 59.8 percent, 30.5 percent, 4.5 percent, 2.8 percent, and 2.3 percent. *Malone & Hyde* was reversed on other grounds by the Sixth Circuit, but it did not address risk distribution. The Rent-A-Center opening brief stated that there were four insureds in the first year. See also *Rent-A-Center* and *Securitas. Avrahami* stated that three or four insureds is inadequate, but that the number of risk exposure units was more important.

38. Rev. Rul. 2002-90, 2002-2 C.B. 985.

39. *See Malone & Hyde*, 62 F.3d 835 (1995), Philadelphia Manufacturers Mutual Insurance Company v. Commissioner, 284 F.2d 296 (1960), Rent-A-Center, Inc. & Affiliated Subsidiaries v. Comm'r, 142 T.C. 1 (2014), Humana Inc. & Subs. v. Comm'r, 88 T.C. 197, Hospital Corp. of Am. v. Comm'r, TC Memo 97-482, Kidde v. United States, 40 Fed. Cl. 42 (1997) and Securitas TC Memo 2014-225.

40. Rev. Rul. 2005-40, 2005-2 C.B. 4.

41. *Id.*

42. *Humana*, 88 T.C. 197.

43. Disregarded refers to entities viewed by taxing authorities as not separate from their owner for income tax purposes.

44. It should be noted that the concept of disregarded entities has recently been brought up in Healthmark Grp. LTD Gregory Lentz a Partner Other Than Tax Matters Partner v. Comm'r (Docket No. 8269-14). In *Healthmark* the taxpayer had eight single member LLCs that were disregarded entities, that is, not regarded as separate from their owners for income tax purposes. The Service disallowed deductions for premiums paid to a sister captive, as risk had not been distributed through disregarded entities. On March 27, 2015, a decision was entered, stipulating entry of judgment pursuant to which all deductions were allowed. The Service has not identified the reason for this apparent concession, and has not taken any action with respect to Rev. Rul. 2005-40, situation 3.

45. Treasury Regulation Sections 301.7701-2(c)(2)(iv) and 301-7701-2(e)(5).

46. Pierre v. Commissioner, 133 T.C. 24 (2009), supplemented by TC Memo 2010-106.

47. Rev. Rul. 2002-89, 2002-2 C.B. 984.

48. AMERCO, Inc. v. Comm'r, 96 T.C. 18 (1991), *aff'd*, 979 F.2d 162 (9th Cir. 1992) (with more than 50 percent unrelated risk, where the court held that a parent and its subsidiary insurance company could shift risk where that insurer had significant unrelated business); The Harper Grp. v. Comm'r, 96 T.C. 45 (1991), *aff'd*, 979 F.2d 1341 (9th Cir. 1992) (with 29 percent unrelated risk, where the court held it is possible to have a true insurance transaction between a corporation and its wholly owned insurance company if the captive has substantial unrelated insurance business); Sears, Roebuck & Co. v. Comm'r, 96 T.C. 61 (1991), *aff'd*, 972 F.2d 858 (7th Cir. 1992) (with 99 percent unrelated risk, where the court held payments by the taxpayer to its subsidiary for insurance policies constituted insurance premiums for tax purposes, including deductibility by the taxpayer).

49. Ocean Drilling & Exploration Co. v. United States, 24 Ct. Cl. 714 (1991), aff'd per cur. 988 F.2d 1135 (Fed. Cir. 1993).

50. Avrahami v. Comm'r, 149 T.C. No. 7 (2017).

51. 142 T.C. at 38. While the opinion does not discuss this, petitioner's brief provides as a proposed finding of fact that in one year four subsidiaries of RAC were charged approximately 15.8 percent, .9 percent, 13.6 percent, and 69.7 percent, respectively, of the Legacy premiums. Petr. Br., Prop. FOF, ¶ 58. Likewise, the Service's brief acknowledges that risk was concentrated in mainly three subsidiaries: RAC East, RAC West, and RAC Texas. *See Resp. Br.* at 31.

52. 142 T.C. at 38 (emphasis added).

53. *Id.* at 39. The holding in *Rent-A-Center* is significant because it indicates that risk distribution may be viewed in a manner similar to the dicta in Gulf Oil Corp. v. Comm'r, 89 T.C. 1010, where, as noted earlier, risk distribution was not dependent on the number of insured entities, but rather, "that a single insured can have sufficient unrelated risks to achieve adequate risk distribution." *Gulf Oil*, 89 T.C. at 1026 (dictum).

54. T.C. Memo. 2014-225. Even though the arrangement in *Securitas* included over 25 subsidiaries in one of the years, the Tax Court did not focus on this in analyzing whether risk was distributed. Instead, the Tax Court focused on the activities of the insureds.

55. *See* Kidde Industries v. United States, 40 Fed. Cl. 42, 50–51 (1997).

56. TAM 200827006.

57. *See Kidde Industries*, 40 Fed. Cl. at 51–52.

58. *Id.*

59. *Id.* at 52–53.

60. *Harper Grp.*, 96 T.C. 45, *aff'd*, 979 F.2d 1341 (9th Cir. 1992).

61. *Id.* at 60.

62. 149 T.C. No. 7, slip op. at 76 (italics in the original text).

63. Rev. Rul. 2007-47, I.R.B. 2007-30.

64. *Id.*

65. IRS Letter Ruling 201511021 (December 1, 2014).

66. ILM 201511021.

67. Rev. Rul. 89-96, 1989-2 C.B. 114.

68. R.V.I. Guaranty Co, LTD. & Subsidiaries v. Comm'r, 145 T.C. 9. *See* TAM 201149021.

69. *Id.* at 35.

70. *Id.* at 45.

71. Statement of Financial Accounting Standards No. 113 (December 1992).

72. I.R.C. § 831(b)(1).

73. Per I.R.C. § 816(a), a life insurance company means an insurance company which is engaged in the business of issuing life insurance and annuity contracts.

74. I.R.C. § 831(b)(2)(A).

75. H.R. 2029 114th Cong. (Dec. 18, 2015).

76. I.R.C. § 831(b)(2)(B)(i).

77. I.R.C. § 831(b)(2)(B)(ii)(I).

78. I.R.C. § 831(b)(2)(B)(ii)(II).

79. *See* I.R.C. § 1563 for controlled group rules, where for the purposes of Section 831(b)(2)(B), "at least 80 percent" is replaced by "more than 50 percent."

80. "Abusive Tax Shelters Again on the IRS 'Dirty Dozen' List of Tax Scams for the 2015 Filing Season." IR-2016-25, Feb. 16, 2016; *see also* IR-2015-19, Feb. 3, 2015, and IR-2017-31, Feb. 14, 2017.

81. It should be noted that if any employee of the company, or a member of the employee's family (as defined in I.R.C. § 2032A (e)(2)), is an employee of another company exempt from taxation by reason of this paragraph (501(c)) (or would be so exempt but for this sentence), such company will not be granted exempt status under I.R.C. § 501(c).

82. Treas. Reg. § 301.7701-3(a). See Rev. Rul. 93-132. On December 20, 2017, the House of Representatives and the Senate each passed H.R.1 (the Tax Cuts and Jobs Act), and the legislation (the "2017 Act") was signed into law by the President on December 22, 2017. Modifications of the law described herein are noted where appropriate below. The 2017 Act does not change the text of either section 831(a) or 831(b), but many of its provisions affect domestic C corporations generally, or domestic insurance companies generally. The graduated corporate rate structure with a top rate of 35 percent was replaced with a flat 21 percent rate. The corporate alternative minimum tax was repealed. The 2017 Act generally eliminates net operating loss carrybacks and permits net operating loss carryovers to offset only 80 percent of taxable income, but there is a special rule for non-life insurance companies. An insurance company taxed under section 831(a) can carry a net operating loss back two years and forward 20 years; the net operating loss an offset 100 percent of taxable income. The dividends received deduction has been tightened.

83. Rev. Proc. 2015-52. The computation of reserves for all P&C insurance companies (including captives) has been amended. This will generally result in a smaller reserve deduction. As a transition, the December 31, 2017, reserve balance will be recalculated using the rules applicable in 2018. Any adjustment will be includible in income over eight years. Under the 2017 Act, discounting of reserves will use the corporate bond yield, rather than the AFR. Short-tail business will continue to use three years, but longer tail business will generally use fourteen years, not ten, as the discounting period. The 2017 Act eliminates the ability of a taxpayer to use its own loss expense in discounting. Before the 2017 Act, reserves were reduced by 15 percent of the amount of tax exempt income, dividends received deduction and change in cash surrender value. Numerically, this equals 5.25 percent divided by 35 percent, the highest corporate rate. Under the 2017 Act, the statute provides this "proration factor" will continue to be 5.25 percent divided by the top corporate rate. For 2018, with a top rate of 21 percent, the proration factor is 25 percent.

84. Footnote 9 of the *Rent-A-Center* opinion states that the taxpayer typically paid its premium for the policy incepting in December of a given year in September of the next year, and deducted its premium in the inception year under the recurring deduction election. I.R.C. § 461(h)(3)(A)(iii).

85. Cf. Rev. Rul. 2007-47.

86. Crawford Fitting Co. v. United States, 606 F. Supp. 136 (N.D. Ohio 1985).

87. *Id.*

88. *Id.*

89. *Id.* at 38.

90. *Id.*

Chapter 4: U.S. Taxation of Non-U.S. Captives

1. The description of the law contained in this chapter is current as of December 19, 2017. On December 20, 2017, the House of Representatives and the Senate each passed H.R.1, and the

legislation, an Act to provide for reconciliation pursuant to titles II and V of the concurrent resolution on the budget for fiscal year 2018, which is commonly referred to as the Tax Cuts and Jobs Act (the "Act"), was signed into law by the President on December 22, 2017. Modifications of the law described herein are noted where appropriate below. In addition to these modifications, the Act also imposes a base erosion anti-abuse tax ("BEAT") on certain deductible payments (including reinsurance premiums, and presumably insurance premiums) made by a U.S. person to a related non-U.S. person. The rate of tax is 5 percent for 2018 and 10 percent for 2019 through 2025. For a short description of the BEAT see the Appendix.

2. A discussion of this topic is beyond the scope of this chapter.

3. For purposes of this discussion, the term "U.S. person" means (1) a citizen or resident of the United States; (2) a partnership or corporation created or organized in or under the laws of the United States or organized under the laws of any political subdivision thereof; (3) an estate, the income of which is subject to U.S. federal income taxation regardless of its source; (4) a trust if either (x) a court within the United States is able to exercise primary supervision over the administration of such trust and one or more U.S. persons has the authority to control all substantial decisions of such trust or (y) the trust has a valid election in effect to be treated as a U.S. person for U.S. federal tax purposes; or (5) any other person or entity that is treated for U.S. federal tax purposes as if it were one of the foregoing.

4. A captive that is characterized as an insurance company for U.S. federal tax purposes will be characterized as a corporation for such purposes. Section 7701(a)(3) of the Internal Revenue Code of 1986, as amended (the Code). A non-U.S. captive not characterized as an insurance company for U.S. federal tax purposes may be able to elect to be characterized as a partnership or disregarded entity depending on the captive's particular circumstances. *See* Treas. Reg. § 301.7701-3.

5. Unless noted otherwise, section references are to the Code.

6. Under these constructive ownership rules, certain individuals and entities are considered to own the stock owned by another individual or entity: (1) an individual is treated as owning stock owned by his spouse, children, grandchildren, and parents (provided any such person is a U.S. citizen or resident alien); (2) a partner or beneficiary is treated as owning his proportionate share of stock owned by a partnership or non-grantor trust; (3) a grantor is treated as owning stock owned by a grantor trust; (4) a shareholder who owns 10 percent or more of the value of a corporation is treated as owning his proportionate share of stock owned by the corporation; (5) a corporation will be treated as owning stock owned by its 50 percent or greater shareholders; (6) a partnership will be treated as owning stock owned by its partners (the "partner to partnership attribution rule"); (7) stock owned by beneficiaries of a non-grantor trust generally will be treated as owned by the trust; and (8) a person with an option to acquire stock will be treated as owning the stock subject to the option. Section 958(b), which incorporates by reference section 318, with certain modifications. In addition, the Act modifies the application of section 958(b) so that a U.S. person can be attributed ownership downward from a non-U.S. person. For example, a U.S. subsidiary of a non-U.S. parent will be characterized as owning the stock the parent owns in its non-U.S. subsidiaries (*see, e.g.,* Figures 4.3, 4.6, and 4.7).

7. Section 957(a). The Treasury Regulations under section 957 provide that in determining the amount of voting power held by a shareholder all the facts and circumstances will be considered. Trea. Reg. § 1.957-1(b). Accordingly, the consideration of the quantum of voting power held will be based on qualitative considerations as well as quantitative considerations.

8. Section 951(b). The Act modifies the definition of 10% U.S. Shareholder to include a U.S. person who owns 10 percent or more of the total value of all classes of stock of a non-U.S. corporation.

9. The Act removes the 30-day requirement.

10. This direct or indirect requirement means that a person characterized as a 10% U.S. Shareholder purely as a result of constructive ownership will not have income inclusions.

11. Section 951(a).

12. Treas. Reg. § 1.951-1(e).

13. Section 952. There are other categories of subpart F income, such as "foreign base company services" and "foreign base company sales" income, that are not typically earned by a captive.

14. Section 952(c) of the Code. A detailed discussion of rules applicable to the use of prior year deficits in earnings and profits are outside the scope of this chapter.

15. The rule only applies if the gross amount of premiums or other consideration for the reinsurance or the issuing of insurance or annuity contracts (other than certain insurance or reinsurance related to same country risks written by certain insurance companies) exceeds 75 percent of the gross amount of all premiums or other consideration in respect of all risks. In the case of a captive, this requirement would be expected to be met.

16. We note that for U.S. federal income tax purposes, there are special rules for insurance companies to calculate their income, including the allowance of certain reserves as deductions. A discussion of these rules is outside the scope of this chapter.

17. Section 951(a). Although unlikely to apply in the context of a captive, section 953(a)(2) creates an exemption to subpart F insurance income for income characterized as "exempt insurance income," and section 954(i)(1) provides a similar exemption for "qualified insurance income." A discussion of these exemptions is beyond the scope of this chapter. Generally, the exemptions require that the captive write a certain amount of home country risks and provide that only income from non-U.S. risks can be exempt. In addition, although originally enacted in 1998 and repeatedly extended, these provisions of the Code have not yet been made permanent.

18. Non-insurance income, if any, will not be subject to tax under these rules unless the non-U.S. captive is also characterized as a "general" CFC, and the income is characterized as subpart F income.

19. The RPII rules, however, are applicable to any entity earning insurance income not just to group captives.

20. *See* section 953(c)(1)(A).

21. Section 953(c)(2).

22. Control is measured by either more than 50 percent in value or more than 50 percent in voting power of stock applying certain constructive ownership principles. Section 954(d)(3).

23. Section 953(c)(6).

24. Section 953(c)(1).

25. These RPII inclusions will be limited by each such U.S. person's share of the non-U.S. corporation's current-year earnings and profits. In addition, the use of losses in prior years may be available as deficits to offset earnings in later years in the same manner as described under the general CFC rules discussed earlier.

26. The one main exception to this would be an agency captive, which might not write any RPII business.

27. Non-RPII income (e.g., premium and investment income allocable to coverage of persons other than RPII shareholders and their related persons) would not be subject to U.S. federal income tax.

28. If the captive were characterized as a life insurer, the appropriate form would be an 1120-L.

29. There is an exception to this general rule if the dividends are characterized as "debt financed." Sections 512(b)(3), 512(b)(4), and 514 of the Code; *see also* section 512(b)(13)(A) and (C).

30. *See* PLRs 9407007, 9027051, 9024086, 9024026, 8922047, 8836037, and 8819034. However, in PLR 9043039, the IRS ruled that subpart F income inclusions of a tax-exempt 10% U.S. Shareholder of a CFC should not be treated as non-taxable dividends; rather, such income should be treated as if the underlying income was realized by such shareholder for purposes of computing its UBTI. The IRS gave no reason for the departure from its position in prior rulings; and subsequent rulings (*see, e.g.*, PLR 200315032), as well as the congressional committee reports to the 1996 act that enacted section 512(b)(17) (discussed next), expressed the view that the IRS's position in PLR 9043039 was incorrect.

31. Section 512(b)(17) achieves this result by applying a "look-through" rule that takes into account how the income would be treated if earned directly by the tax-exempt entity.

32. Section 512(b)(17)(B) of the Code. The exceptions to the rule apply on a shareholder-by-shareholder basis. For example, if the subpart F insurance income that was allocable to a tax-exempt organization included income attributable to insuring the risks of both the tax-exempt organization itself and other shareholders that were not tax-exempt affiliates of the organization, only the subpart F insurance income attributable to the insurance of risks of the other shareholder would be characterized as UBTI. H. R. Rep. No. 104-586, at 137, 1996-3 C.B. at 475.

33. Section 959(e).

34. The reduced tax rates applicable to dividends received by individuals under section 1(h)(11) are not available with respect to dividend distributions by captives domiciled in jurisdictions that are not characterized as having comprehensive tax treaties with the United States, such as many typical captive jurisdictions. Notice 2011-64, 2011-37 I.R.B. 231.

35. Earnings and profits of non-U.S. corporations must be determined under U.S. federal income tax principles for purposes of applying U.S. federal tax rules. For purposes of section 1248, in calculating earnings and profits certain modifications to the general rules are applied.

36. With respect to this second group of shareholders, if they hold their interests through a non-U.S. holding company that owns the shares of the insurance company and the transferred shares are those of the holding company and not the insurance company, section 1248 is not expected to apply.

37. A U.S. shareholder is defined under section 953(c) as a U.S. person who owns any stock in a non-U.S. corporation pursuant to section 958(a). Section 958(a) defines stock ownership as (1) direct ownership or (2) indirect ownership through a non-U.S. entity. Section 953(c)(1)(A) of the Code. However, the prefatory language of section 953(c)(1) of the Code provides "[f]or purposes only of taking into account related person insurance income."

38. Section 6038(b).

39. Section 6501(c)(8).

40. The federal insurance excise tax, commonly referred to as the "FET" (discussed later), would be applicable if the shareholder pays premium to the captive and the transaction is characterized as insurance for U.S. federal tax purposes. In addition, the Act (new section 965) includes provisions that generally require U.S. persons characterized as 10% U.S. shareholders of non-U.S. corporations to include in their taxable income for the last taxable year beginning before December 31, 2017 their pro rata share of the non-U.S. untaxed earnings of the non-U.S. corporation, even if it was, and is, not a CFC. The Act corresponding includes an expanded dividends received deduction (new section 245A) for the foreign source portion of certain dividends.

41. Section 316. If the non-U.S. captive does not determine its earnings and profits on a U.S. basis, all distributions from the captive will be characterized as dividends.

42. Section 1(h)(11).

43. *See* sections 243(a) and 245.

44. Section 1297(d).

45. Section 1297. The PFIC provisions also contain a look-through rule under which a non-U.S. corporation shall be treated as if it "received directly its proportionate share of the income" and as if it "held its proportionate share of the assets" of any other corporation in which it owns at least 25 percent of the value of the stock. Section 1297(c).

46. Sections 1297 and 954.

47. The exception is intended to ensure that income derived by a bona fide insurance company is not treated as passive income, except to the extent such income is attributable to financial reserves in excess of the reasonable needs of the insurance business.

48. Section 1297(b)(2)(B). The Act modifies the insurance company exception, and provides that income "derived in the *active* conduct of an insurance business by a *qualifying insurance corporation*" is not passive income. In order to be a "qualifying insurance corporation," (i) a corporation must be treated as an insurance company for U.S. tax purposes if it were a U.S. domestic corporation; and (ii) its "applicable insurance liabilities" must constitute more than 25 percent of its total assets (or it must meet an alternative facts and circumstances test). For these purposes, "applicable insurance liabilities" include loss and loss adjustment expenses, and reserves (other than deficiency, contingency or unearned premium reserves). The alternate facts and circumstances test allows a non-U.S. corporation that does not meet the 25 percent test to otherwise qualify for the exception, if (i) the corporation is predominantly engaged in an insurance business, (ii) at least 10 percent of its total assets comprise "applicable insurance liabilities," and (iii) the reason for the failure to meet the 25 percent test is solely due to run-off or ratings-related circumstances.

49. Section 831(c). The legislative history of section 831(c), which codifies the definition of a property, casualty insurance company by a cross reference to section 816(a) (the definition of an insurance company for life insurance purposes) indicates that an insurance company in runoff should retain its status as an insurance company even if it has little or no premium.

50. Comments by various IRS representatives have indicated a willingness to modify the employee rule.

51. In general, a shareholder receives an "excess distribution" if the amount of the distribution is more than 125 percent of the average distribution with respect to the shares during the three preceding taxable years (or shorter period during which the taxpayer held the shares).

52. Section 1291.

53. They may also consider making a protective QEF election instead.

54. Section 1295. In order for a shareholder to be able to make a QEF election, the captive must provide an annual information statement.

55. Section 1293(c).

56. Premium paid to a 953(d) electing company is also not subject to the FET (discussed later). Although, if it pays premium for reinsurance coverage to a non-U.S. insurance company, such premium would be subject to the FET.

57. As noted earlier, for U.S. federal income tax purposes there are special rules for insurance companies to calculate their income, including the allowance of certain reserves as deductions.

58. 2003-2 C.B. 55.

59. The "all earnings and profit amount" attributable to a shareholder is generally such shareholder's pro rata share of the earnings and profits of the electing entity reduced by the amount of previously taxed subpart F income. Treas. Reg. § 1.367(b)-3(b)(2).

60. A discussion of the consequences of section 367 are beyond the scope of this chapter.

61. There is a special tax applicable to non-U.S. companies that have pre-1988 earnings and that make the election. It was included as a transition rule when the election provision was added to the Code as part of the 1986 federal tax changes.

62. Rev. Proc. 2003-47, 2003-2 C.B. 55.

63. Section 953(d)(2)(A) and (B).

64. As noted earlier, a discussion of the consequences of section 367 are beyond the scope of this chapter.

65. Section 953(d)(3).

66. In general, U.S. income tax treaties contain provisions indicating the requirements that must be met in order for a resident in the treaty partner's jurisdiction to be eligible for benefits under the treaty. For corporate entities these requirements often include meeting one of the following: an ownership and base erosion test, a publicly traded test, an active business test, or an EU or NAFTA ownership test. A comprehensive discussion of the U.S. income tax treaty rules is beyond the scope of this chapter.

67. To the extent that income is subject to U.S. federal income tax under these rules it will be excluded from subpart F income and, accordingly, would not also be included by shareholders as income on their U.S. federal tax returns. Section 952(b).

68. The branch profits tax was put in place to equalize the treatment of non-U.S. companies that operated in the United States through branches with those that operated through subsidiaries, by imposing a tax on "dividend equivalents" that is consistent with the imposition of a withholding tax on dividends.

69. Section 864(c)(2).

70. Section 864(c)(3).

71. The income from U.S. situs risks is generally characterized as U.S. source.

72. Section 842(b) was intended to prevent a non-U.S. insurance company from avoiding U.S. income tax on investment income derived from reserves attributable to its U.S. business by investing the reserves outside the U.S. Based on the reasoning of North West Life Assurance Co. of Canada, 107 T.C. 363 (1966), section 842(b) may be deemed inapplicable in determining investment income attributable to a captive entitled to the benefits of a U.S. income tax treaty. The Tax Court concluded in the *North West Life Assurance* case that section 842(b) and the U.S. tax treaty with Canada were in conflict, and thus that a Canadian insurer was not required to apply section 842(b) to treat a minimum amount of net investment income as ECI.

73. Section 864(c)(4)(C) of the Code.

74. Section 832(b)(4) of the Code.

75. Treas. Reg. § 1.882-4(a)(4); Swallows Holding, Ltd. v. Comm'r 515 F.3d 162 (3rd Cir. 2008), remanding 126 T.C. 96 (2006). Additionally, if a U.S. federal income tax return is not filed, the period of limitations will not begin to run.

76. *See* Spermacet Whaling & Shipping Co. v. Comm'r, 30 T.C. 618 (1958), *aff'd*, 281 F.2d 646 (6th Cir. 1960). We note that bills have been introduced in Congress that would treat certain non-U.S. companies that are managed and controlled in the United States as U.S. domestic companies. To date, the bills have only applied these provisions to publicly traded corporations, or private corporations with significant assets (e.g., gross assets of $50 million or more).

77. *See* De Amodio v. Comm'r, 34 T.C. 894, 906 (1960) *aff'd*, 299 F.2d 623 (3d Cir. 1962) (non-U.S. taxpayer owning U.S. income-producing real property held to be engaged in a U.S. trade or business where such property was managed through real estate agents who collected rents, arranged for repairs, paid taxes, and negotiated leases).

78. *See, e.g.*, Griffin v. United States, 588 F.2d 521 (5th Cir. 1979); Esmond Mills v. Comm'r, 132 F.2d 753 (1st Cir. 1943), *cert. denied*, 319 U.S. 770 (1943) (courts applied common law agency principles).

79. *Id.*

80. *See* InverWorld, Inc. v. Comm'r, T.C. Memo. 1996-301. In InverWorld, Inc., T.C. Memo 1996-301, the Tax Court concluded that InverWorld, Ltd. (LTD), a Cayman Islands exempted company, was engaged in a trade or business in the United States because a substantial part of the activities that produced LTD's income occurred in the United States.

81. *See, e.g.*, Linen Thread Co., Ltd. v. Comm'r, 14 T.C. 725 (1950); Scottish American Investment Co. v. Comm'r, 12 T.C. 49 (1949). Please note that these cases were decided before the enactment of the trading safe harbor under section 864(b).

82. 14 T.C. 725 (1950).

83. *See also* Abegg v. Comm'r, 50 T.C. 145 (1968), *aff'd*, 429 F.2d 1209 (2d Cir. 1970) (holding that "searching for business activities with a view to undertaking them does not constitute engaging in a trade or business"); Pasquel v. Comm'r, 12 T.C.M. (CCH) 1431 (1953) (acquiring an interest in U.S. property from a U.S. person already under contract to purchase that property and participating in the proceeds of its resale abroad does not constitute a trade or business).

84. Rev. Rul. 56-165, 1956-1 C.B. 849.

85. These cases were decided prior to the enactment of the trading safe harbor under section 864(b) (discussed immediately following).

86. *See also* (1) Rev. Rul. 77-231, 1977-2 C.B. 241 (implied that a non-U.S. reinsurance company was not engaged in a U.S. trade or business where the non-U.S. reinsurer: (a) was not authorized to do business in the United States; (b) did not have any office or permanent establishment in the United States in which the reinsurance could be negotiated; (c) had U.S. insurance companies travel to foreign countries to negotiate any reinsurance transactions with the non-U.S. reinsurance company; and (d) did not solicit reinsurance business at any U.S. office); and (2) PLR 8110048 (concluded that a non-U.S. insurance company was not engaged in a U.S. trade or business because the non-U.S. insurance company (a) maintained no office or fixed place of business in the United States; (b) did not execute policies of insurance or maintain its books and records in the United States; (c) had rating and claims work required to be performed in the United States performed by independent service organizations on a fee basis; and (d) was not authorized by any state to perform any insurance business in that state (e.g., as a surplus lines insurance company)).

87. 1980-2 C.B. 318.

88. *Compare*, Rev. Rul. 80-222 (premiums paid to a non-U.S. reinsurer which had no U.S. contacts other than the location of its reinsured and the situs of the risks being insured are not subject to U.S. income tax).

89. Section 864(b)(2)(A). Additionally, courts have consistently held that mere investing is not the carrying on of a trade or business. *See* Higgins v. Comm., 312 U.S. 212 (1941); *see also* FSA 200224003.

90. Treas. Reg. § 1.864-2(c)(2)(i). Proposed Treas. Reg. § 1.864(b)-1.

91. The proposed regulations provide that if the taxpayer is an eligible nondealer, the term engaged in a trade or business in the United States does not encompass effecting transactions in derivatives for the taxpayer's own account, including hedging transactions within the meaning of Trea. Reg. § 1.1221-2. The regulations, although they are still in proposed form and not final, provide that taxpayers may take positions consistent with the proposed regulations.

92. Although an investor is not eligible for the trading safe harbors, courts have consistently held that mere investing is not the carrying on of a trade or business. *See* Higgins v. Comm., 312 U.S.

212 (1941); *see also* FSA 200224003. Thus, it may be possible to fall within the scope of this common law rule with respect to mere investment activities, even if a taxpayer is characterized as a dealer with respect to another portion of its activities.

93. Treas. Reg. § 1.864-2(c)(2)(iv).

94. *Id.*

95. *See, e.g.*, Kemon v. Comm'r, 16 T.C. 1026 (1951).

96. "Independent" status may turn on whether the agent is economically and legally independent from the principal. *See* Taisei Fire & Marine Ins. Co. v. Comm'r, 104 T.C. 535 (1995).

97. In addition to tax considerations, a non-U.S. captive should consider state regulatory constraints on its doing business in any U.S. state. Generally, if the captive is doing a reinsurance business instead of direct business, there will be wider latitude from a regulatory perspective.

98. In Rev. Rul. 2008-15, 2008-1 C.B. 633, the IRS took the position that premiums paid by a non-U.S. person not engaged in a U.S. trade or business to a non-U.S. insurance company, including from one non-U.S. insurer to another, were subject to the FET. This position was invalidated by the Court of Appeals for the District of Columbia Circuit in Validus Reinsurance, Ltd. v. U.S., 786 F.3d 1039 (2015), and the IRS revoked Rev. Rul. 2008-15 in Rev. Rul. 2016-3, 2016-3 I.R.B. 282.

99. Treas. Reg. § 46.4374-1.

100. The FET is not imposed, however, on premiums that (1) are paid to a non-U.S. insurer that is engaged in a U.S. trade or business and (2) are characterized as effectively connected income. It also is not imposed on premiums written by a captive that makes a 953(d) election.

101. Section 4371(1).

102. Section 4372(d).

103. Section 4371(2).

104. Section 4372(e).

105. Section 4371(3). The FET applies in addition to the BEAT. For a short description of the BEAT see the Appendix.

106. Please note that there is an additional depository period in September.

107. Sections 881(a) and 1442(a).

108. For example, the withholding tax does not apply to "portfolio interest," interest on U.S. bank deposits, interest related dividends received from regulated investment companies, and insurance premiums. *See* sections 881(c), 881(d) and 871(k); Treas. Reg §§ 1.1441-1(c) and 1.1441-2(a)(7).

109. Section 865. Additionally, Treas. Reg. § 1.1441-2(b)(2) provides that, for purposes of the withholding at source rules, capital gain is generally not characterized as FDAP.

110. "FATCA" stands for the "Foreign Account Tax Compliance Act," which was enacted as part of the Hiring Incentives to Restore Employment Act enacted in March 2010.

111. Treas. Reg. § 1.1473-1(a)(1)(i).

112. For these purposes, U.S. risks will include property located in the United States, liability arising out of an activity in the United States, and risks in connection with the lives or health of U.S. residents. Section 861(a)(7).

113. Treas. Reg. § 1.1473-1(a)(1)(ii).

114. A comprehensive discussion of these rules is beyond the scope of this chapter.

115. In certain circumstances, "withholding agents" are required to file IRS Form 8966 with the IRS.

116. Captives properly making a 953(d) election would be required to provide IRS Form W-9 indicating that it is a U.S. person for FATCA purposes.

117. A "substantial U.S. owner" is generally a U.S. person that owns more than 10 percent (by vote or value) directly or indirectly. There are certain exceptions to the indirect ownership rule so that if shares are held indirectly through certain types of entities an indirect owner may not be characterized as a "substantial U.S. owner."

118. There are a number of exceptions to the NFFE information reporting requirements, including for members of a publicly traded group. It is also possible for a passive NFFE to elect to be a direct reporting NFFE and thereby provide the information with respect to its "substantial U.S. owners" directly to the IRS instead of on the IRS Form W-8BEN-E.

119. Cash value contracts are insurance contracts (*other than indemnity reinsurance contracts* and term life insurance contracts) that have an aggregate *cash value* greater than $50,000. Treas. Reg. § 1.1471-5(b)(3)(vii)(A). Cash value means any amount that (1) is payable to any person upon termination, cancellation, or withdrawal, or (2) any person can borrow under the contract; certain amounts are excluded from cash value, such as amounts returned for certain premium deposits. Treas. Reg. § 1.1471-5(b)(3)(vii)(B).

120. A non-U.S. entity is also characterized as an FFI if it is a depository institution, custodial institution, or investment entity. Treas. Reg. § 1.1471-5(e)(1). In addition, certain holding companies may be characterized as FFIs. Treas. Reg. § 1.1471-5(e)(1).

121. If the FFI is domiciled in a country that has an intergovernmental agreement (IGA) with the United States, the requirements would be specified in the IGA; and if not domiciled in a country with an IGA, the requirements are set forth in the U.S. Treasury Regulations and include registering with the IRS and providing information to the IRS about the FFI's "U.S. account holders."

122. A U.S. shareholder is defined under section 953(c) as a U.S. person who owns any stock in a non-U.S. corporation pursuant to section 958(a). Section 958(a) defines stock ownership as (1) direct ownership or (2) indirect ownership through a non-U.S. entity. Section 953(c)(1)(A) of the Code. However, the prefatory language of section 953(c)(1) of the Code provides "[f]or purposes only of taking into account related person insurance income."

123. Sections 6038(b) and 6501(c)(8).

124. Sections 6038B.

125. Section 6038D.

126. In order to begin the running of the period of limitations with respect to a year, some non-U.S. companies that are not engaged in a U.S. trade or business choose to file protective/$0 U.S. federal income tax returns.

127. Table 4.3 does not consider RPII or PFIC status.

128. One level of tax imposed at the shareholder level.

129. Two levels of tax may be imposed, one at the corporate level, and another at the shareholder level if dividends are paid.

Chapter 5: Employee Benefits

1. News Release, Bureau of Labor Statistics, Employer Costs for Employee Compensation—June 2017 (Sept. 8, 2017), http://www.bls.gov/news.release/ecec.nr0.htm.

2. Conning; MarketStance analysis; Insurance Information Institute.

3. IRS Rev. Rul. 92-93.
4. IRS Rev. Ruls. 2002-89, 2002-90, and 2002-91.
5. Wells Fargo & Co. v. Comm'r, 224 F.3d 874 (8th Cir. 2000).
6. Savings are estimated from CICA 2009 International Conference.

Chapter 6: The Role of Corporate Counsel

1. www.springgroup.com, May 23, 2016.

2. I am generically going to refer to captive insurance companies, but the topics in this chapter will apply to single parent captives, group captives, cell captives, and risk retention groups alike.

3. Or your company must be committed to spending the time and effort on risk management programs that will reduce losses.

4. Statement of Financial Accounting Standard No. 113 defines certain criteria that reinsurance contracts must meet in order for the contracts to qualify for reinsurance accounting treatment. For a reinsurance contract to qualify for reinsurance accounting treatment the contract must indemnify the ceding company against loss or liability relating to insurance risk (commonly referred to as "transfer of risk"), as defined by the Statement. The Statement includes the following two conditions, both of which must be met, for a transfer of risk to occur: (1) the reinsurer must assume significant insurance risk (the "9a test"), and (2) it is reasonably possible that the reinsurer may realize a significant loss (the "9b test").

In order for the 9a test to be satisfied, a reinsurance company should be subject to some degree of variability in both the timing and amount of underwriting results. In addition, the financial results of the reinsurance company should vary inversely to some degree with the results of the ceding company for each claim (i.e., a claim for reinsurance should result in a loss for the reinsurer and an offset to loss for the reinsured). Reinsurance contracts that contain provisions that limit the amount of insurance risk to which the reinsurer is subject (experience refunds, cancellation provisions, etc.) or delay the timely reimbursement of claims by the reinsurer (payment schedules, etc.) are not considered to have transferred "significant" insurance risk and therefore do not meet the 9a test.

In order for the 9b test to be satisfied, a cash flow analysis should be performed comparing the present value of the reinsurer's cash outflows (claims paid, ceding commissions, experience refunds, etc.) to the present value of the related cash inflows. Under most reinsurance contracts an actuary can accurately estimate loss, and the premiums charged by the reinsurer will generally approximate the estimated claims payable. Therefore, if the present value of the cash inflows for a given contract exceeds the present value of the related cash outflows, the likelihood that the reinsurer will realize significant loss is not considered "reasonably possible," and the 9b test is not satisfied.

5. I do want to acknowledge and thank a few individuals for whom without I could not have written this chapter. First David Smith, former general counsel for ADM who gave me the opportunity to join the captive insurance industry. Second there are three individuals—Mike Lusk, former vice president of Insurance and Risk Management at ADM; John Lower, senior vice president at Arthur J Gallagher; and Peter Joy, vice president of Aon. These three gentlemen have over 100 years combined experience in the captive insurance industry and have been my mentors, teachers, and friends. Most of what I know about the captive insurance industry comes from them sharing their knowledge with me. Finally, my wife, Michelle Mosby-Scott, whose love and support make everything possible.

Chapter 8: Closing the Captive

1. Global Insurance Run-off Survey 2018. https://www.pwc.com/gx/en/insurance/assets/pdf/global-insurance-run-off-survey-2018.pdf.

2. It should be clearly noted that workers' compensation is one of the most tightly regulated areas of run off, and options for commutation and accelerated closure reflect this. The accelerated options we explore in this chapter are confined to knowledgeable parties—they are insurers themselves or large commercial enterprises; they are not private individuals or corporate employees.

3. A transfer process is available in Vermont but it applies only to non-admitted business, thus Vermont domiciled captives are excluded. Additionally, other states, including Pennsylvania and Connecticut, have statutory provisions that allow insurers to divide their business, subject to regulatory review and approval.

4. *Alternative Mechanisms for Troubled Insurance Companies*, NAIC, 2009, http://www.naic.org/store/free/AMT-OP.pdf.

5. https://www.courts.ri.gov/Courts/DecisionsOrders/10-3777.pdf.

6. Regulation 68 is referred to now as 230-RICR-20-45-6.

7. *Alternative Mechanisms, supra* note 6.

8. https://www.courts.ri.gov/Courts/DecisionsOrders/10-3777.pdf.

9. Rhode Island Commutation Plan Statute, ch. 27-14.5-1 (6)(ii).

Chapter 9: Captive Insurance Tax Controversy

1. Notice 2016-66, Transaction of Interest—Section 831(b) Micro-Captive Transactions (Nov. 1, 2016).

2. Note that these audits generally include the captive insurance company and the operating company that is insured, which has some relationship to the captive. If the operating company is a flow-through entity such as an S corporation, the IRS often places those shareholders under examination as well.

3. *IRS Audits*, IRS, https://www.irs.gov/businesses/small-businesses-self-employed/irs-audits (last updated Oct. 26, 2017).

4. Large Business and International Directive on Information Document Requests Enforcement Process, LB&I Control No: LB&I-04-0214-004 (Feb. 28, 2014).

5. It is important to note that in many IDR requests, the IRS may not specifically mention e-mail correspondence as a document it is seeking. However, in the definition section of the IDR it will likely define "document" to include various items, including any sort of electronic correspondence.

6. *Large Business and International Directive on Information Document Requests Enforcement Process*, LB&I Control No: LB&I-4-0214-004 (Feb. 28, 2014); IRM Exhibit 4.46.4-2.

7. I.R.C. § 7402(b); I.R.C. § 7604.

8. IRM 4.10.3.3(2) (Feb. 26, 2016).

9. IRM 8.2.1.2 (June 28, 2012).

10. IRS Publication 5, Cat. No. 460741 (Rev. Jan. 1999).

11. IRM 8.2.1.5 (Aug. 11, 2015).

12. *Appeals*, IRS, https://www.irs.gov/individuals/appeals-resolving-tax-disputes (last updated Sept. 15, 2017).

13. *Appeals Independence*, IRS 2014 IRS Nationwide Tax Forum, https://www.irs.gov/pub/irs-utl/04-AJAC%20Part%201%20Exam%20Cases.pdf; *Appeals—An Independent Organization*, IRS, https://www.irs.gov/individuals/appeals-an-independent-organization (last updated Aug. 31, 2017).

14. IRM 8.1.1.1(1) (Oct. 1, 2016).

15. IRM 8.1.1.1 (2) (Oct. 1, 2016).

16. Rev. Proc. 2003-41, Appeals Fast Track Mediation Procedure.

17. *Fast Track Settlement—Large Business & International*, IRS, https://www.irs.gov/compliance/appeals/fast-track-settlement-large-business-international} (last updated Sept. 30, 2017).

18. IRS Pub. 3605, Cat. No. 29749Q, Fast Track Mediation: A Process for Prompt Resolution of Tax Issues (Rev. Sept. 2002).

19. *Fast Track Mediation*, IRS, https://www.irs.gov/individuals/fast-track-mediation (last updated Aug. 26, 2017).

20. *Appeals*, *supra* note 12.

21. Memorandum for Appeals Employees, AP-9-0713-03, attachment 5 (July 18, 2013).

22. IRM 8.1.1.1(3) (Oct. 1, 2016).

23. *Id.*

24. IRM 8.6.1.4 (Oct. 1, 2016).

25. *Id.*

26. IRM 8.6.1.4.1 (Oct. 1, 2016).

27. *See* IRM 8.7.11.7 and .8 for new emphasized guidance to appeals officers, which promote the use of pre-conference meetings. Note that in certain cases, appeals will allow the examination team to be present for the conference.

28. Rev. Proc. 2012-18, 26 C.F.R. § 601.106, Ex Parte Communications between Appeals and Other Internal Revenue Service Employees.

29. Rev. Proc. 2000-43, Prohibition of Ex Parte Communications between Appeals Officers and Other Internal Revenue Service Employees.

30. *Post-Appeals Mediation*, IRS, https://www.irs.gov/compliance/appeals/post-appeals-mediation (last updated Aug. 27, 2017).

31. *See* Avrahami v. Comm'r, 149 T.C. No. 7 (Aug. 21, 2017). *See* Chapter 3 for more on *Avrahami.*

32. Securitas Holdings, Inc. v. Comm'r, T.C. Memo 2014–225, at 18 (T.C. 2014).

33. *See, e.g.*, Helvering v. Le Gierse, 312 U.S. 531 (U.S. 1941); Clougherty Packing Co. v. Comm'r, 812 F.2d 1297 (9th Cir. 1987) *aff'g* 84 T.C. 948 (1985); Harper Grp. and Includible Subsidiaries v. Comm'r, 96 T.C. 45 (Jan. 24, 1991).

34. Black Hills Corp. v. Comm'r, 101 T.C. 173 (1993) (citing Amerco & Subsidiaries v. Comm'r, 96 T.C. 18, 38 (1991), *aff'd*, 979 F.2d 162 (9th Cir. 1992)).

35. R.V.I. Guar. Co., Ltd. & Subsidiaries v. C.I.R., 145 T.C. 209, 231; *see also Securitas*, T.C. Memo 2014–2015 at 27.

36. *R.V.I.*, 145 T.C. at 232.

37. *Id.* at 236.

38. *Id.* (citing *Black Hills Corp.*, 101 T.C.).

39. *Id.*

40. *Securitas,* T.C. Memo 2014–2015 at 19.

41. *Id.* at 27.

42. *R.V.I.*, 145 T.C. at 228.

43. *Id.*

44. Humana, Inc. v. Comm'r, 881 F.2d 247, 257 (6th Cir. 1989).

45. *Id.*

46. *See* Rent-A-Center, 142 T.C. 1, 24 (Jan. 14, 2014); *Harper Grp.*, 96 T.C. 45.

47. Rev. Rul. 2002-90, I.R.B. No. 2002-52 (Dec. 30, 2002).

48. Rev. Rul. 2002-89, I.R.B. No. 2002-52 (Dec. 30, 2002).

49. *See, e.g.*, PLR 200724036 (six insureds does not sufficiently distribute risk).

50. *R.V.I.*, 145 T.C. at 225 (citing *Harper Grp.*, 96 T.C. at 59).

51. *Id.*

52. *See* Kidde Industries, Inc. v. U.S., 40 Fed. Cl. 42, 52 (Fed. Cl. 1997), *dismissed*, 194 F.3d 1330 (Fed. Cir. 1999).

53. *See Rent-A-Center*, 142 T.C. at 14.

54. *See, e.g.*, Avrahami v. Comm'r, T.C. No. 17594-13, Answering Brief for Respondent, p. 250.

55. I.R.C. § 7701(o).

56. Coltec Indus., Inc. v. United States, 454 F.3d 1340, 1347 (Fed. Cir. 2006).

57. Frank Lyon Co. v. United States, 435 U.S. 561, 584 (1978).

58. *Coltec*, 454 F.3d at 1353; *see* Klamath Strategic Inv. Fund ex rel. St. Croix Ventures v. United States, 568 F.3d 537, 543 (5th Cir. 2009) ("The economic substance doctrine allows courts to enforce the legislative purpose of the [Tax] Code by preventing taxpayers from reaping tax benefits from transactions lacking in economic reality.").

59. *Frank Lyon*, 435 U.S. at 583–84.

60. United States v. Cumberland Pub. Serv. Co., 338 U.S. 451, 456 (1950); Rice's Toyota World v. Comm'r, 752 F.2d 89, 91–92 (4th Cir. 1985).

61. Klamath Strategic Investment Fund ex el. St. Croix Ventures v. U.S., 568 F.3d 537 (5th Cir. 2009).

62. *Rice's Toyota World*, 752 F.2d at 91–92; Bails Bonds by Marvin Nelson, Inc. v. Comm'r, 820 F.2d 1543, 1549 (9th Cir. 1987).

63. Sochin v. Comm'r, 843 F.2d 351, 354 (9th. Cir. 1988); *see also* Pasternak v. Comm'r, 990 F.2d 893, 898 (6th Cir. 1993).

64. I.R.C. § 6662(b).

65. *Id.* § 6662(h).

66. *Id.* § 6662(i).

67. *Id.* § 6662(d)(2)(B).

68. United States v. Rylander, 460 U.S. 752, 757 (1983); United States v. Treadstone, et al., Order Clarifying Summons, No. CV-15-01733-PHX-ROS (Oct. 2, 2015).

69. *Rent-A-Center*, 142 T.C. at 13; Sears, Roebuck & Co. v. Comm'r, 96 T.C. 61, 101 (1991).

70. *R.V.I.*, 145 T.C. at 46–37.

71. New Colonial Ice Co. v. Helvering, 292 U.S. 435, 440 (1934).

Appendix

The Base Erosion Anti Abuse Tax ("BEAT")—Overview

Saren Goldner and P. Bruce Wright

The BEAT (section 59A) imposes a 10 percent minimum tax (5 percent for 2018 and 12.5 percent after 2025, with the rates increased for banks and "registered securities dealers") on corporate U.S. taxpayers (not including RICs, REITs and S corporations) by adding back into the U.S. tax base of an "applicable taxpayer" any "base erosion payments" made to a "foreign person" that is a related party. The minimum tax rate is then applied to this modified taxable income amount. The difference between this minimum tax amount and the taxpayer's regular corporate tax liability (taking into account certain credits) is the base erosion minimum tax amount.

The definition of related party for this purpose is very broad and a "foreign person" is any person that is not a U.S. person. An "applicable taxpayer" includes only a U.S. corporate taxpayer that is included in a "controlled group" that has (i) average annual gross receipts of a least $500 million for the three-year taxable period ending with the preceding taxable year, and (ii) a "base erosion percentage" of 3 percent (i.e., the percentage of "base erosion payments" relative to total deductible payments) or higher for the taxable year.

"Base erosion payments" generally include amounts that are deductible by an applicable taxpayer, specifically include reinsurance premium payments and presumably include insurance premium payments as well as loss payments. The BEAT essentially applies to deductible amounts on a gross basis, even if the amount would typically be reduced in arriving at net income; for example, premium plus investment income, less loss payments generally equals underwriting income subject to U.S. tax, whereas, the BEAT applies to the gross amount of premium paid by a U.S. applicable taxpayer to a non-U.S. related party.

In addition, the BEAT applies to a deductible amount (e.g., premium) even if the corresponding income of the non-U.S. person is subject to U.S. tax on a net basis, for example as subpart F income or effectively connected income. The BEAT also applies in addition to the FET. Because the BEAT operates to add back the deductible amounts/base erosion payments into the U.S. tax base, it is only the excess of the deductible amount over the net income amount that is potentially subject to the BEAT minimum tax (assuming the net income amount is included in the U.S. income of the same applicable taxpayer generating the deduction).

The BEAT provisions authorize the IRS to issue regulations to implement broad anti-abuse provisions to prevent the use of intermediaries and conduits to avoid the tax.

Index

Achievement of, 115
Actuary, 6, 11–12, 17, 75, 77, 99, 121, 123, 131–132, 153
Affiliates, 23, 25, 30, 50, 139, 141, 147
Availability, 98

Bank records, 122
Brother-sister, 25–26, 28, 66, 141–142
business owner, 5
Business Plan
Capitalization, 11
owner, 11
purpose, 11
reinsurance, 11
underwriter, 12

Captive Insurance
Affiliated businesses, 1–2
Agency captives, 3
branch captive, 4
Capitalization, 11
cash inflow, cash outflow, 153
Categories
alien captive, 4
deductibles captive, 3
domestic captive, 4
domicile, 4, 15, 73, 102
excess captive, 3
foreign captive, 4
Group captive, 2–3, 40, 47, 66, 79–80, 99, 111, 146, 153
offshore captive, 4
Life, 2
Non-life, 2
primary captive, 3
property-casualty captives, 3
Pure captive, 2, 14–15, 66, 72–73, 79
Reinsurance, 79
rental captive, rent-a-captive, 3
Risk retention groups, 3, 101, 153
special purpose captives, 3
sponsored-cell captives, cell captives, 3, 73, 80, 153
workers comp captive, 3
claims administrators, 6
Commercial insurance, 1, 3, 5–7
components of, 9, 10, 99
confidential, 126
Consumer, 2, 97, 115
consumer protection focus, 97
California, 30
Colorado, 26
Communications,123, 128–129, 155

defined, 4, 27, 42, 47, 52, 56–58, 60, 70, 144, 147, 152–153
pre-defined, 19
dialogue, 126
Domicile
European Union (EU), 15
onshore-U.S. domiciles, 15
offshore domiciles, 15
Delaware, 105
Diversity, 4, 39, 67

Earnings of the non-U.S. corporation, 53, 147
Exceptions, 48–50, 128, 147, 152
Exemption, 49, 59, 70, 77, 146
Extended warranties, 32
Exit strategies, 117

Feasibility Study
contribution of business owner's business units, 10
Domiciles, 10
Federal tax issues, 12
Federal claims, 28–29
Federal income tax consequences, 9
Federal income tax purposes, 12, 21–22, 27, 29, 31, 33–34, 36, 40–41, 44, 47–48, 53, 56, 66, 140, 146, 148
Federal tax Rules, 41, 147
FFI, 61, 152
Financial benefits, 10, 21, 67, 79, 139
formal, 7, 75, 91–92, 114, 121, 123–124, 126, 136
framework, 9, 15

General captive theory, 10

Hiring Incentives to Restore Employment Act, 2010, 151

Internal Revenue Code of 1986 (IRC), 21, 145
IRS Taxation
administrative appeals, 125
appeals conference, 124, 128
arms length, 13, 31, 136
delinquency notice, 123
examination function, 125
fast track, 119, 125–127, 129
interview, 124
mediation, 125, 127, 129, 155
oath, 124
Insurance Risk, 12, 22, 24, 27, 31–33, 36, 40, 130, 153

Liability Risk Retention Act of 1986, 3
Life Insurance companies, 2, 34, 144
Limited liability Company, LLC, 3, 28, 112, 142
Limitations, 38, 50, 61, 114, 149, 152
Liquidity, 115, 131, 136
and capitalization, 131

Management, in Summary, 4
Managers, management, 4
Micro captive, 12, 35, 154
mutual insurance companies, 3, 36
Merging Captive Companies, 110
Money, 6, 77, 80, 93, 99, 107, 136
Montana, *See* Dormancy, 105

New York, 110
NFFE, 60, 152

Ohio, 144

Penalties, *See* IRC Section 6662, 132
PFIC, 51–53, 61, 148, 152

Possession, 51, 121, 133–134
Post-Appeals Mediation (PAM), 129, 155
Pre-audit, 134
Preliminary consideration, 33–34
Prepaid, 37
pre-summons letter, 123
Protest, 125, 128
Public policy concerns, 7, 115
  parent-subsidiary, parent-subs, 24–25
  Premium, 13–14, 85–86, 136

Regulations
  Risk distribution, risk shifting, risk transfer, 23
  federal, 115
  state, 11–14
Regulators, 3, 75, 90, 101, 107
Rhode Island, 110–113, 116, 117, 154

Small Insurance Companies, 2, 34
Service providers
  Actuary, 12
  Attorney and corporate secretary, 12
  Auditors, 12
  Bankers, 12
  Captive manager, 12
  Other roles, 12
  Registered office, 12
Stop loss, 8, 65, 67, 69, 74, 76–81
  Aggregate, 76, 78
  Medical, 76–77, 79–80

Targeted, 68
Texas, 143
Three-pronged test, 22, 40
Threshold, 24, 26, 34–35, 77, 80

Vermont, 16, 88, 97–101, 103, 105, 111, 116–117, 154

Witness, 114, 124, 133
Written agreement, 30